## Praise for *Why We Love Middle-earth*

"One could not ask for a more congenial pair of guides to Middle-earth than Alan Sisto and Shawn E. Marchese. The combination of learning and fun that has made *The Prancing Pony Podcast* such a delight shines through in this tour of the Middle-earth experience. *Why We Love Middle-earth* is a great resource for readers and film-viewers who are new to Tolkien and curious about all things Middle-earth."

—Corey Olsen, The Tolkien Professor and president of Signum University

"Alan and Shawn bring the same love for Tolkien and the fandom to this book that they've brought to *The Prancing Pony Podcast* for years. I would expect nothing less, but I can also think of no higher praise."

—Matt Graf, *Nerd of the Rings*

"This delightful read is accessible, humorous, and informative, with the appropriate dash of nostalgia. Perfect for both new and veteran Tolkien fans alike, it is sure to entertain, enlighten, and just maybe help you step out your front door and meet other members of the Tolkien community."

—K.M. Rice, author of the Afterworld series

"An absolutely phenomenal read. Sisto and Marchese perfectly encapsulate the spirit of Tolkien's legacy and bring it to the page. A heartfelt look at the passion found in the Professor's stories and why Middle-earth remains such a beloved fantasy world. Tolkien fans of all ages will certainly want to add this book to their collections."

—Don Marshall, Obscure Lord of the Rings Facts Guy

"You will not find a friendlier, more informative-yet-easygoing introduction to Tolkien's world than this book. Alan and Shawn are like wisecracking Hobbits, simultaneously goofing off and admiring every song and story shared in Elrond's Hall of Fire. Come for the groanworthy dad jokes; stay for the deep love of the lore."

—Jeff LaSala, author of *The Silmarillion Primer*

"*The Prancing Pony Podcast* has established itself as an institution among those of us who like to live, breathe, and dream J.R.R. Tolkien's magnificent Middle-earth legendarium. Approachable yet knowledgeable, fan-friendly yet scholarly, the *PPP* is one of those rare podcasts that successfully bridges the gap between the absolute Tolkien beginner and the serious devotee. This has clearly also been their intention with this book, and they have definitely succeeded in that aim. *Why We Love Middle-earth* is an entertaining read, but it also offers in-depth commentary on Tolkien's works, the various film adaptations, and the fan responses to those works, guiding the novice through approaching the books as well as offering new insights for the serious reader. Maintaining the balance between the disparate audiences is no mean feat, but the result is a delightful and fascinating read that I would heartily recommend to all fans of Middle-earth."

—Dr. Sara Brown, language & literature department chair, Signum University

"From erudition to entertainment, from comedy to camaraderie, *The Prancing Pony Podcast* is the *Car Talk* of Tolkien podcasts. Whether you are a Tolkien beginner or were there 300 episodes ago, Alan and Shawn are always worth listening to. *Why We Love Middle-earth* is a great introduction to Tolkien and the podcast. By treating the books, adaptations, and fandom individually, Alan and Shawn have once again proven themselves excellent guides for those wanting to enter Middle-earth. (Pre-order now and get a free Gollum GPS.)"

—Thomas Hillman, author of *Pity, Power, and Tolkien's Ring: To Rule the Fate of Many*

PRESENTS

# WHY WE LOVE MIDDLE-EARTH

PRESENTS

# WHY WE LOVE MIDDLE-EARTH

An Enthusiast's Book about Tolkien, Middle-earth, and the LotR Fandom

## SHAWN E. MARCHESE
## & ALAN SISTO

PUBLISHING

CORAL GABLES

For permission requests, please contact the publisher at:
Mango Publishing Group
2850 S Douglas Road, 2nd Floor
Coral Gables, FL 33134 USA
info@mango.bz

For special orders, quantity sales, course adoptions and corporate sales, please email the publisher at sales@mango.bz. For trade and wholesale sales, please contact Ingram Publisher Services at customer.service@ingramcontent.com or +1.800.509.4887.

Why We Love Middle-earth: An Enthusiast's Book about Tolkien, Middle-earth, and the LotR Fandom

Library of Congress Cataloging-in-Publication number: 2023937111
ISBN: (paperback) 978-1-68481-209-7, (hardcover) 978-1-68481-418-3,
(eBook) 978-1-68481-210-3
BISAC category code SOC022000, SOCIAL SCIENCE / Popular Culture

Shawn: For Lisa, Lucian, and Vesper—my Sun, my Moon, my Evening Star

Alan: For Heidi, Jai, and Elanor—thank you for your never-ending belief in me

And to J.R.R. Tolkien, for decades of inspiration and enchantment

# TABLE OF CONTENTS

# INTRODUCTION

If any historical society ever starts putting up blue plaques at the places where podcasts were born, the blue plaque marking the birthplace of *The Prancing Pony Podcast* would be on Facebook. (We realize that's an oddly Brit-centric reference for two Americans to make at the beginning of a book, but we are Anglophiles through and through. It comes with the territory of Tolkien fandom, to a certain degree, a fact which also explains the many references in our podcast and in this book to Monty Python, Douglas Adams, and Top Gear...but we digress.)

We are Alan and Shawn, the hosts of *The Prancing Pony Podcast* and the authors of the book you are now holding—upon whom should be placed all of the blame for anything you don't like, but only a small amount of the credit for anything you do—and we met in a Facebook group. It was the year 2015; Peter Jackson's *The Hobbit: The Battle of the Five Armies* was still a recent addition to our home media shelves, we had babies at home, and we found our escape from dirty diapers and sleepless nights in a Facebook group for Tolkien fans, to which we still belong and which we still serve as admins for, as of the date of writing this book.

We had both been Tolkien fans for many years. Perhaps we should start there.

# ALAN'S STORY

I first read *The Hobbit* in 1978 after seeing the Rankin/Bass animated version on television the year before. In fact, my first edition of the book was a softcover that used still images from that film. I didn't discover *The Lord of the Rings*, though, until high school about five years later. But judging from the Dwarvish runes all over my Pee-Chee folders (remember those?), I'd already begun to sink deep into Tolkien fandom. Not deep enough for *The Silmarillion* quite yet, but that's another story.

# SHAWN'S STORY

I discovered Tolkien in 1991, after a childhood spent buried in the pages of *Dungeons & Dragons* sourcebooks and mass-market fantasy paperbacks cowritten by twenty-sided dice rolls. After reading about how Tolkien first wrote *The Hobbit* (told in the first chapter of this book), I went right out and bought a box set of all four books of *The Hobbit* and *The Lord of the Rings*. I read it all as quickly as I could that summer, and unlike Alan, I went straight on into *The Silmarillion*. I didn't understand it right away, but I read it.

# OUR STORY

For both of us, Tolkien fandom was a major part of our identity through adolescence and young adulthood. It wasn't exactly cool at the time; we might get sideways looks at parties when we made a reference to Elrond or Pippin Took or Túrin Turambar, and virtually no one could read the loopy Elvish letters or blocky Dwarvish runes we'd scribble on our notebooks in class... but it was *ours*. Though we didn't know each other at the time, we both took similar paths (just on different timeframes) from *The Hobbit* on into *The Lord of the Rings* to *The Silmarillion*, *Unfinished Tales*, and beyond, understanding less and less of the arcane prose and complex story threads as we went deeper...and we both reread *The Lord of the Rings* every year, long before anyone knew that an indie horror filmmaker from New Zealand was about to kick off the next century with a blockbuster adaptation of Tolkien's magnum opus starring the video game kid from *Back to the Future Part II* and Mikey from *The Goonies*.

And then Peter Jackson did just that, and it was phenomenal. Not just "phenomenal" in the sense of "really awesomely good," but "phenomenal" in the sense that it was a *phenomenon*. Suddenly everyone knew these characters and this world, and friends and family who'd never taken interest before came to us, the longtime fans, for answers to their Middle-earth questions: Who is Gandalf really? Just how old is Galadriel? What's this "Númenor" place that people keep mentioning? And while the mainstream popularity of Middle-earth waned over time (the lackluster reception of the *Hobbit* films didn't help), still Frodo, Gollum, and Aragorn had been established as household names, and there was no going back.

And that's more or less where the world was when we met in 2015, in a Facebook group with the finger-achingly long name of "The Silmarillion/ Children of Húrin/The Hobbit/The Lord of the Rings." Seeking to generate some interesting content and discussion in the group, the admins of this Facebook group launched a series of "Book Weeks" in which users were encouraged to write a post about their favorite passage, theme, or aspect of that week's assigned book: it was a bit like an informal book club. We took to this like hobbits to mushrooms, and started participating immediately. And, being the loquacious, attention-seeking prats we are, our posts got longer and longer, with quotes from the text, analysis, and citations of secondary sources like Tolkien's biography. We weren't the only people in the group who took the Book Week exercise so seriously, but something (probably our own vanity...no, definitely our own vanity) drew us into a friendly competition with each other to write longer posts, and—who are we kidding?—get more likes than the other. And while we were at it, just plain *more posts* than the other, too. There were weeks when we'd post a new essay every single day.

This continued for months, and then in January 2016, when Alan decided he wanted to start a Tolkien podcast to get a little practice for his budding career as a voiceover artist, he reached out to Shawn to be his cohost. We hadn't spoken voice-to-voice before, nor met in person; we were only friends through text posts and comments online. But we luckily found that our chemistry extended to vocal banter as well as social media one-upmanship, and less than two months later, *The Prancing Pony Podcast* launched at the end of February.

Our early listener base was largely drawn from the Facebook group we met in, with our fellow Book Week participants being some of our earliest supporters and subscribers. We recorded our first episode with the intention of covering two of Tolkien's written works, "On Fairy-stories" and "Mythopoeia," and a bit of a biographical overview from Humphrey Carpenter's *J.R.R. Tolkien: A Biography*. Our plan was to release it and wait a month until our second episode. But, as it turned out, we ended up covering only half the material we'd intended to cover, in about double the time (see above re: loquacious and attention-seeking), so we decided to cover the rest of it in our second episode and release that episode two weeks later. We kept a biweekly schedule through the entire first season, covering *The Silmarillion* chapter by chapter, all the while expanding our listener base through a lot of social media outreach, honing our podcaster chops with not only reading-and-discussion episodes on *The Silmarillion* but also interviews with Tolkien scholars (and even one member of the Tolkien family).

At the start of our second season, we launched a Patreon campaign and set as our first goal "get us to this number, and we'll start doing weekly episodes." Well, we blew through that number in about forty-five seconds, and from then on we were a weekly podcast. We covered *The Hobbit* in season two, and then started covering *The Lord of the Rings*, in season three. We didn't actually meet in person until near the end of season two, twenty-eight months after beginning our podcast together, when we both attended Mythmoot V (hosted by Signum University in June 2018), where we had a chance to speak and to record a live podcast episode.

Tolkien fan conferences, or "moots," have always been important to us. Maybe it's because we met in person at a moot. Maybe it's just because they're a lot of fun: a day or more spent in the company of fellow Tolkien fans, talking about Tolkien, hearing presentations, and just generally geeking out. But we have actively participated in as many moots as possible, ever since that first one. We had the honor of keynote speaking at Signum University's annual regional (and not exclusively Tolkien-oriented) moot in Texas—TexMoot—in 2019. Later that year, we attended, and had a chance to record another live podcast at, Tolkien 2019, held in Birmingham, England, as a celebration of fifty years of the Tolkien Society. We finally leaned into our love of moots and fan gatherings when we started hosting our own PPP Moots, first online in 2021, and then in person in Milwaukee, Wisconsin (home of the impressive Tolkien archives at the Raynor Memorial Libraries at Marquette University), in 2022.

# THE STORY OF THIS BOOK

We weren't always sure we wanted to write a book. It was certainly something we had thought of, and figured we'd end up doing someday; but we had so much we wanted to do with *The Prancing Pony Podcast* itself that it wasn't a priority for many years. Amazon Prime's *The Rings of Power* changed all that.

Just as we saw twenty years ago with the response to Peter Jackson's movies, we knew that *The Rings of Power* was going to once again put Tolkien's works near the top of the pyramid of pop culture. We knew that there would be lots of new fans discovering Tolkien's world through the show, interested in reading the books, but not sure where to start—particularly since *The Rings of Power* covers material from *The Silmarillion* and *Unfinished Tales*, which might lead some optimistic viewers to those books first...which is absolutely *not* where a new Tolkien reader should start. Trust us on this.

In fact, this entire book is one big exercise in "trust us on this." We've written this book with the goal of sharing our knowledge of the books, the adaptations, and the Tolkien fandom as a whole, with a new group of fans: people who may not have ever read a single word of Tolkien's writing. And we also have filled this book with preemptive answers to questions that, in our many years as Tolkien podcasters, we've found that new fans often have: not "Why did Sauron make the One Ring?"-type questions, but questions about becoming a Tolkien fan, like "What book should I read next?" "Which adaptations are worth my time?" and "Where can I find other Tolkien fans?" The goal is to share our love of Tolkien with this new audience, entice them to read—and keep reading, and keep watching—and deepen their love of Tolkien, to welcome them into this world of Tolkien fandom that has meant so much to us.

With that in mind, this book is—just like the Elvish race—divided into three parts (don't understand what we mean? You'll get there). Part One—Stepping Into the Road: Discovering Tolkien's Books provides readers with a roadmap to guide them on their Tolkien reading journey, to help them determine where to start and which book to read next. Although reading order is not as hotly debated a topic among Tolkien fans as it is among fans of the Professor's friend C.S. Lewis's Narnia series, we still think there's a right order in which to approach the books, and we often get the question from new readers about which books to read in which order. We'll cover all of this, with our explanations as to why.

Of course, we know that not everyone reading this book is going to read all of Tolkien's books (though we will never stop saying that you really, really should), and adaptations of Tolkien are an absolutely wonderful way to get deeper into Tolkien's world without cracking a book. For that reason, Part Two—Other Minds and Hands: Middle-earth in Adaptation covers the major adaptations of Tolkien's works: the Peter Jackson films, as well as the animated adaptations that came before it. We'll discuss what makes them great, what (occasionally) makes them not so great, how they measure up to Tolkien's vision, align with Tolkien's thematic interests, and more, and who knows? Maybe you'll find a new favorite movie or other adaptation you didn't know existed.

Finally, reading the books and watching the movies is only part of the fun of being a Tolkien fan. When we're not reading or watching something Tolkien-related, many of us are enjoying the company of other Tolkien fans and getting deeper into some aspect of the appreciation of Professor Tolkien's masterpiece. There are many niches available for fans to explore, such as collecting books and other memorabilia, studying Tolkien's invented languages, academic study, fan organizations, and more. We explore some of the more popular niches of the fandom in Part Three—Concerning Fandom: Express Yourself as a Tolkien Fan. We hope newcomers who find themselves drawn toward the Tolkien fandom will find a place to call home in this section.

But this book isn't just for newcomers to Tolkien's work. We hope that longtime Tolkien fans will also learn much within these pages. Casual fans will hopefully find in this book a handy guide to help them deepen their fandom through further reading, even beyond the obvious entries in Tolkien's catalog of published works. For more intense fans, we hope this book will provide a quick reference to new aspects of the fandom that maybe you just haven't had a chance to get around to yet, and push you over the line from hardcore fan to true Tolkien obsessive (it's not so bad; again, trust us on this).

There's always a chance that you're a serious OG Tolkien fan who's been steeped in this stuff for so long that you've seen it all. You know your Fingolfin from your Finarfin and can parse out the Elvish words that form the root of each of those names. You've been to every major moot since 1992, and all your secondary source books are signed by the authors with personal notes only the two of you understand, like "Thanks again for helping me hide the you-know-what before you-know-who arrived. Best wishes." If that's you, you may very well know more about all this Tolkien stuff than *we* do; but we think that even the most seasoned fans can find something to love in reading this book, as we've found much to love in writing it. For us, writing this book has been an exercise—not just in "trust us on this"—but in all seriousness, in *recovery*. To borrow Tolkien's own phrasing from "On Fairy-stories," writing this book has helped us with "regaining a clear view" on Tolkien's work. Often on our podcast, we've lamented the fact that we can't read a particular favorite passage again for the first time, or discover Tolkien's work anew like someone just coming to the books. In taking upon ourselves the role of guides through Tolkien's world—Strider to the hobbits of the world, if you will—we have tried to see Tolkien's legendarium and the fandom surrounding it through the eyes of a newcomer again, and we hope that others out there who love these works and this community will gain that clear view as well, and possibly find enchantment afresh in our beloved Middle-earth.

Last, but most certainly not least, this book is a gift to our fans: to the many thousands of listeners who've downloaded our podcast, supported us on Patreon, joined us in our social media spaces, and become our companions on this journey—and, in a few cases, cherished friends. We've attempted, as much as possible, to replicate the *Prancing Pony Podcast* experience in printed form. This hasn't always been as possible as we'd like it to be; those who know our podcast and our particular style of banter know that we really do keep it conversational, talking with (and often over) and reacting to each other. There are aspects of this that are simply impossible to capture on the printed page, and it wouldn't be quite as fun to read as you think it would be. But we have done our best; while much of the book is in a combined voice (after all, our longtime fans know we agree on pretty much everything anyway), our individual voices as authors will come through on occasion, and we trust that those who know our work best will recognize those voices when they emerge, even if they aren't labeled as such on the page. But keeping this book true to *The Prancing Pony Podcast*, and to the identity that we have established—collectively and individually—as voices in the Tolkien community, has been of the utmost importance to us, especially since the announcement in 2022 that Shawn would no longer be a permanent cohost on *The Prancing Pony Podcast*. We want to assure our fans that, although Shawn is no longer a part of the podcast every single week, just as he remains an occasional guest on the show, he remains a part of all that we've built together, and is very much a part of this book. And though some things must inevitably change, the spirit and passion that drove Alan and Shawn to this point remains the same: *Plus ça change, plus c'est la même chose.* "The more things change, the more they stay the same." Which is not Elvish, but French, and from a Rush song[1] (you knew it was coming).

So wherever you are on your Tolkien journey—whether you've been a fan for decades, or have only just discovered *The Hobbit*, or are somewhere in between—you are most welcome, and we thank you for letting us be your guide. Now follow us, on the road that goes ever on and on.

---

1    The song in question is "Circumstances," from Rush's 1978 album *Hemispheres*, though in actuality the quote comes originally from the French writer Jean-Baptiste Alphonse Karr. We just aren't smart enough to have heard of Karr before Rush's lyrics pointed us to him, and anyway, we bet he never belted those words out as epically as Geddy Lee did.

## PROLOGUE

# WHO WAS J.R.R. TOLKIEN?

*"I do not feel inclined to go into biographical detail.
I doubt its relevance to criticism."*

—*J.R.R. Tolkien, from a 1957 letter to Caroline Everett*[2]

Any good Tolkien-related book needs a prologue. *The Lord of the Rings* has one, at least, and so, despite the protestations of the Professor above, we believe ours needs to start with an introduction to the man himself in order to help you understand who he was and what motivated, encouraged, and drove him to create the vast tapestry of his Middle-earth legendarium.

## HIS WHAT?

His legendarium. Say it with us: Legend. Dairy. Um.

In the common parlance of Tolkien obsessives like us and the well-respected scholars whose books we pore over in the wee hours of the night, the

---

2   Carpenter, Humphrey, ed. *The Letters of J.R.R. Tolkien*. William Morrow, 2000, No. 199.

"legendarium" is the umbrella term for Tolkien's writings about Middle-earth: *The Hobbit*, *The Lord of the Rings*, *The Silmarillion*, and the host of other works in varying stages of incompletion that we will tell you about as you make your way through this book. This was a term Tolkien used himself in various of his letters, though he often defined it more narrowly to refer just to the mythology of Middle-earth. As used by most fans today, it includes everything Tolkien wrote relating to Middle-earth, whether finished or unfinished: fiction, poetry, linguistic notes and commentaries, philosophical essays on the ethics and metaphysics of his fantasy world, and the many maps, family trees, and philological diagrams that fill in the corners.

It is certainly possible to become a fan of J.R.R. Tolkien without diving into the deep end and reading all of the bits and pieces that make up the greater legendarium. But we hope that, over the course of this book, we will whet your appetite to do just that. We find the hobby of studying, learning, loving, and living Tolkien's world—in all its detailed, world-built, and realistic glory— to be not only incredibly rich and rewarding, but also far more accessible than many people realize; and we want everyone reading this to fall in love with Middle-earth the way we have. But first, as we said, we think some introduction to the author himself is in order.

# SHALL WE GET ON WITH IT THEN?

Indeed we shall.

John Ronald Reuel Tolkien was born on January 3, 1892, in the city of Bloemfontein in the Orange Free State, at the time a British colony in what is now the nation of South Africa. Ronald, as he was known, was the elder of two sons born to Arthur Tolkien, an English banker living in the colony, and his wife Mabel (née Suffield). But the South African climate proved hard on young Ronald's health, so in early 1895 Mabel took Ronald and his little brother Hilary back to England, settling in a village near Birmingham. The boys' father planned to join the family in England as soon as his work would allow, but sadly, it never happened; Arthur got sick in late 1895, delaying any chance of travel, and died in February 1896. Ronald was four years old.

Now raising two boys as a widow, Mabel turned to religion for comfort and community. She converted to Roman Catholicism in 1900 and raised her sons Catholic. She taught them how to read and write Latin and French as well as English, and awakened in young Ronald a love of language. Both this love of language and a deep devotion to the Catholic faith would stay with Ronald for the rest of his life. But tragedy struck the Tolkien family again in 1904, when Mabel became ill from complications relating to her diabetes, which at the time was not nearly so easily treated as today. She died in November 1904, leaving the boys in the care of the local parish priest, Father Francis Morgan. Tolkien would later write of his mother that she "was a martyr indeed, and it is not to everybody that God grants so easy a way to His great gifts as He did to Hilary and myself, giving us a mother who killed herself with labour and trouble to ensure us keeping the faith."[3]

Father Francis initially put the boys up with an aunt who proved somewhat disinclined to take proper care of them, then in 1908 moved them into a boarding house where the teenage Ronald met a charming young woman named Edith Bratt, a fellow orphan lodging in the house who made beautiful music on the landlady's piano, and in Ronald's heart. Ronald and Edith became friends quickly, and eventually decided they were in love. When Father Francis found out about their mutual affection, he was none too happy about it, not least because Edith was a Protestant. They kept the teenage romance on the down-low as much as possible, though eventually Father Francis found out, and forbade Ronald from seeing Edith again until his twenty-first birthday.

---

3   Carpenter, *Biography*, 1977, 31.

Why We Love Middle-earth

During this time, Tolkien was attending King Edward's School for boys in Birmingham, where he proved an excellent student, particularly in language and literature. He played rugby, performed in the annual school play (in Greek) every year, and befriended a group of boys who formed an informal "club" called the "Tea Club and Barrovian Society," or TCBS. The principal members of the TCBS, and Ronald's closest friends for the next several years, were the "immortal four" of Robert Quilter Gilson (the son of King Edward's headmaster), Geoffrey Bache Smith, and Christopher Wiseman. The boys shared a love of poetry and art and had big dreams of changing the world.

The "immortal four" of the TCBS remained friends as they went off to college: two to Oxford and two to Cambridge. Tolkien himself began his college career at Exeter College, Oxford, in 1911. He initially majored in classics (i.e., ancient Greek and Latin studies), but soon changed his concentration to English Language and Literature, with a focus on Old and Middle English. It was while at Oxford that he first discovered a piece of Old English poetry that inspired him to write the first poem that would become part of the Middle-earth legendarium, though we'll get to that later. He was also well underway working on the invented languages that would become the Elvish tongues of his invented world.

But while Ronald was in school falling in love with Beowulf and Cynewulf and all the other 'wulfs, Edith nearly became the one that got away. She moved away from Birmingham, and over time believed that Ronald no longer loved her, so she accepted an engagement to another local boy in Cheltenham, where she was living. But Tolkien, unafraid to chase what he really wanted, raced *Good Will Hunting*-style to Cheltenham in January 1913 to declare his love once again and ask for Edith's hand in marriage. She said yes, though he had to finish school first.

And he did, in 1915, graduating with First Class Honours. But blissful married life with Edith was not to be his just yet, for by that time, World War I had started. All four of the TCBS resolved to enlist, which Tolkien did less than three weeks after graduating in June 1915. It was several months before he was to ship out, though, and he made good on his promise to marry Edith, in March 1916, before going to France in June of that year. Luckily for Tolkien and for all of us fans of his work, he survived the war; he was overcome by trench fever just a few months after arriving on the front, and was hospitalized in October 1916. His friend Wiseman also made it back alive, though Gilson and Smith were not so fortunate. In the foreword to the second edition to *The Lord of the Rings*, written nearly fifty years later, Tolkien would reflect poignantly that "by 1918 all but one of my close friends were dead."[4]

Back in England, Ronald reunited with Edith, recovered from his illness, and began the next phase of his life as a husband and father. The Tolkiens had four children: John (born 1917), Michael (1920), Christopher (1924), and Priscilla (1929). Tolkien took a job briefly working as a lexicographer for what would become the *Oxford English Dictionary* (yes, he actually worked at a dictionary) in 1919 before being hired to teach English at the University of Leeds in 1920. In 1925, though, Tolkien moved his family back to Oxford to take a position as a professor of Anglo-Saxon at Pembroke College. All this time, Tolkien was writing the stories that would become the First Age of Middle-earth (which, again, we'll get to later)...but hobbits were still not in his wildest imaginings.

In the late 1920s or early 1930s, Tolkien started writing the story that would become *The Hobbit*, primarily to amuse his children.[5] He maintained a healthy work-life balance through all these years, spending ample time teaching and doing academic work on *Beowulf, Sir Gawain and the Green Knight*, and other medieval literary works, while setting aside time to work on his writing, spend time with his family...aaannd hang out with the boys down at the pub. Every Thursday evening, Tolkien would meet his good friend C.S.

---

4   Tolkien. J.R.R. *The Lord of the Rings: The Fellowship of the Ring.* HarperCollins, 2020, xiii.

5   Tolkien did a lot of writing for his children, much of which has been published since his death, such as *The Father Christmas Letters* and *Mr. Bliss.*

Lewis (at the time a fellow Oxford professor) and a larger group of like-minded writers and scholars[6] called the "Inklings" at one of the local pubs for an epic but highbrow boys' night of beer, tobacco, poetry or prose readings, and no doubt incredibly vivacious conversation. The Inklings would prove to be a top-notch writing workshop for Tolkien's future compositions.

*The Hobbit* was eventually published in 1937 and became quite a success; Tolkien's publishers begged him for a sequel, which became *The Lord of the Rings*, published in three volumes between 1954 and 1955. But while he was writing to meet the demands of his publishers (and his audience), Tolkien was constantly at work on other writings, within the Middle-earth legendarium and without. The sheer literary output is staggering, as is the fact that so much of it was never published until after his death.

Which is, to be fair (and not to be a downer), probably a good place to leave this breakneck biographical sketch, so we can get on with the real story in the chapters to come. Though Tolkien achieved fame with *The Hobbit* and *The Lord of the Rings*, he continued writing stories, epic poems, essays, linguistic sketches, and philosophical treatises about Middle-earth and its denizens until his death in September 1973.[7] His third son, Christopher—who had always been Middle-earth's number-one fan, even as a child, and had followed in his father's footsteps as a war veteran and English professor—was appointed his literary executor, and started the work that would define the rest of his *own* life, of editing and publishing his father's many incomplete manuscripts: *The Silmarillion*, *Unfinished Tales*, The History of Middle-earth, and many, many others.

There's much more to tell, but that's what the rest of this book is for. As Tolkien himself said in narrating the first chapter of *The Hobbit*, "Now you know enough to go on with." So come with us, and we'll go on together.

---

6    Though Tolkien and Lewis are the two most well known Inklings, other members of the group made names for themselves in literature and scholarship: Charles Williams, Owen Barfield, Roger Lancelyn Green, Nevill Coghill, and others.

7    Edith preceded him in death, passing in November 1971.

# PART I

# STEPPING INTO THE ROAD: DISCOVERING TOLKIEN'S BOOKS

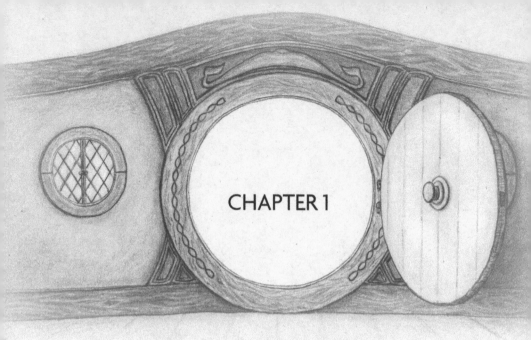

# CHAPTER 1

# AN UNEXPECTED BURGLAR: *THE HOBBIT*

*"In a hole in the ground there lived a hobbit. Not a nasty, dirty, wet hole, filled with the ends of worms and an oozy smell, nor yet a dry, bare, sandy hole with nothing in it to sit down on or to eat: it was a hobbit-hole, and that means comfort."*

—*J.R.R. Tolkien*, The Hobbit, *Chapter 1, "An Unexpected Party"*[8]

These are the first words of J.R.R. Tolkien's *The Hobbit*, and the first words of Tolkien's writing that many people ever encounter. For many of us lifelong Tolkien fans, our obsession with Middle-earth begins right here at the doorstep of Bilbo Baggins, Esq.

And with good reason: they're the words that introduced the world to Middle-earth when the first edition of *The Hobbit* was published on

---

8    Tolkien, J.R.R. *The Hobbit*. HarperCollins, 2020, 3.

September 21, 1937. Not that anyone was calling it "Middle-earth" just yet (we'll get to that later). Much like the effect these words can have on the individual fan, it's quite fitting that the introduction of Middle-earth to the world was at Bilbo's front door, on the precipice of an adventure that would change the life and perspective of this ordinary hobbit forever.

But we're getting ahead of ourselves.

*The Hobbit* is the perfect place to start on one's journey through Middle-earth, in part because of its accessibility, no matter who you are or when you approach it for the first time. While *The Lord of the Rings* can be a bit scary and intense for younger readers, and *The Silmarillion* has been known to make even full-grown adults scratch their heads trying to make sense of the quasi-biblical diction and the arcane Elvish family trees with all their Fingolfins and Finarfins, *The Hobbit* is aimed squarely at younger readers. Tolkien wrote it with his own children in mind, and read it to his children while it was in development. It was intended for children when it was published, but it remains a favorite for many readers well into adulthood, even among those who read it for the first time as adults. Put another way: long before Harry Potter and Katniss Everdeen were reaching beyond the boundaries of their young adult demographic to appeal to Mom, Dad, and even the college-aged babysitter, Bilbo Baggins was doing the same.

# BUT WHAT MAKES BILBO SO APPEALING?

Despite his diminutive stature and hairy feet, Tolkien's everyman protagonist Bilbo Baggins—who finds adventure literally knocking on his door and answers the call (against his better judgment) to find himself in a world of goblins, dragons, magic rings, and necromancers—is a familiar trope to anyone who's picked up a classic children's fantasy tale. Alice, take a good hard look in that looking glass; you'll see Bilbo. Dorothy, we're looking at you and your little dog, too. Pevensie kids, you're just a bunch of little Bilbos—move to the back of the lion (don't groan; go with it).[9] Okay, granted, Bilbo's not a child, and he doesn't step through a mirror or a wardrobe into a literal alternate world...but otherwise, *The Hobbit* fits comfortably in the classic "portal" fantasy mold. Yes, the Shire (not yet called that in this book) is part of the same plane of existence as Middle-earth; but the world Bilbo lives in behind the round door of his hobbit-hole is as different from that of Gandalf and Thorin Oakenshield and the Elvenking of Mirkwood as Kansas is from Oz. And Tolkien takes pains to separate Bilbo's civilized digs from "the Wild": that is, everything roughly east of Rivendell, which is reached in only three chapters. From that moment on, Bilbo is thrust into a world of what Tolkien called (in his seminal essay "On Fairy-stories") "arresting strangeness," and we see the world of Middle-earth through his outsider's eyes, much as we see Hogwarts through Harry's eyes in his first year there. This makes Middle-earth instantly accessible to the new reader, despite its strangeness, and we discover it along with Bilbo as the terrifying and dangerous and wonder-filled place that it is.

*The Hobbit* would be an impressive fantasy world-building achievement on its own, and for nearly two decades, until the publication of *The Lord of the Rings*, it was. But peeking through the cracks of this standalone story is a much larger world and mythology. Who were the Elves of Gondolin? Why were they at war with the goblins, and why is their king's sword in an untidy troll-cave? Who are the Wood-elves? Why does their king hate the Dwarves of the Lonely Mountain so much, and why didn't their ancestors travel to "Faerie in the West"? What is "Faerie in the West" anyway? And who is this Necromancer? Though these things are all mentioned in the pages of *The Hobbit*, not one of them is fully explained—and many aren't explained at all! But they don't *need* to be in order for the story to make sense. Their inclusion makes the world seem larger, somehow, and more *open* in a way than simply tying up every loose end and "textual ruin" (to borrow a phrase

---

9   Also, fair warning: this won't be the last awful pun.

from Tolkien scholar Michael D.C. Drout that we'll explain elsewhere—yes, we are introducing a textual ruin to tell you this) would *close* to make the world feel smaller. And these questions do have answers elsewhere in Tolkien's published writings...they just hadn't been published in 1937, when *The Hobbit* came out.

That's because, when Tolkien started writing *The Hobbit* around 1930, he had already been working on a mythology of Middle-earth for nearly twenty years, and he drew on this mythology to add color to the world of Bilbo and the Dwarves. But, once again, we're getting ahead of ourselves.

## Okay, Then Start at the Very Beginning.

It is, as someone once said, a very good place to start.

According to the most commonly told version of the story, relayed by Humphrey Carpenter in his authorized *J.R.R. Tolkien: A Biography*, Tolkien was grading exam papers one summer day when he found a blank page in a student's exam book. Nature abhors a vacuum, and apparently so did Professor Tolkien; he filled the emptiness of the blank page by writing a single sentence: "In a hole in the ground there lived a hobbit." At the time, he had no idea what a "hobbit" was or why it would live in a hole in the ground, but, as he later wrote, "Names always generate a story in my mind. Eventually I thought I'd better find out what hobbits were like. But that's only the beginning."[10]

Tolkien thought he might have the genesis of a good story for his kids, so he wrote it for them (thanks for making the rest of us dads look bad, Professor!). Tolkien developed the story between 1928 and 1933, telling it to his four children—John, Michael, Christopher, and Priscilla—in the

---

10    Carpenter, Humphrey. *J.R.R. Tolkien: A Biography*. Houghton Mifflin, 1977, 172.

evenings after dinner in the winter. Tolkien filled the book with things he knew his children would want to see. For example, the Tolkien children really, *really* liked bears, so many of the stories he wrote for them—including posthumously published works like *Mr. Bliss* and his annual letters to the kids from Father Christmas (an ongoing saga of goblins, elves, magic, and mayhem at the North Pole)—featured bears. Talking bears, fighting bears, friendly bears, intimidating bears...the children's teddy bears even make an appearance in some of these stories. And wouldn't you know, in Chapter 7 of *The Hobbit*, right between a chapter about murderous goblins and a chapter about murderous spiders, Bilbo and his friends meet...a bear. And he's no ordinary bear, either; he's Beorn, a human living in one of the few friendly places to be found on his side of the Misty Mountains, who by night shapeshifts into a bear who's somewhat less murderous than all those other nasty things—as long as one stays on his good side. In keeping with the lighter tone and the aim of making it accessible to children, *The Hobbit* also contains some interesting anachronisms in the narration, like references to "the whistle of an engine coming out of a tunnel," and not one but two instances in which someone or something is likened to a football. While this kind of thing would be absolutely unheard of in, say, *The Silmarillion*, with its elevated mythological/biblical diction, or even *The Lord of the Rings*, they fit in perfectly within the pages of *The Hobbit*, and it is largely because of Tolkien's deep insertion of his own narrative voice, as though he were speaking to children, that they do.

Whether it was the bears or something else that won them over, Tolkien's children seem to have enjoyed their winter reads with Dad and Bilbo. Later in life, after Middle-earth had been revealed to the world through the publication of *The Hobbit* and later *The Lord of the Rings*, Tolkien's sons and daughter reminisced about the story sessions they had when they were children. Christopher Tolkien later shared a recollection from his brother Michael that "Father would stand with his back to the fire in his small study of the house in North Oxford... and tell stories to my brothers and me; and [Michael] said that he remembered with perfect clarity the occasion when my father said that he was going to start telling us a long story about a small being with furry feet, and asked us what he should be called—then answering himself, said, 'I think we'll call him a Hobbit.' "[11]

All the Tolkien children had a close relationship with their father's literary creation, but none more so than Christopher. Even as a child, Christopher proved to be an excellent continuity supervisor—he would later recount also that he "was greatly concerned with petty consistency as the story unfolded, and that on one occasion I interrupted: 'Last time, you said Bilbo's front door was blue, and you said that Thorin had a golden tassel on his hood, but you've just said that Bilbo's front door was green and that Thorin's hood was silver.' " Tolkien *père*'s response, by Christopher's own admission, was, "Damn the boy."[12] But when they weren't pointing out continuity errors, the children had a tendency to mimic their father, making up their own stories in imitation of the story being told to them every night, with characters like "Philpot Buggins, Ollum the giant frog...the wizards Kimpu, Mandegar, and Scandalf the Beanpiper."[13] We don't know about you, but we're hoping Amazon will make *The Scandalf the Beanpiper Chronicles* their next big fantasy series.

But we digress.

Despite the fact that his kids were the intended audience, Tolkien wasn't the sort of writer to remain content with writing a simple children's story filled with silly dwarves and shapeshifting ursines. There were other stories in his mind, and *they were banging down the door trying to get out*. Back in 1916, he had begun making up languages and myths for a race of Elves whom he imagined to have inhabited the isle of Great Britain in the remote past. We'll

---

11   Quoted in Christina Scull & Wayne G. Hammond's *The J.R.R. Tolkien Companion and Guide: Reader's Guide, Part 1*. HarperCollins, 2017, 512.

12   Scull & Hammond, *Reader's Guide Part 1*, 2017, 512-13. This close relationship with and attention to detail regarding his father's published works was one Christopher Tolkien would maintain until his own death in 2020, as he oversaw the posthumous publication of numerous unfinished manuscripts (including *The Silmarillion, Unfinished Tales,* and many more) as his father's literary executor.

13   Rateliff, John D. *The History of The Hobbit*. HarperCollins, 2011, xvi.

talk more about these stories in a few chapters—after all, on the surface they don't seem to have much in common with the world of Bilbo Baggins, and when Tolkien first started writing, they weren't meant to. But the longer Tolkien kept writing, references to those "lost tales" began appearing more and more in the manuscript. Swords left over from ancient wars with the goblins would end up being found in troll-caves not far from Bilbo's hobbit-hole. Descendants of the heroes of those ancient wars would enter the story to give counsel to Thorin and company...or to imprison them. It was as though the world of the Elves began intruding into the world of the hobbit, despite Tolkien's best intentions, and in fact against his "original will," as he would put it in one of his letters.[14] In a 1964 letter, Tolkien wrote that "by the time *The Hobbit* appeared (1937) this 'matter of the Elder Days' was in coherent form. *The Hobbit* was not intended to have anything to do with it.... It had no necessary connexion with the 'mythology,' but naturally became attracted toward this dominant construction in my mind, causing the tale to become larger and more heroic as it proceeded. Even so it could really stand quite apart, except for the references."[15]

And while the mythology influenced *The Hobbit*, the latter influenced the former as well, as Tolkien elaborated in a 1955 letter to the British-American poet W.H. Auden: "*The Hobbit* was originally quite unconnected, though it inevitably got drawn in to the circumference of the greater construction; and in the event modified it."[16]

But perhaps the best summation of the relationship between *The Hobbit* and the mythology that preceded it, and came to be published as *The Silmarillion*, is captured in a 1951 letter to Milton Waldman,[17] a representative of Collins publishing house to whom Tolkien was pitching *The Lord of*

---

14   Carpenter, *Letters*, No. 31.

15   Carpenter, *Letters*, No. 257.

16   Carpenter, *Letters*, No. 163.

17   Carpenter, *Letters*, No. 31. Listeners to *The Prancing Pony Podcast* will recognize this as a letter referenced so frequently by the authors of this book that it has its own drinking game and would be pretty much a free space on a PPP Bingo card.

the Rings and The Silmarillion at the time: "The Hobbit, which has much more essential life in it, was quite independently conceived: I did not know as I began it that it belonged. But it proved to be the discovery of the completion of the whole, its mode of descent to earth, and merging into 'history.' As the high legends of the beginning are supposed to look at things through Elvish minds, so the middle tale of The Hobbit takes a virtually human point of view—and the last tale [The Lord of the Rings] blends them."

We'll get to that last tale in the next chapter.

In addition to the kid stuff and the mythology stuff, though, there was yet another major thread of, uh, stuff weaving its way through the fabric of The Hobbit: Tolkien's day job. By the early 1930s, when he started writing The Hobbit, Tolkien was already making a name for himself as a leading scholar of Anglo-Saxon language and literature from his position at Oxford University's Pembroke College.[18] In 1936, he delivered a groundbreaking lecture on the Anglo-Saxon poem Beowulf that forever changed scholarship on that poem; if he hadn't gone on to write stories about hobbits and elves, it's very likely he would have gone down in history anyway among a smaller and more specialized group of academics.

As it turned out, though, Tolkien let that stuff seep into his fantasy writing. Anglo-Saxon linguistic and literary influences appear all over his work, even The Hobbit. For example, the name Beorn, which Tolkien gave to his bear-human shapeshifter character, doesn't just look an awful lot like the modern word bear; it is actually related to it. The word bear in English comes from the same ancient Germanic root word as the Old Norse word björn, which

---

18   That is to say, the language and literature of England between about AD 410 and 1066, before the Norman Conquest. The language of the Anglo-Saxons of this period was a Germanic language they brought over with them when they migrated from northern Germany, and contained far fewer words "borrowed" from other languages like French and Latin than English does today. Word-nerds like us and the scholars we idolize call this "Old English." In 1066, when William the Conqueror "william-the-conquer"ed England, he brought over his own French dialect, resulting in a massive influx of French words into English and starting the next phase of the language, known as Middle English. Tolkien studied and wrote papers on both Old and Middle English, but is more well known for his work in Old English.

gives us the modern word for bear in Scandinavian languages like Swedish. The cognate[19] of *björn* in Old English was *beorn* (the name of the friendly fellow in Chapter 7).

And that would be interesting enough in and of itself, but it's more complicated than that, because, in Old English, *beorn* was *not* the common word for bear. *Beorn*, even though it came from the word *bear*, actually meant "warrior" or "hero." In Tolkien's story, Beorn is both of these things: a warrior and a bear. Tolkien combined the two diverging meanings of the root word into one character: a human *beorn* by day who transforms into a *björn* by night. According to Peter Gilliver, Jeremy Marshall, and Edmund Wiener— three lexicographers working for the *Oxford English Dictionary* who've analyzed the lexicographical aspects of Tolkien's work in their book *Ring of Words*—"the etymological ambivalence of Beorn's name is translated by Tolkien into narrative."[20] (It's perfectly okay to have your mind blown by stuff like this. We have a feeling it will happen a lot as you make your way through this book.)

This is just one particular example that we think is pretty amazing. *The Hobbit* is full of inspirations from Tolkien's day job, with allusions to everything from Old English and Middle English poetry to Norse eddas. For a more complete list, look for not only John Rateliff's *The History of The Hobbit* (mentioned previously), but also Douglas A. Anderson's *The Annotated Hobbit*.

And, as with most of the stories he wrote, Tolkien's Catholicism was a thread of influence as well. Cosmologically speaking, the world of Tolkien's

---

19  To word-nerds and the scholars we idolize, a *cognate* is a word derived from the same root as another word in another language, like *father* in English and *padre* in Spanish, both of which derive from a common ancient word for your old man that's been lost to time but was probably pronounced something like *peter. Think of them as the siblings and first-cousins-x-times-removed of the linguistic world. In some cases, two words that are cognate may have the same or similar meaning, but not always. In some cases, cognate words can develop opposite meanings, like English *black* and Spanish *blanco*. Linguistic etymology is a funny thing.

20  Peter Gilliver, Jeremy Marshall, and Edmund Weiner. *The Ring of Words: Tolkien and the Oxford English Dictionary.* Oxford University Press, 2009, 95.

legendarium is monotheistic, having a single eternal creator ("big G") God while functioning much like a polytheistic mythology, with lots of created angelic-type "demiurges" playing the role of "little G" gods.[21] Neither Tolkien's big-G God Eru Ilúvatar nor the little-g gods the Valar are ever named in *The Hobbit*, but there are aspects of the story that make it obvious divine powers are pulling the strings. The most obvious example may be the question of Bilbo's extraordinarily good luck: from the accidental winning of a riddle-game, along with a certain magic ring, from a particularly *nassssty* competitor to his party's good fortune in arriving at the Lonely Mountain at exactly the right time on exactly the right day to be able to find the astronomically aligned lock on the door, the characters of *The Hobbit* are profoundly lucky, to a degree that would have lots of ordinary people in the real world calling them up to pick lottery numbers. It honestly stretches believability at times, and in many a lesser story might have the reader rolling their eyes.

But Tolkien makes it work, partly because it's not hidden in the workings of the story; as "Tolkien Professor" Corey Olsen says in his book *Exploring J.R.R. Tolkien's The Hobbit*, "the narrator draws our attention to it quite forcefully on several occasions."[22] And not only does he make it work, but the more one reads, the more obvious it becomes that Bilbo's "luck" is actually something deeper: a special fate, the hand of providence. Bilbo turns out to be an agent of a master plan, fulfilling prophecies and allowing events to unfold in Middle-earth, in ways he doesn't quite understand, orchestrated (a deliberate word choice on our part; we'll get to that later) by the divine powers that move the world, right on up to big-G God Ilúvatar. It's not all explicit how and why things unfold the way they do, until one reads past *The Hobbit* into the other books of the legendarium, but it's all there in Bilbo's story...and the genius of Tolkien is that he makes it work as part of an excellent story, even for those who don't share in his Catholic faith.

We hope you'll agree with us, after all of this, that *The Hobbit* is no mere children's tale.

---

21    We'll cover this more fully in Chapter 3.

22    Olsen, Corey. *Exploring J.R.R. Tolkien's The Hobbit*. Mariner Books, 2012, 7.

## Noted. So What Happened Then?

Once he had a complete manuscript of *The Hobbit* written, Tolkien did the exact opposite of what most of us would do with our first children's book manuscript: he started showing it to his friends. One of these friends was C.S. Lewis, future author of The Chronicles of Narnia, fellow professor at Oxford, and de facto leader of the Inklings. Lewis would write in a 1933 letter to a friend about reading *The Hobbit* for the first time: "Since term I have had a delightful time reading a children's story which Tolkien has just written... Reading his fairy tale has been uncanny—it is so exactly like what we [would] both have longed to write (or read) in 1916: so that one feels he is not making it up but merely describing the same world into which all three of us have the entry. Whether it is really good (I think it is until the end) is of course another question: still more, whether it will succeed with modern children."[23]

Tolkien also showed the draft to another colleague, philologist Elaine Griffiths. Griffiths, as it turned out, had a book deal with a publishing house called George Allen & Unwin to revise a translation of *Beowulf*, and after a 1936 meeting with her publishers, connected her A&U rep Susan Dagnall to Ronald Tolkien for a copy of the book *he* was working on—a deflection trick we will certainly be trying the next time we're in trouble with a deadline. Dagnall visited Tolkien, read the story, and loved it...and on October 3, 1936, he sent a typescript copy to Allen & Unwin for consideration.

Sir Stanley Unwin (the Unwin of Allen & Unwin) handed the typescript to his ten-year-old son Rayner, who reviewed children's books for his father at the rate of one shilling per report (not quite four British pounds today). Young Rayner wrote, complete with pre-teen misspellings: "Bilbo Baggins was a hobbit who lived in his hobbit-hole and never went for adventures, at last Gandalf the wizard and his dwarves perswaded him to go. He had a very exiting time fighting goblins and wargs. at last they got to the lonley

---

23    Quoted in Rateliff, *The History of The Hobbit*, 2011, xvii.

Why We Love Middle-earth

mountain; Smaug, the dragon who gawreds it is killed and after a terrific battle with the goblins he returned home—rich!"[24] Then the boy added, with (we can only imagine) all the smug superiority of a kid who's just hit double digits himself, "This book, with the help of maps, does not need any illustrations it is good and should appeal to all children between the ages of 5 and 9." You know, *little* kids (sure, little Rayner).

The book was accepted for publication, and the rest, as they say, is history. *The Hobbit* was published on September 21, 1937, in an initial print run of 1,500 copies that sold so quickly that a second printing was needed before Christmas. It's so popular that it's been translated into over sixty languages as of the writing of this book. It's all very impressive, of course, but that would be the end of the story, if Allen & Unwin hadn't asked for a sequel.

## So, on to Frodo and the Fellowship?

Not quite. Because the revisions to *The Hobbit* didn't stop there. As Tolkien further developed the sequel to *The Hobbit* that we would eventually call *The Lord of the Rings*, he started realizing that there were changes he needed to make to *The Hobbit* to make it better fit the story as it was developing and aligning further with the mythological material from the First Age. He started making those changes in 1951 for what would become the second edition of the book, which makes first-edition *Hobbits* quite a prize among collectors. We'll talk more about those changes in detail when we get to the next chapter, but we want to point that out here because it's proof that Tolkien was retconning before it was cool.

Interestingly, Tolkien also started a from-the-beginning rewrite of *The Hobbit* in 1960, to retell the entire story in language not "overtly addressed

---

24    Quoted in Carpenter, *Biography*, 1977, 180-81. The fact that young Rayner Unwin struggled with the spellings of some common English words as seen in the excerpt above, but spelled *wizard, goblin,* and *warg* perfectly, puts him in the category of Kids We Would Be Proud to Call Our Son.

to children."[25] The idea would have been to tell the story in a more epic-fantasy style, consistent with *The Lord of the Rings*. But he gave up this endeavor quickly, "recognizing, perhaps, that for better or worse, he had created it as a children's book and a fairytale, and to make it otherwise would be to deny its essential nature and destroy much of its charm."

# So, Why Do We Love It?

Humphrey Carpenter described Tolkien himself in his authorized biography as "a man of antitheses." *The Hobbit* is a bit like that: a book of antitheses. It's a children's book filled with references to literary works found in graduate-level syllabuses. It's a lighthearted tale of adventure with a darkly tragic streak running through it. It's a standalone work that's perfect for introducing new readers to Tolkien's Middle-earth, with a few Easter eggs hidden within that will only be found by readers familiar with works published later on.

But what is it that ultimately makes it worth reading as an adult, or as a longtime fan of Middle-earth going back and rereading Tolkien's "grown-up" books again? Based on the conversations we've had with listeners of our podcast, the reasons to revisit *The Hobbit* are many: from the lighthearted tone and charming humor of the narration, to the intriguing interplay of fate and free will that drives Bilbo's adventures through his so-called "luck," to the non-sanitized fairy-tale sense of enchantment that pervades its most mysterious passages, to the "coming of age" quality of the story (despite the fact that its protagonist is actually fifty-one years old), to Bilbo himself: an everyman who finds his courage in the least likely places.

And also, there's a dragon in it.

---

25    Scull & Hammond, *Reader's Guide Part 1*, 2017, p. 397.

So, if you haven't already, pick up *The Hobbit* and give it a read. Or read it again. Join Bilbo as he walks out his front door into an adventure that will change his life, and the lives of his family and friends for generations to come...not to mention the fate of Middle-earth itself. We can't think of a better place to start your journey.

# WHY ALAN LOVES IT

The fantasy worlds I grew up with were set in space, not in Middle-earth: I grew up on the original *Star Trek*, and saw the first Star Wars film in a drive-in theater on my ninth birthday, just a couple of days after it debuted in 1977. I knew nothing of the Elves, Hobbits, or of Middle-earth, until one fateful day later that year when I sat down in front of my television set and was absolutely mesmerized by an animated story called *The Hobbit*. When I found out that this story was also a *book*, I knew what I wanted to find under my Christmas tree that year, and Santa happily obliged. I read that volume, complete with stills from the Rankin/Bass adaptation, over and over again until the binding failed. But—and this still makes me sad—I simply *did not know* that there were more stories set in this world.[26]

Bilbo's adventure intrigued nine-year-old me: the trolls, the stone-giants, the shapeshifting bear, the giant eagles, and the mighty dragon! I wanted to know more about *all* of them. I read and reread the story, filling in some of the gaps in my mind—developing a "head canon"—and just absorbing as much as I could of this charming story. Little did I know the impact that this time spent with Bilbo, Gandalf, Thorin, and the rest would have on the rest of my life.

---

26    Oddly, there was no "also by the author..." or "if you liked this, be sure to pick up..." at the back of the book.

# WHY SHAWN LOVES IT

I don't remember ever *not* being aware that there was a book called *The Hobbit*. Even in my youth, in the distant age of Trapper Keepers and *Garbage Pail Kids* (the 1980s, in the Shire Reckoning), I always knew *The Hobbit* was a thing. I'm sure my first exposure to the idea was a commercial for the 1977 Rankin/Bass adaptation, which for some reason didn't excite me...at least, not enough to put down my Star Wars action figures and actually watch the cartoon. But I had a vague awareness of the name "J.R.R. Tolkien," and a place called Middle-earth (which I assumed was underground—like the *middle* of the *earth*) that was the setting of some story or other...and there my knowledge stopped for many years.

Thanks to *Dungeons & Dragons*, I learned all about elves, dwarves, and halflings long before my tenth birthday, but I never actually read *The Hobbit*, even as my love for fantasy deepened through roleplaying games and the sword-and-sorcery movies of my childhood.

All that changed when I was fifteen, and I learned the story of how Professor Tolkien wrote the first sentence of *The Hobbit* on a student's exam book: a rebellious spark on the part of an otherwise diligent professor that started a fire. I was entranced by the idea that an errant word-doodle by a bored teacher could lead to the creation of an entire world, with books upon books of story to be discovered. I knew I must read this book, and so I went out and spent some saved-up allowance on a Ballantine paperback box set of *The Hobbit* and *The Lord of the Rings* (complete with legit '80s-style cover art).

I read *The Hobbit* in three days. I'm a slow reader, so reading a book that fast is, for me, a feat as epic as Bilbo's battle with the spiders of Mirkwood. From the very first pages I was hooked, and by the time Bilbo, Gandalf, Thorin, and company arrived at Elrond's Last Homely House in Chapter 3, I couldn't put it down. It's hard to say what really grabbed me. I certainly had no idea that I was taking my first steps onto a long road that would forever dominate my destiny (sorry, Star Wars references still creep into my writing sometimes).[27] But that's exactly what happened—though it's safe to say that *The Hobbit* really was a prelude to a much deeper enchantment that I would discover when I opened to the first page of the next book we'll be talking about.

---

27    *Alan:* he's not sorry.

# CHAPTER 2

# SEQUEL, SCHMEQUEL:
# *THE LORD OF THE RINGS*

*"One Ring to rule them all, One Ring to find them,*
*One Ring to bring them all and in the darkness bind them*
*In the Land of Mordor where the Shadows lie."*

—*J.R.R. Tolkien*, The Lord of the Rings, *Book I, Chapter 2,*
*"The Shadow of the Past"*[28]

It's the granddaddy of all fantasy novels, and generally seen as responsible more than any other for the vaguely Northern European look and feel that overlays the vast majority of high fantasy properties from books to video games to *Dungeons & Dragons*. Generations of high fantasy authors would go on to either be inspired by it, or attempt some grand refutation of it, from Terry Brooks and Terry Goodkind to Terry Pratchett (a lot of Terrys

---

28    Tolkien, J.R.R. *The Lord of the Rings; The Fellowship of the Ring.* HarperCollins, 2020, 51.

writing fantasy, aren't there?) and Ursula K. Le Guin, to Michael Moorcock and George "the Other" R.R. Martin. And it's safe to say there would be no Horcruxes in Harry Potter without Sauron's One Ring, no Dothraki language without two (arguably more) Elvish languages, and we'd like to think no grizzled old Ben Kenobi whispering wisdom to young Luke, even from beyond the grave for three episodes, without Gandalf doing pretty much the exact same thing to Frodo for three volumes.

But don't call it a trilogy—in fact, we'd like your help in making #NotaTrilogy trend. Tolkien intended *The Lord of the Rings* to be published as one book; it was only split into three by his publishers in order to sell them separately and recoup the costs of printing nearly 1,200 pages, an ungodly count for a novel in 1954. Based on the evidence of his letters, Tolkien struggled with the decision, especially with what to name each volume, before settling on the now-iconic titles *The Fellowship of the Ring*, *The Two Towers*, and *The Return of the King*. But there's no doubt that the three form a single story and must be read together, and that was intentional.

We know there's a lot to unpack there.

# THEN LET'S UNPACK IT

Indeed, we shall!

A few weeks after the publication of *The Hobbit*, Stanley Unwin of Tolkien's publishing house Allen & Unwin wrote to Tolkien in apparent excitement, saying that "a large public" would be "clamouring next year to hear more from you about Hobbits!"[29] (Yes, he used that exclamation point—and we're pretty sure that people in the 1930s tended to use exclamation points only when they were very, very excited about something.) It seems clear that

---

29   Carpenter, *Letters*, No. 17.

Allen & Unwin were ready for a sequel to the adventures of Mr. Bilbo Baggins, Esq., and had a very sly way of letting the Professor know this.

Tolkien wrote back to his publisher on October 15 of that year, in a letter published as Letter 17 in Humphrey Carpenter's *The Letters of J.R.R. Tolkien*. The professor was understandably quite happy about the overwhelmingly positive reaction to *The Hobbit*, but he was also "perturbed":

> I cannot think of anything more to say about hobbits. Mr Baggins seems to have exhibited so fully both the Took and the Baggins side of their nature. But I have only too much to say, and much already written, about the world into which the hobbit intruded. You can, of course, see any of it, and say what you like about it, if and when you wish. I should rather like an opinion, other than that of Mr. C.S. Lewis and my children, whether it has any value in itself, or as a marketable commodity, apart from hobbits. But if it is true that *The Hobbit* has come to stay and more will be wanted, I will start the process of thought, and try to get some idea of a theme drawn from this material for treatment in a similar style and for a similar audience—possibly including actual hobbits. My daughter would like something on the Took family. One reader wants fuller details about Gandalf and the Necromancer. But that is too dark...[30]

The above-mentioned "world into which the hobbit intruded" is that of *The Silmarillion*, the book that Tolkien really wanted to write. In this letter, he is clearly saying that he doesn't really *want* to write another book about hobbits (but hey, guys, uh...how about all that Gondolin stuff I mentioned writing a whole mythology about?) but, perhaps recognizing that publishing any book was better than publishing none, he basically said he'd see what he could come up with. But he didn't seem to want anything about Gandalf. Or the Necromancer in the south of Mirkwood, whom Gandalf dealt with

---

30    Ibid.

offstage during the important bits of Bilbo's story. I guess we'll see how well that ended up working out for him.

A month later (in November 1937), Tolkien delivered several manuscripts to Stanley Unwin in London for publication consideration. Among them were *Farmer Giles of Ham* (a fun short story about a farmer and a dragon, filled with tongue-in-cheek humor and linguistics jokes, because Tolkien), *The Lost Road* (an epic but unfinished time-travel story about genetic memory[31] and the myth of Atlantis)...and some of the manuscripts that would become *The Silmarillion*. But we don't mean a cleanly typed, nicely bound and formatted manuscript of that magnum opus in a fancy three-ring binder. Humphrey Carpenter describes the "Silmarillion"[32] material submission as:

> [a] bundle of manuscripts [that] had arrived in a somewhat disordered
> state, and the only clearly continuous section seemed to be the long
> poem 'The Gest of Beren and Lúthien'. So this poem was passed to a
> publisher's reader. The reader did not think much of it; in fact in his
> report was very rude about the rhyming couplets. But he hastened to
> say that he found the prose version of the Beren and Lúthien story
> enthralling—Tolkien had presumably attached it to the poem for the
> purpose of completing the story, for the poem itself was unfinished.[33]

---

31  The idea that memories can be inherited from birth from one generation to the next is like the Bene Gesserit "Other Memory" (for you *Dune* fans). In the case of *The Lost Road*, the genetic memory concerned the collapse of Atlantis, in the form of common dreams dreamed by a father and son for thousands of years throughout history down to the twentieth century. The story was never finished, but some of these ideas would find their way into Tolkien's legendarium in the form of the history of the island kingdom of Númenor, which Aragorn's remote ancestors ruled thousands of years before the events of *The Lord of the Rings*. It's also noteworthy that Tolkien himself had dreams of Atlantis for many years; something he called his "Atlantis-haunting"... and that, unbeknownst to him at the time he was writing *The Lost Road* or even *The Lord of the Rings*, these dreams were also shared by his son Michael.

32  Note: When italicized, *The Silmarillion* refers to the book edited by Christopher Tolkien and published in 1977. When speaking of the broad collection of manuscript material on the First Age from which Christopher Tolkien compiled the final book, we follow the younger Tolkien's own convention of calling it the "Silmarillion" (in quotation marks).

33  Carpenter, *Biography*, 1977, 183-84.

That unfinished "Gest" later became *The Lay of Leithian*, a long-form epic "lay" (lyrical poem telling a tale of adventure and romance, popular in the Middle Ages) about the obstacle-ridden love of a mortal Man and an Elvish woman, which preceded the more popular story of Aragorn and Arwen, and, in fact, is directly related to it within the universe. We'll talk more about it in Chapter 5. For now, it's enough to know that it was never finished, but that Tolkien fans today have the ability to read the *Lay* in as-close-to-its-entirety as Tolkien ever got it, because his son Christopher published it in the third volume of The History of Middle-earth series, collecting most of his father's unfinished Middle-earth works and commentaries.

Of course, in 1937, having just published the wildly successful tale of the exploits of a droll little three-foot-tall fellow with a long pipe and hairy toes, Tolkien's publishers were having none of it. In fact, it's probably fair to say that they weren't quite sure what to make of the "Gest," let alone the disordered bundle of papers full of backstory and world-building attached to it. But Stanley Unwin was apparently as supportive as he could be, graciously saying to Tolkien in a letter that "The Silmarillion contained 'plenty of wonderful material' which might be mined to produce 'further books like The Hobbit rather than a book in itself.' "[34] That's as kind a rejection as we can think of, really.

Tolkien, for his part, played it cool. He wrote back in December 1937 to explain that he never expected any of it to be published, really:

> I did not think any of the stuff I dropped on you filled the bill. But I did want to know whether any of the stuff had any exterior non-personal value. I think it is plain that quite apart from it, a sequel or successor to The Hobbit is called for. I promise to give this thought and attention. But I am sure you will sympathize when I say that the construction of elaborate and consistent mythology (and two languages) rather occupies the mind, and the Silmarils are in my heart. So that goodness knows what

---

34    Ibid., 184.

will happen. Mr Baggins began as a comic tale among conventional and inconsistent Grimm's fairy-tale dwarves, and got drawn into the edge of it—so that even Sauron the terrible peeped over the edge. And what more can hobbits do? They can be comic, but their comedy is suburban unless it is set against things more elemental. But the real fun about orcs and dragons (to my mind) was before their time.[35]

It's not entirely clear whether this was completely accurate, or a bit of posterior protection on Professor Tolkien's part. Despite his assertion that he didn't really expect any of the "Silmarillion" material to be fit for publication, as we will see, Tolkien never let go of the idea of having it published. As it stands, The Lord of the Rings is very much an exercise in the kind of "mining" Unwin recommended: using the stories of the "Silmarillion" material as backstory and legend behind another story more or less like The Hobbit (more at first, and less as it went on, it must be said). So from that perspective, Tolkien played the part of the obedient author and followed his publisher's recommendation. But from another perspective, it seems that Tolkien was never quite comfortable with The Lord of the Rings being the only window into those stories that his readers would ever get, and as his magnum opus took shape, as we will see, he did end up spending a great deal of time and energy trying to push for The Silmarillion to be published alongside it.

But that was all yet to come. In 1937, Tolkien was happy enough to try his hand at something with a bit more mainstream appeal. He even asked Unwin if Tom Bombadil of all people/things—at that time a whimsical character from a nonsense poem, another literary creation for his children based on one of their toys—"could be made into the hero of a story," which is a concept that intrigues us and sends us into uncontrollable fits of laughter.[36]

---

35   Carpenter, Letters, No. 19.

36   Ibid. Tom Bombadil would end up getting his "own book" in a sense, in 1962. However, The Adventures of Tom Bombadil is not quite Tom's own story but rather a collection of poems, two of which he features prominently in. The rest are an assortment of delightfully silly rhymes, meditations, and tongue-twisters meant to exemplify hobbit-poetry from the land of the Shire.

Perhaps it was this that prompted Tolkien to include Tom Bombadil in the eventual draft of *The Lord of the Rings*, where he never became much more than a whimsical character full of nonsense poetry, who has nonetheless managed to perplex readers and podcast listeners ever since. However it came about, Tolkien wrote back to his publisher again just a few days later to inform them that he had just begun work on—wait for it—a new book about hobbits.

And there was much rejoicing. (Yayyy.)

## Back to Hobbiton

The rejoicing by Allen & Unwin cooled pretty quickly...once Tolkien started writing, the actual completion of the manuscript took twelve years. Tolkien had a tendency to write in "waves": great big bursts of creative activity separated by breaks, often tied to the demands on his time of the academic year at Oxford. Tolkien being Tolkien, he stopped to restart and/or rewrite what he'd already written several times as well. According to Christopher Tolkien, writing in *The Return of the Shadow* (Book Six of The History of Middle-earth, and the first of four books in the series which focus on the composition and textual history of *The Lord of the Rings*), he went back and rewrote the first chapter of *The Lord of the Rings* a total of *three times* before the hobbits even got out of Hobbiton. But once he got past whatever block was troubling him there, he went on and wrote all the way up to Rivendell—what we would come to know in the finished publication as Book I and a bit of Book II—before "the impulse failed," and he would eventually go back and start again from the beginning.[37]

But let's not get the wrong idea from all of this. This "First Phase" of composition was structurally enough like the finished book to be

---

37    Tolkien, J.R.R., edited by Christopher Tolkien. *The Return of the Shadow* (*The History of Middle-earth, Vol. VI*), HarperCollins, 1988, 3.

recognizable; it's just not *quite* the story we would come to know and love. At first, the character we know as Frodo was named "Bingo Bolger-Baggins" (yes, you read correctly: Bingo was his name-o). Aragorn, first introduced to the hobbits as Strider, actually made his first appearance in this earliest draft as a world-weary, "queer-looking, brown-faced hobbit" ranger named Trotter (so named on account of the fact that he wore wooden shoes, a most un-hobbity thing with which to accessorize).

And yet, despite these often-hilarious differences in detail, the story was surprisingly consistent with the story that was later published. Take, for example, this passage from Chapter 10 of Book I in the published *The Lord of the Rings*, upon the meeting of Frodo and Strider:

> Frodo turned and looked at him thoughtfully, wondering about Gandalf's second postscript. 'Why didn't you tell me that you were Gandalf's friend at once?' he asked. 'It would have saved time.'
>
> 'Would it? Would any of you have believed me till now?' said Strider. 'I knew nothing of this letter. For all I knew I had to persuade you to trust me without proofs, if I was to help you. In any case, I did not intend to tell you all about myself at once. I had to study you first, and make sure of you. The Enemy has set traps for me before now. As soon as I had made up my mind, I was ready to tell you whatever you asked. But I must admit,' he added with a queer laugh, 'that I hoped you would take to me for my own sake. A hunted man sometimes wearies of distrust and longs for friendship. But there, I believe my looks are against me.'
>
> 'They are—at first sight at any rate,' laughed Pippin with sudden relief after reading Gandalf's letter. 'But handsome is as handsome does, as we say in the Shire; and I daresay we shall all look much the same after lying for days in hedges and ditches.'[38]

---

38    Tolkien, *Fellowship*, 2020, 171-72.

In *The Return of the Shadow*, the "first phase" form of this revelation appears like so:

> 'Well, I must admit I am glad to have a word from him,' said Bingo. 'And if you are a friend of Gandalf's then we are lucky to meet you. I am sorry if I was unnecessarily suspicious.'

> 'You weren't,' said Trotter. 'You weren't half suspicious enough. If you had had previous experience of your present enemy, you would not trust your own hands without a good look, once you knew that he was on your track. Now I am suspicious: and I had to make quite sure that you were genuine first, before handing over any letter. I've heard of shadow-parties picking up messages that were not meant for them—it has been done by enemies before now. Also, if you want to know, it amused me to see if I could induce you to take me on—just by my gifts of persuasion. It would have been nice (though quite wrong) if you had accepted me for my manners without testimonial! But there, I suppose my looks are against me!'

> 'They are!' said Odo laughing. 'But handsome is as handsome does, we say in the Shire, and anyway I daresay we shall all look much the same before long, after lying in hedges and ditches.'[39]

This is just one example, but it can be seen that the general structure, outcome, and even some dialogue (like Pippin's "hedges and ditches") existed in more or less their final form, even in the first draft. For what it's worth, it's not always this clear. A full history of the text has been painstakingly reconstructed by Christopher in the pages of The History of Middle-earth volumes VI-IX, and is well beyond our abilities to recapture here. But it's fascinating stuff: for our part, it reminds us that, however superhuman Tolkien's abilities as a writer may seem to wide-eyed fanboys like us, he

---

39    Tolkien, *Return of the Shadow*, 1988, 155.

Why We Love Middle-earth

revised and over-edited just like the rest of us. And frankly, it's at least as impressive that Christopher was able to make as much sense of it as he was.

Very early on, Tolkien had worked out in his mind that the plot of the new *Hobbit* book (as he was still thinking of it) was going to revolve around that little magic ring that Bilbo "found" (though Mr. S. Gollum may disagree on the correct verb to use here) in the caves below the Misty Mountains. He knew that the ring was going to be an artifact of much greater power and evil than originally envisioned, that it was going to be linked to the Necromancer whose fate was sealed offscreen by Gandalf and some unnamed friends during the timeline of *The Hobbit*, and that Bilbo would hand it off to an heir to get rid of it. In one very enticing note written early on, Tolkien wrote of the ring that "You must either lose it, or yourself."[40] This, of course, turned out to be a guiding theme of the story that was eventually published, and a central motif in Tolkien's sub-creation.

## Sub-What?

Sub-creation. Oh, yeah, we'd better pause to explain that before we go much further.

See, between the initial drafting of *The Hobbit* in the early 1930s and when *The Lord of the Rings* really got going at the end of the decade, he had been working at his day job. A lot. As we mentioned previously, he delivered a lecture on *Beowulf* in 1936 called "Beowulf: The Monsters and the Critics" which changed the nature of *Beowulf* studies to this day, and which would have secured his legacy anyway, even if he had never invented hobbits. In 1939, he delivered another very different lecture, called "On Fairy-stories," in which he discussed fairy tales as a literary form, and in the making essentially laid out his template for what makes a fantasy story "work." Among the

---

40   Ibid, 42.

criteria he called out as essential is the inner consistency of reality (i.e., it must be something that feels real to the reader, so that the reader may engage in "Secondary Belief"—none of that "suspension of disbelief" stuff that Samuel Taylor Coleridge wrote about, when he wasn't writing about mariners killing albatrosses.)[41] It must possess "arresting strangeness" (as we mentioned in the previous chapter), and many more criteria that frankly merit their own chapter, which we may or may not get to in this book.[42] But among the ideas discussed in "On Fairy-stories" is the idea of writing, or any artistic act, as an act of *sub-creation*.

In the lecture, though, this term is a bit of a loose thread; Tolkien doesn't explain in these pages his rationale for calling it "sub-creation" as opposed to simple "creation." That idea is more fully explored in a poem Tolkien wrote and dedicated to his friend C.S. Lewis called "Mythopoeia,"[43] which explains how human beings' desire to make up stories is a reflection of their own creation by God. But, as he hinted in the quote from the Waldman letter we just mentioned, Tolkien believed that only the divine creation was *true* Creation; anything created by him as a human (and anything created by the characters in his stories, from the little-g gods called the Valar, to Sauron and his jewelry projects, to the Dwarves and their amazing mithril coats, to Mrs. Maggot's delicious mushroom and bacon dinners) is subordinate to that true Creation; thus, sub-creation. In many ways, *The Lord of the Rings* was an exercise in putting into practice many of the ideas of fantasy and heroic literature that Tolkien explored in these two lectures, which may be why it feels so much more immersive and real to most readers than *The Hobbit*.

Certainly, the "inner consistency of reality" Tolkien spoke of in "On Fairy-stories" was achieved to a much greater degree than previously, and much of this has to do with the way Tolkien leaned into the "Silmarillion" material,

---

41 A reference we will forever be indebted to the '80s metal band Iron Maiden for explaining to us.

42 Most likely *not*, but have a listen to the very first episode of *The Prancing Pony Podcast* where we discussed this essay/lecture in detail.

43 The poem was in fact inspired by a conversation between Tolkien and Lewis in 1931.

Why We Love Middle-earth

"mining" it, as Stanley Unwin suggested, to provide depth, history, and backstory for the world. Much like the Necromancer and the swords of Gondolin popping up in *The Hobbit*, references to tales from his decades-old mythology began appearing in the nascent text of *The Lord of the Rings;* but this time around Tolkien was deliberate about linking back to the mythology he had been writing. Instead of using the mythology to provide a few interesting Easter eggs that ultimately didn't impact the larger story, as he had in *The Hobbit*, the references to the larger mythology in *The Lord of the Rings* are signposts of a much deeper story below the surface. Now, the wise "Elrond the master of the house" who aided Thorin and company on their quest to retake the Lonely Mountain became the son of one of the most important—but also most mysterious—heroes of the First Age, Eärendil the Mariner, and one of an ancient line of heroes descended from both Men and Elves, with even a little divine blood in the mix. The Men of the once-great realm of Gondor, we are told in *The Lord of the Rings*, are descended from the humans who allied with the Elves in the wars of the First Age (though the story in between, the tale of Númenor—so frequently referred to as "Westernesse" in *The Lord of the Rings*—was a later addition to the "Silmarillion" material). And the romance of Aragorn—himself a descendant of the Men of Númenor—and Elrond's daughter Arwen is both a sequel to, and practically a nostalgia reboot of, the tale of Beren and Lúthien, the most personal to Tolkien of all the early stories of the legendarium.

And, as he continued to write, the world of "the Silmarillion" which his publishers emphatically labeled "not ready for prime time" began to break through more and more. Need a supremely terrifying baddie to inhabit an abandoned Dwarf ruin beneath the mountains? How about a Balrog, one of Morgoth's[44] old special forces troopers still hanging around for thousands of years after the First Age? And that beautiful, otherworldly Elf-queen hiding in the enchanted forest? Yeah, we'll make her a former princess of the Noldor. The guy who made the titular Rings, too (not counting the One): he's not just

---

44   Who's Morgoth, you ask? Oh, just wait for the next chapter.

any Noldorin prince, but the grandson of, like, the greatest Elven smith who ever lived, who, by the way, just happened to make the magic jewels that the "Silmarillion" is named for... so, uh, Allen & Unwin, are you sure you don't want to publish both books together?

## Keep Trying, Professor...

Oh, he tried. But in the meantime, he kept on working on *The Lord of the Rings*, which along the way turned out to be two things he hadn't expected: for starters, it was a much more "mature" book than the previous one. By the time Tolkien reached the end of Book IV (that's four of six, the end of *The Two Towers*), he realized that his original ideas for the end of the book were too "juvenile," and would have to be reworked. Without a doubt, the stakes do get much higher—*The Lord of the Rings* is a sober meditation on temptation and corruption, the nature of evil, the destructive impact of war on the earth and its people, and the decline of human civilization, with the world itself hanging in the balance. This is much headier stuff than the "there and back again" jaunt to help a few vagabond Dwarves regain their lost treasure that is *The Hobbit*.

But this more mature work of fiction was turning out to be much longer than Tolkien had ever expected, too. He got through most of the first book (that's Book I of Six within *The Fellowship of the Ring*—splitting the single novel into separate volumes would come later) by the fall of 1938, before going back and making some changes. Still, he thought he was close to finishing. In February 1939, Tolkien sent a letter to his publishers saying he thought he could put a few things in his life on the back burner in an effort to finish the new book off by June.[45] "I think I shall make a special effort, at the expense of other duties, to finish it off before June 15." He must have been assuming that Mount Doom was a bit closer than it ended up being—his mistake was to our

---

45    This projection, now hilarious in hindsight, can be found in Carpenter's *Letters of J.R.R. Tolkien* in Letter 36.

Why We Love Middle-earth

benefit, because there ended up being a lot more story to tell. By December 1939, he had only gotten as far as Moria, and had to take a break.

These sorts of starts and stops (with a lot of communication back-and-forth to his publishers at Allen & Unwin) would continue until 1948—a full twelve years after he started writing what started out as a slightly darker sequel to *The Hobbit*.[46] By that time, the original readers of the adventures of Bilbo, assuming they were in Rayner Unwin's target demo of children aged five to nine, would have been between seventeen and twenty-one. When all was said and done, it's probably a very good thing that the new book took on a much darker epic-fantasy tone than its predecessor did, because it's hard to imagine those now-adult readers getting quite as into the adventures of Bingo and Trotter, many of them having got jobs and families and having lived through (and many of them having fought in) another world war in the interval.

The reasons for Tolkien's lengthy writing process were many, according to his biographer Humphrey Carpenter. He was a perfectionist, for starters, and according to Carpenter "felt he must ensure that every single detail fitted satisfactorily into the total pattern. Geography, chronology, and nomenclature all had to be entirely consistent."[47] He was also spending a great deal of time on his invented languages, primarily the Elvish languages Quenya and Sindarin, which had been the impetus for creating his grand mythology in the first place (more on this next chapter). And, like any writer worth his salt, he got sidetracked by other projects, including an aborted attempt at a standalone time-travel novel of Númenor, and completed fan-favorite short story "Leaf by Niggle," which was in many ways a mirror into Tolkien's own sub-creative process. So we're certainly not complaining about it taking him so long to finish *The Lord of the Rings*, especially not now that so much of this other stuff (even the incomplete drafts) has been published

---

46   Readers interested in learning all about this in detail should listen to Episode 93 of *The Prancing Pony Podcast*, and pick up Volumes VI-IX of The History of Middle-earth, where Christopher Tolkien discusses the textual history in exhaustive detail.

47   Carpenter, *Biography*, 1977, 194.

posthumously. And of course, it was his perfectionism (or "niggling") that made the world of Middle-earth so much more real for us.

And, by this time, World War II was in full swing. Though Tolkien's oldest son John trained for the priesthood during the war, his two younger sons Michael and Christopher both served in the military during this time. The fates of his sons were also clearly weighing heavily on Tolkien's mind, if the number of letters he wrote to his boys while they were away is any indicator: in Carpenter's *Letters* volume, the vast majority of Tolkien's letters published in the compendium for the years 1940 to 1941 were to Michael, who was serving as an anti-aircraft gunner. Similarly, *virtually all* of the letters published in the volume for the period of late 1943 to late 1945 were to Christopher—more than fifty letters in this roughly two-year period to his son that we know about, and only a few in that time period to anyone else, like his publishers at Allen & Unwin. As fathers ourselves, whose sons are nowhere near fighting age yet, we can only imagine what he must have been feeling...and how it must have weighed on his soul.

Through all of this, Tolkien continued to stay in touch with his publishers. He gave another extremely optimistic estimate to Allen & Unwin in early 1945, saying that he'd probably get it done in about three weeks, "with nothing else to do—and a little rest and sleep first."[48] We'll give you two guesses whether he met that target or not, and the first guess won't count. But he also kept subtly-not-subtly hinting to his publishers that what he really wanted to publish was *The Silmarillion*—alongside *The Lord of the Rings*, perhaps, but certainly not the latter without the former. Frankly, we think the old Professor deserves a heap of credit for taking Stanley Unwin's words to heart about "mining" the "Silmarillion" material for *The Lord of the Rings* at all, when he so clearly wanted to just publish the First Age material on its own.

---

48    Carpenter, *Letters*, No. 98.

Finally, in February 1950, Tolkien wrote to Unwin to inform him that *The Lord of the Rings* had finally been completed ("if still partially unrevised," he said). But he was beginning to try a new tactic in luring Unwin into publishing it alongside *The Silmarillion.* The tactic? Self-deprecation.

And now I look at it [*it* being the finished typescript of *The Lord of the Rings*], the magnitude of the disaster is apparent to me. My work has escaped from my control, and I have produced a monster: an immensely long, complex, rather bitter, and very terrifying romance, quite unfit for children (if fit for anybody); and it is not really a sequel to *The Hobbit,* but to *The Silmarillion...* [which has] bubbled up, infiltrated, and probably spoiled everything (that even remotely approached 'Faery') which I have tried to write since.

It has captured *The Lord of the Rings,* so that that has become simply its continuation and completion, requiring the *Silmarillion* to be fully intelligible—without a lot of references and explanations that clutter it in one or two places.

Ridiculous and tiresome as you may think me, I want to publish them both—*The Silmarillion* and *The Lord of the Rings*—in conjunction or in connexion.[49]

Very smooth, Professor.

See, Tolkien had (according to famed Tolkien chroniclers Wayne G. Hammond and Christina Scull, in their *The Lord of the Rings: A Reader's Companion*) spent the last twelve years not just writing, teaching, and worrying about the war (and, you know, sleeping and eating and all that), but also getting progressively angrier at Allen & Unwin for "rejecting" *The*

---

49  Carpenter, *Letters,* No. 124.

*Silmarillion.*[50] By now, Tolkien was actively trying to talk Allen & Unwin out of publishing any of it, because he had found someone else who had expressed an interest in publishing both, to his preferences. Enter Milton Waldman.

Milton Waldman worked for another publishing house, the Scottish firm William Collins, Sons.[51] He was introduced to Tolkien through a mutual friend and expressed an interest in publishing the sequel to the wildly popular *The Hobbit.* So, when he asked Tolkien to send him a manuscript for his review, Tolkien sent him...*The Silmarillion.* And believe it or not, Waldman ate it up. "It was like nothing else Waldman had ever seen," Carpenter writes, "a strange archaically worded tale of Elves, evil powers, and heroism." Some of it was typed, but much was in finely lettered manuscript.[52] Waldman told Tolkien he would love to publish it, if he could finish it, and if he had no "commitment" to Allen & Unwin to let them publish it. After informing Waldman that he had, in his eyes, no "legal" obligation, but perhaps a "moral" one, from which he would try to remove himself, he told him that, if he could talk Allen & Unwin out of publishing *The Lord of the Rings,* he would do it.

This kicked off a round of back-and-forth between Tolkien, Unwin, and Waldman, which lasted a little over a year. It's quite comical to read now, in the pages of the *Letters* and Carpenter's *Biography,* and we've discussed it quite a bit on *The Prancing Pony Podcast.* At one point in spring of 1950, Tolkien gave Unwin an ultimatum: agree to publish them both immediately, or he would walk. Unwin's answer was a reluctant no. Apparently publishers don't like it when you hold their feet to the fire.[53]

---

50    In reality the publishers had done no such thing. According to Humphrey Carpenter, they'd merely said (repeatedly) that *The Silmarillion* was not the *Hobbit* sequel they were looking for.

51    Incidentally, the "Collins" in the name of the modern publishing house HarperCollins, which publishes Tolkien's works today. Collins merged with the American publisher Harper & Row in 1990. The same year, Unwin Hyman (itself formed from a merger of Allen & Unwin and Bell & Hyman in 1986) was sold to HarperCollins as well.

52    Carpenter, *Biography,* 1977, 208.

53    To our publishers: We'll be good. We promise.

Why We Love Middle-earth

But as it turned out, Waldman was starting to have some ideas of his own. For starters, he wanted *The Lord of the Rings* substantially cut, which Tolkien wasn't too keen to do. Secondly, he wanted Tolkien to finish the nowhere-near-ready-for-prime-time *Silmarillion* soon, so they could both be published. And for a third, when Tolkien informed Waldman that *The Silmarillion* was nowhere near completion, as he'd projected it to be almost as long as *The Lord of the Rings* when all was said and done, Waldman was confused to say the least...and apparently publishers don't like it when writers confuse them, either.[54]

By March 1952, there was still no agreement inked with Collins, and Tolkien wrote to Collins demanding an answer, yes or no (because it had worked so well with Stanley Unwin). The answer, unsurprisingly, was no—not just because they didn't want their feet held to the fire, either; the cost of paper had gone up in the postwar period, and they were quite nervous about the length of these two books together. After a solid two years, Tolkien had nothing to show for his gambit and was no closer to publishing either of his masterworks. But around that time, he received a letter from Rayner Unwin—all grown up now—inquiring about one of his poems, and just sorta checking in friendly-like to see the progress on those *Hobbit* books. Tolkien wrote back in June of 1952:

> As for *The Lord of the Rings* and *The Silmarillion*, they are where they were. The one finished (and the end revised), and the other still unfinished (or unrevised), and both gathering dust... But I have rather modified my views. Better something than nothing! Although to me all are one, and the 'L of the Rings' would be better far (and eased) as part of the whole, I would gladly consider the publication of any part of this stuff. Years are becoming precious... When I have a moment to turn round I will collect the *Silmarillion* fragments in process of completion—or rather the original outline which is more or less

---

54   To our publishers: See previous footnote.

complete, and you can read it... But what about *The Lord of the Rings*?
Can anything be done about that, to unlock gates I slammed myself?[55]

Humphrey Carpenter sums up the response best: "Rayner Unwin did not
need to be asked twice."[56]

# SO, MISSION ACCOMPLISHED?

Well...not quite.

Allen & Unwin agreed to publish the book, but there were—insert Robin
Williams's Genie voice from Disney's *Aladdin*—"a few, uh, provisos, a couple
of quid pro quos." As we noted above, the price of paper was quite high
at the time, and publishing a book that long was a risky proposition for the
publisher. But they were really keen on *The Lord of the Rings* (and more than
happy to have it without any ultimatums from some presumptuous Oxford
professor), so they gladly took the deal, under the condition that the book
be separated into—you guessed it—three volumes, each sold for the price
of a standalone book. Which may seem perfectly natural to us now, because
*The Lord of the Rings* has been considered a *horrified gasp* "trilogy" by
casual readers and filmgoers ever since. But this is where it started. Professor
Tolkien never envisioned his book as a trilogy, and—while we hesitate to
come across as gatekeepers in any way, shape, or form—most Tolkien fans
eventually come to view it as Tolkien intended: as a single novel.

Tolkien was so dead-set against the idea of the book being published as a
trilogy that, for a long time, he resisted Rayner Unwin's provocations to give
each volume his own title. He originally wanted the six books to have titles
which would be printed on the cover like so: *The Lord of the Rings, Volume*

---

55   Carpenter, *Letters*, No. 133.
56   Carpenter, *Biography*, 1977, 213.

Why We Love Middle-earth

1, *The Ring Sets Out and the Ring Goes South*. Rather a mouthful, not to mention hard to fit on a book cover along with any kind of art. So, eventually, Rayner Unwin convinced Tolkien to give each volume its own title, and after a fair bit of back-and-forth, the two came up with the three titles we know today: *The Fellowship of the Ring*, *The Two Towers*, and *The Return of the King*.[57]

The first of the newly defined volumes, *Fellowship*, was published on July 29, 1954, with only 4,500 copies ordered for the first print run. Allen & Unwin thought this would be enough for the "moderate interest" (according to Carpenter) they expected in the new book...but as it turned out, just as with *The Hobbit*, demand exceeded their expectations. A second printing was ordered only six weeks after the initial publication of *Fellowship*. It seems Tolkien and the folks at Allen & Unwin had another hit on their hands; and the rest, as they say, is history.[58]

# SPEAKING OF HISTORY...

During the writing of *The Lord of the Rings*, as the story developed in Tolkien's mind, he gradually began to realize that the simple tale of how Bilbo found the ring (not yet capitalized) in the published edition of *The Hobbit* simply wouldn't suffice. Fine for a simple invisibility ring, perhaps; but not sufficient for an artifact of evil crafted by the Necromancer, who would become an embodiment of evil and a tyrannical Dark Lord, former lieutenant of Morgoth (who had been in Tolkien's mind for decades, as we'll discuss in the next chapter). As early as the second phase of writing, when

---

57  Tolkien actually preferred *The War of the Ring* for the third volume instead of *The Return of the King*, on account of the pretty obvious spoiler in the title. But he eventually relented, wanting to just see the blasted thing in print. *The War of the Ring* would eventually become the title given by Christopher Tolkien to the volume of The History of Middle-earth that covers the draft manuscripts for much of what would become part of the third volume.

58  *The Two Towers* had a similar initial print run of 4,250 when it was published on November 11, 1954, though *The Return of the King* ended up with a much larger initial print run of 12,000 when it was released on October 20, 1955.

Tolkien went back and rewrote some of his earliest drafts of Book I of *The Lord of the Rings* (when Frodo is just making his way to Rivendell), Tolkien realized that the story of the Ring's previous owner Gollum would need to be substantially rewritten, to make the creature much more corrupted and contemptible than he had been in the original story. These changes originally started making their way into the draft of *The Lord of the Rings* in the second chapter, originally titled "Ancient History" but now part of the chapter we know as "The Shadow of the Past." In these revisions, Gollum's dark past was discussed in grave detail so as to set up the murderous, treacherous, and ultimately irredeemable (though he is so close at times—no spoilers here) creature that would provide much of the conflict to Frodo's storyline. But in so doing, it became painfully obvious to Tolkien that some changes would have to be made to Gollum's previous incarnation in Chapter 5 of *The Hobbit*, the chapter titled "Riddles in the Dark," as well.

Douglas A. Anderson, editor of *The Annotated Hobbit*, explains the changes in a footnote to this chapter in *The Hobbit*: "As Tolkien wrote the sequel, *The Lord of the Rings*, he found it necessary to revise *The Hobbit* in order to bring it in line with the sequel. The portrayal of Gollum has been substantially altered; in the first edition [published in 1937] he is not nearly as wretched a creature. And the stakes of the riddle contest are slightly different: It was still Bilbo's life if he lost, but if he won, Gollum would give him a present."[59]

If you guessed that that present was round, gold, and roughly hobbit-finger-sized, then you're spot on. And if you know the story well enough to wonder how Gollum could ever willingly give away his precious, the Horcrux-like (sorry, Rowling; Tolkien did it first) piece of the Dark Lord's fallen but immortal soul that eroded Gollum's will and identity for five centuries, reducing him to an addict craving only a sight of his favorite fix, to a wandering hobbit as a reward for winning a riddle contest...well, then perhaps you understand why Tolkien had to make those changes to

---

59    Tolkien, J.R.R., edited by Douglas A. Anderson. *The Annotated Hobbit*. Houghton Mifflin, 2002, 128.

Why We Love Middle-earth

*The Hobbit*. As first published, Gollum was all too ready to kill and eat our little hobbit hero Bilbo, but still, in the words of Tolkien scholars Scull and Hammond, "nonetheless treats the riddle contest as sacred; and when he loses and cannot give Bilbo the present he had promised him (the magic ring that confers invisibility), he apologizes and shows the hobbit a way out of the caverns."[60]

You read that right. *He apologizes and shows Bilbo the way out of the caverns*. None of that "thief, we hates it" stuff we see in the later edition.

The new Gollum was first introduced to readers with the 1951 printing of *The Hobbit*, in which we see the Gollum we know and love/loathe: he offers to show Bilbo the way out if he wins, but when Bilbo does win, Gollum attempts to go invisible and kill him. And needless to say, he certainly doesn't want to give his "precious" to the nasssty hobbit. Not wanting to see fourteen years of published books suddenly become obsolete, though, Tolkien came up with an absolute stroke of genius. From the beginning, Tolkien had (with his tongue firmly in his cheek) presented *The Hobbit* not as his original creation, but a translation of an ancient manuscript that he had discovered.[61] Tolkien would end up doubling down on this blink-and-you-miss-it frame narrative in *The Lord of the Rings*, but for future editions of *The Hobbit*, the party line would be that the first edition had published a false version of the story which had been told by Bilbo to his friends and written in his memoirs; the story now told in the 1951-and-forward editions of *The Hobbit* was the truth.

In other words, Bilbo lied. The Ring—no longer just a piece of magic jewelry but a soul-corrupting artifact of evil—had sunk its metaphorical claws into Bilbo from the moment he'd found it, and it caused him to lie to his friends about how it had come into his possession.

---

60   Scull & Hammond, *Reader's Guide Part 1*, 2017, 525.

61   For example, the dust jacket of the first edition of *The Hobbit* featured this inscription in runes around the border: "*The Hobbit or There and Back Again*, being the record of a year's journey made by Bilbo Baggins of Hobbiton, compiled from his memoirs by J.R.R. Tolkien and published by George Allen and Unwin Ltd."

Tolkien even addressed this brilliant little retcon in the prologue to *The Lord of the Rings*, in a section titled "Of the Finding of the Ring" that serves as a kind of "Last Season on..." for readers entering Middle-earth for the first time. After relaying the version of the story that we know from the 1951 *Hobbit* and everything since, Tolkien writes in the prologue:

> Now it is a curious fact that this is not the story as Bilbo first told it to his companions. To them his account was that Gollum had promised to give him a present, if he won the game; but when Gollum went to fetch it from his island he found the treasure was gone: a magic ring, which had been given to him long ago on his birthday... This account Bilbo set down in his memoirs, and he seems never to have altered it himself, not even after the Council of Elrond. Evidently it still appeared in the original Red Book [of Westmarch; the fictional multi-volume manuscript written by Bilbo, Frodo, and the other Hobbits and from which Tolkien "translated" all of these stories], as it did in several of the copies and abstracts. But many copies contain the true account (as an alternative), derived no doubt from notes by Frodo or Samwise, both of whom learned the truth, though they seem to have been unwilling to delete anything actually written by the old hobbit himself.[62]

In our humble opinions, this deserves an Ent-sized round of applause.

There were other changes made to the original text of *The Hobbit* at this time as well, all generally in the spirit of leaning into the newly expanded world of Middle-earth that took shape beneath Tolkien's pen during the drafting of *The Lord of the Rings*. A few references to the earlier mythology were fleshed out or revised to make them more consistent with the now-developed lore—such as changing the reference to the "Gnomes" of Gondolin to the "High Elves" (yes, they were originally called Gnomes). And the more Tolkien leaned into his fantasy sub-creation, the more he sought to

---

62    Tolkien, *Fellowship*, 2020, 13.

make it feel internally consistent, and remove it from our world: so an early reference to "tomatoes" (a New World crop) in *The Hobbit* was changed (in a still later edition) to "pickles," a vegetable preparation known in the Old World. Strangely, references to another New World crop, tobacco, remained throughout *The Hobbit* referred to as "tobacco"—despite Tolkien's insistence on almost universally referring to the Halflings' leaf as "pipe-weed" throughout the text of *The Lord of the Rings*.[63]

## Oh, Yeah. Pipe-Weed. What's Up with That, Anyway?

Despite what you may have read on the internet, or inferred from certain admittedly hilarious scenes in Peter Jackson's movies, it's tobacco. Nothing more or less than that.

How do we know, you may ask?

For starters, Tolkien smoked a pipe. According to Carpenter's *Biography*, he traced his own "addiction" (his word) to his childhood guardian Father Francis Morgan, who would hang around the oratory smoking a large cherrywood pipe.[64] And he smoked tobacco in it. We even know his favorite tobacco, thanks to an invoice from the smoke shop in Dorset he frequented during the last years of his life which was sold at an auction (yes, Tolkien fans will buy *anything* with his autograph on it).[65]

---

63  References in *The Hobbit* to modern games like "golf" and "football" were also retained, adding to *The Hobbit's* generally more colloquial, informal, and modern feel while still being more or less consistent with the world of *The Lord of the Rings*. These references generally can be seen as "Tolkien the translator" coming through, and relating the source material of the Red Book of Westmarch to his twentieth-century audience, but they nonetheless have led to a lot of spirited discussion and excitement among longtime Tolkien fans.

64  Carpenter, *Biography*, 1977, 30.

65  Capstan Medium Navy Cut. And he was apparently late in paying for it.

And he really loved smoking. In a 1966 interview with the *Daily Telegraph* magazine, he was recorded as saying, "Every morning I wake up thinking, 'Good, another 24 hours' pipe-smoking.' "[66] He was even smoking during the interview (not so strange for the sixties, perhaps)—which Tolkien apologized for in a 1967 letter to the authors of the article,[67] as it apparently made understanding his responses rather difficult. So it stands to reason that he would make one of his own favorite hobbies a favorite hobby of Middle-earth as well.

And, besides all that, *he told us so.* No less than four times in *The Hobbit*, the leaf Bilbo smokes is referred to as "tobacco." The word "tobacco" also appears twice in *The Lord of the Rings*: once in the text itself, and once in the Prologue...though he does usually refer to it as "pipe-weed." Elsewhere in the Prologue, he says pipe-weed was "a variety probably of *Nicotiana*," which is the genus that contains various species of tobacco plants, but not cannabis.

We think the Cheech and Chong stuff with Merry and Pippin in the movies is funny, too, but there's really no question about this: pipe-weed is tobacco, nothing more, nothing less. Whether that's a relief or a disappointment is entirely up to you.

But we digress. Back to *The Lord of the Rings*, and the all-important question:

# SO, WHY DO WE LOVE IT?

Well, we're pretty sure you're reading *this* book (and if you're not, who are we addressing right now? Spooky!), which means it's almost certain that you've either read, or heard of, or viewed some blockbuster media with

---

66  Charlotte and Denis Plimmer, "The Man Who Understands Hobbits," *The Daily Telegraph Magazine*, March 22, 1968.

67  As noted in previous footnote, Charlotte and Denis Plimmer, and the letter as published in Carpenter's *Letters* collection is 294. The article was published on March 22, 1968: "The Man Who Understands Hobbits."

the name *The Lord of the Rings* on it. You don't need us to tell you that Tolkien's not-a-trilogy became a sensation. It was published to generally positive reviews, though a few of his Oxford colleagues said things to him like, "Now we know what you have been doing all these years!" (according to Humphrey Carpenter) and expressed relief that Ronald would now be getting back to some real work.[68] It's safe to say that, thanks to his academic work (particularly the *Beowulf* lecture/essay we mentioned in the previous chapter), Tolkien would have secured his legacy amongst a more selective group of individuals who study medieval English literature. But it was the sensation that *The Lord of the Rings* became that made him a household name.

And it remains a sensation today as of the publication of this book, with a new streaming series out (and more adaptations on the way), games, fan clubs, literary societies, annual conventions, and more. A 1997 readers' poll conducted by Waterstones bookshops and BBC Channel Four found *The Lord of the Rings* named the greatest book of the twentieth century.[69]

If you are reading this and are already a Tolkien fan, it's likely the reason you are a Tolkien fan too. Even if you're not a Tolkien fan yet, we are willing to bet that the reason you know about Tolkien's work—and take it seriously as a work of modern fantasy—is because of *The Lord of the Rings*. It's certainly the book that made both of us Tolkien fans. Nothing against *The Hobbit*, but we (and much of the world) would not have become Tolkien fans if

---

68 In reality the Professor was incredibly busy with his day job, despite his side hustle, as a quick glance through Christina Scull and Wayne G. Hammond's *Chronology* will quickly show. These two unparalleled Tolkien chroniclers have assembled a seemingly exhaustive list of the many lectures, faculty meetings, research projects, and more that occupied the Professor's daily life. So take that, Oxford scholars!

69 This wasn't a decision that was universally praised or agreed with. Prominent Tolkien scholar Tom Shippey, who wrote about the phenomenon in his 2000 book *J.R.R. Tolkien: Author of the Century*, recalled a story from a London *Sunday Times* reporter who relayed the response of a colleague who had just been told that *The Lord of the Rings* had won the award. The response: "Oh hell! Has it? Oh my God. Dear oh dear. Dear oh dear oh dear." Shippey himself received some backlash for the title of his book, as he would later recall in a BBC Radio Four interview—of a "distinguished professor of literature" shouting about his title over the phone, *"Author of the Century?* Has the fellow never heard of Proust?" Shippey's response as relayed in the interview was "Well yes, the fellow has heard of Proust, actually. Shall we conduct the rest of this interview in French? I bet mine's much better than yours, you monoglot clown."

not for this book. And it is absolutely certain that everything else we know about Tolkien's Middle-earth that's been published in over a dozen volumes and counting since the author's death—from *The Silmarillion* to *The Fall of Númenor* and whatever else may come next—would never have seen the light of day if not for the writing, publication, and spectacular success of *The Lord of the Rings.*

It is the magnum opus, without question. It is the book that, to many people, gives the fantasy universe its name. To our friends in the Tolkien fan community, we are known as podcasters who talk about the "Middle-earth legendarium." But when our cousins and old friends from high school ask what we're up to, we tend to say "a *Lord of the Rings* podcast." And of course, it is the book whose title Amazon Prime has placed in front of the proper title of its new series: *The Lord of the Rings: The Rings of Power,* even though the events of the series take place thousands of years before Bilbo's eleventy-first birthday.

We aren't gatekeepers, and we won't say who is and is not a "Tolkien fan." But from our point of view, it's impossible to really become an appreciator of Tolkien's writing without having read *The Lord of the Rings.* It's not a quick read, but we think you'll find it goes much faster than you think it will when you first behold its thousand pages (plus appendices).

So read it. What have you got to lose?

Read it aloud if you can. Savor it. Listen along with a favorite podcast if you like.

Read the appendices. You'll be glad you did.

Don't skip the poetry. There's a lot of it, and you'll be tempted to skip it, but trust us on this.

This is *The Lord of the Rings*. It is worth your time.

# WHY ALAN LOVES IT

When I explained why I loved *The Hobbit*, I mentioned that when I finished reading it in the first few days of 1978, I didn't know that this J.R.R. Tolkien fellow had written anything else. Thanks to a copy of *The Hobbit* that lacked a section of "Also From the Author," a somewhat culturally isolated youth, and a serious case of shyness,[70] I had no clue that Middle-earth contained other stories. In fact, I didn't even know that Bilbo's world was *called* "Middle-earth."

Fast-forward to the start of my freshman year in high school (1982, for those trying to do the math): I was still a full-blown sci-fi nerd (the *Battlestar Galactica* series, *The Empire Strikes Back*, and the first two *Star Trek* films were my schtick) when I ended up playing D&D for the first time with some friends. When "halflings" were mentioned, I thought back to Bilbo's story and said something like, "These are just *hobbits*, who do they think they're kidding?" That led to a conversation in which I learned of the existence of *three* more incredible books set in the same world. I checked out *Fellowship* from our school library and, a week later, spent my paper route money on a box set of my own, devouring the books in around a week before starting them over again—in what would become an annual tradition of reading *The Lord of the Rings*. Dwarven runes and Elvish script graced my Pee-Chee folders throughout high school, leading inevitably to my becoming the most popular student in my school.[71] With every reading, I fell deeper in love with Middle-earth and was determined to learn more. I pored over the appendices, studying Tolkien's languages (as much as was possible with those limited sources), committing entire family trees to memory, and becoming engrossed in the stories behind *The Lord of the Rings*. This time, the

---

70   Since overcome sufficiently to host a podcast.

71   It is quite possible that I am confusing what *should* have been with what actually *was*.

existence of other books was clear, so I tried *The Silmarillion*, but bounced off of it every time I tried. So I returned to the comfort of the Third Age, year after year...but the deeper legendarium still called.

# WHY SHAWN LOVES IT

As recounted in the previous chapter, my first experience of Tolkien's writing was through a box set of *The Hobbit* and *The Lord of the Rings* (and you really have to see that '80s cover art). I read *The Hobbit* quickly, and went straight on into *The Lord of the Rings* as soon as I was done. So, to be fair, it's hard to separate my initial impressions of the two books, as they were one experience in many ways.

I know I was in love with *The Lord of the Rings* pretty much from the get-go. Here was a book that really delivered on the kind of fantasy stuff I'd grown up on—*Dungeons & Dragons* and stuff like that (at the time, I was only dimly aware of the fact that this was precisely because the kind of fantasy stuff I'd grown up on was pretty much directly inspired by Tolkien's masterpiece). But I remember the moment that I first realized that I was reading my new favorite book. It was in the opening chapters of Book III (the beginning of the volume *The Two Towers*) when the "Three Hunters" Aragorn, Legolas, and Gimli are pursuing their kidnapped friends across the fields of Rohan. There was just something about those chapters that really grabbed me as a teenager: the developing friendship and camaraderie between Aragorn (now captain) and his fellows (an elf and a dwarf, just learning to be friends with each other as well) and their unwavering loyalty to their friends that really helped me through those awkward adolescent years. It presented a kind of masculinity that wasn't "toxic" as we might say now—much like the deep love and friendship of Frodo and Sam in Book IV. And then in Book V, another character (Éowyn, who soon became my favorite) proved to me that the values of loyalty, determination, fellowship, and courage are 100 percent gender-neutral.

By the time I got to the appendices (and yes, I did read them all) I realized that this book was only scratching the surface of the world of Middle-earth. The histories in Appendix A enticed me with their mysterious (and often somewhat repetitive) names of kings and chieftains of the Dúnedain. Appendix D with its calendars showed me how meticulous a world-builder Tolkien really was. And then Appendices E and F, with their language and pronunciation deep-dives, was like fuel on a candle for my lifelong interest in languages and their evolution over time.

I truly believe *The Lord of the Rings* has something for everyone: invented languages, yes; exhaustive historical and mythological world-building, absolutely; but also maps, poetry, breathtakingly gorgeous landscape descriptions, adventure, excitement, bone-chilling moments of terror, inspiring themes, diverse peoples coming together, awesome female characters (okay, not many, but they're there), deeply personal wartime recollections, and *sentient trees marching to war*. Even more than *The Hobbit*, it's a book I recommend everyone at least try to read. Sure, it's long, but it's a lot easier to get through than you think.

Go ahead and take that step. We'll be here waiting for you. We can't wait to welcome you to the fandom.

# CHAPTER 3

# SO YOU THINK YOU CAN WORLD-BUILD: *THE SILMARILLION*

*"And the inner fire of the Silmarils Fëanor made of the blended light
of the Trees of Valinor, which lives in them yet, though the Trees have
long withered and shine no more. Therefore even in the darkness of the
deepest treasury the Silmarils of their own radiance shone like the stars
of Varda; and yet, as were they indeed living things, they rejoiced in light
and received it and gave it back in hues more marvellous than before."*

—*J.R.R. Tolkien*, The Silmarillion, *Chapter 7,
"Of the Silmarils and the Unrest of the Noldor"*[72]

Lone-wolf heroes, twisted monsters, giant bugs, prophecies of impending
doom, immortal gods watching puny mortals from atop a mountain, and
people turned into stars: it may sound like *Clash of the Titans*, but nope. It's
a book Tolkien spent virtually his entire life writing, revising, rewriting, and

---

72   Tolkien, J.R.R., edited by Christopher Tolkien. *The Silmarillion*. HarperCollins, 2021, 57.

re-revising...but that wasn't finally published until four years after his death. Welcome, our friends, to *The Silmarillion*.

One could be forgiven for mistaking Tolkien's epic volume of myths about the Elves of the First Age for a work of Greek mythology, because he started writing the first words of the stories that would become *The Silmarillion* in 1914, while he was studying at Exeter College in Oxford—and incidentally, just about a year after changing his concentration from the study of ancient Greek and Latin classics to the study of English and embarking on the long career as a Germanic philologist that led to all those cool philological Easter eggs in *The Hobbit* and *The Lord of the Rings* that we talked about in the last two chapters. And yes, *The Silmarillion* has been compared to ancient Greek and Roman epics; but it's also been compared to Norse eddas, the Bible, a history book, and even (parts of it, anyway) to a long, drawn-out description of a map. All of these comparisons have some truth to them (even the map one, strange as it sounds), which leads those of us who love it to recognize *The Silmarillion* for what it truly is: a work unlike any other, a book (though it's really not just one book) in a class of its own.

Let's get one thing out of the way: *The Silmarillion* is, in modern fandom and world-building terms, an "in-universe" document. Think of it as something like the Bible or the *Iliad* or *Odyssey* of Middle-earth that was handed down from Elves to Men and eventually to Hobbits. It is very likely meant to be a later volume of the Red Book of Westmarch, containing translations of Elvish myths that Bilbo set down—perhaps during his time in Rivendell between the first and second books of *The Lord of the Rings*. It's very likely that Frodo and Sam heard some of the tales in *The Silmarillion* growing up, as well, probably at the feet of Old Mr. Bilbo because, every time they refer to some ancient hero like Beren or Lúthien, or Túrin or Eärendil, well...they're talking about characters in this book.

But Tolkien was wise enough to connect the ancient mythology as closely as he could to the events of the Third Age. Remember, he was mining these stories for backstory as he was writing *The Lord of the Rings*, and so one should not be too surprised to find some familiar characters in it. Like Elrond's father. Or Galadriel. Or Aragorn's great-great-great-(lots of greats)-grandfather. But we're getting ahead of ourselves.

# BUT ISN'T IT REALLY HARD TO READ?

Well, look...go not to the podcasters for counsel, for they will say both no and yes.

Here's the thing. Yes, *The Silmarillion* takes place thousands of years before anything else that takes place in Middle-earth that was published before it. It's so far before the events of *The Hobbit* and *The Lord of the Rings* that even the term "prequel" is reductive. It's ancient history. Literally.

And the diction is a bit, shall we say, "elevated." "There was Eru, the One, who in Arda is called Ilúvatar; and he made first the Ainur, the Holy Ones..." isn't quite as catchy as "In a hole in the ground there lived a hobbit." And in case it's not clear, yes, *The Silmarillion* actually starts at the beginning. Like, the *very* beginning: the creation of the universe.

And as soon as the universe gets created, the book takes a hard right turn into a chapter that isn't so much a narrative as it is a list of the Valar (or little-g gods) and their domains. It's a bit like that part in the *Mystery Science Theater 3000* theme song that introduces Cambot, Tom Servo, and Crooooww! but instead of a few seconds of footage of Joel's cool homemade robots, it's a full seven pages describing terrifying godlike beings wearing cloaks of seafoam and laughing while they wrestle monsters and stuff.[73]

---

73   But obviously, that's really cool too.

And none of this is helped by the fact that several of these chapters have titles that Sam Gamgee would call "fair jaw-crackers," like *Ainulindalë*, *Valaquenta*, and *Akallabêth*. There are many with titles in English, but let's face it, "Of the Ruin of Beleriand and the Fall of Fingolfin" isn't quite as catchy as "Three is Company" or "Out of the Frying-Pan Into the Fire."

So yes, *The Silmarillion's* very nature—its pure Silmarillionness—has scared away more than a few would-be readers. More even than the poetry in *The Lord of the Rings*. More even than the longest poem in *The Lord of the Rings* (which is the one Bilbo sings in the Hall of Fire in Rivendell, and which, incidentally, retells a story from *The Silmarillion*. Full circle!).

But we think that's a shame. We think everyone should read *The Silmarillion*, and here's why. See, while the world of *The Silmarillion* seeped in through the cracks of *The Hobbit* as Tolkien continued writing it, *The Lord of the Rings* was written with full and complete intention of being the sequel and conclusion to not only *The Hobbit* but *The Silmarillion* as well. A knowledge of these ancient tales, known to Frodo and Sam and the other characters of the Third Age (maybe not Boromir—we're not sure that guy *ever* paid attention in history class), enriches the reader's understanding of Middle-earth and fills in the gaps that Tolkien intentionally left in the narrative of *The Lord of the Rings*, those "textual ruins" that make the world feel more ancient, more complete, and ultimately, more real.

This is so important to a full understanding of the world of *The Lord of the Rings* that we actually did something when we started our podcast back in 2016 that some people told us was crazy: we started with *The Silmarillion*. We knew that a full exploration of the themes and the stories of the First Age (and a little bit of the Second Age near the end) would better inform our reading of *The Hobbit* and *The Lord of the Rings*, and we'd get a lot more out of those books. After all, even though *The Silmarillion* wasn't published until later, those stories were all written (or at least outlined) and were all in

Tolkien's head when he was writing about Bilbo and Gandalf, Frodo and Sam, Legolas and Gimli.

It's not always the easiest nut to crack, but it's worth the effort... and hey, there are podcasts out there that will help you do it. (Hint, hint: we mean ours.)

But we're getting ahead of ourselves.

# SO HERE COMES YOUR "START AT THE BEGINNING" LINE AGAIN, RIGHT?

"You'd like to think that, wouldn't you?" (Read that in your best Wallace Shawn—a.k.a. Vizzini from *The Princess Bride*—voice.)

As mentioned above, starting at the beginning would mean going back to the *very* beginning of the universe. That's because the book published under the title *The Silmarillion* starts with Tolkien's cosmogonical (i.e., creation-of-the-world) myth, *Ainulindalë* or "The Music of the Ainur." It's an awesome myth that involves divine/angelic beings actually *singing* the world into existence, like no other that we know of (though some impressive scholarship has been done by Tolkien biographer John Garth linking it to a Mesopotamian musical creation myth),[74] but we want to save it for later and get into the *Silmarillion* proper—or, more properly, the *Quenta Silmarillion* (which is Quenya, or High-Elven, for "The History of the Silmarils"). For now, it's enough for you to know that, when editing the *Quenta Silmarillion* for publication after his father's death in the 1970s, Christopher Tolkien opted to include four separate standalone writings to contextualize the *Quenta Silmarillion* in

---

74    Garth, John. "Ilu's Music: The Creation of Tolkien's Creation Myth," in *Sub-creating Arda: World-building in J.R.R. Tolkien's Work, its Precursors, and its Legacies*, edited by Dimitra Fimi and Thomas Honegger. Walking Tree Publishers, 2019, 117-51.

the broader scope of Tolkien's legendarium, and help the reader link these ancient stories back to the more familiar Third Age works *The Hobbit* and *The Lord of the Rings*. After we talk about the *Quenta Silmarillion*, we'll come back to these four "bookend" pieces.

## So...the Silmarils. What Are They, and Why Do We Care About Their History?

In short: they are three gems crafted by Fëanor the elf-smith, the greatest craftsman of the Elves who ever lived (and thus the greatest craftsman of any earthly race that ever lived...not to mention the sort of classy guy who'll make something *that beautiful* just to lord it over everyone else that he has them and they don't). They are gems filled with living light, having captured the light of the Two Trees of Valinor before they were destroyed—

## Wait... the Two Trees of *What?*

Valinor. See, before the sun and the moon were created, the light that gave life and illumination to the earth (called Arda by the Elves) came from the Two Trees of Valinor, which glowed with living light. The Two Trees were born of the arts of the Valar in the Undying Lands after they fled the destruction of Almaren, after the Two Lamps were destroyed by Melkor, long before the Noldor returned to Middle-earth—

## "Middle-earth" Is the Only Proper Noun There I Understand...

You're right. Maybe we should have started at the beginning.

Honestly, there isn't any way around it: *The Silmarillion* is a cycle of interconnected tales that form a massive web of mythic scope. The only way to truly understand one of them is to read them all, which is why it sometimes doesn't all make sense until you go back and read it all over again (or, again, read along with an award-winning podcast. Hint, hint). But it's truly worth it, because this was the story that you could say Tolkien was more or less born to write. This was the book he spent his entire life working on and trying to get published.

So let's start at the beginning.

# SIGH.

While studying at Oxford in 1914, J.R.R. Tolkien, then aged twenty-two, came across an Old English ecclesiastical poem called *Crist* (or "Christ"), attributed to an author named Cynewulf. One particular passage of this poem caught his eye:

> *Eala Earendel engla beorhtast*
> *ofer middangeard monnum sended.*

> "Hail, Earendel, brightest of angels
> above middle-earth sent unto men."

According to John Garth, author of *Tolkien and the Great War*—the most authoritative and complete biographical account of Tolkien's youth and wartime experience—the name *Earendel* "struck [Tolkien] in an extraordinary way."[75] Tolkien would later elaborate on this experience in an unfinished story entitled "The Notion Club Papers," in which he gave this

---

75    Garth, John. *Tolkien and the Great War: The Threshold of Middle-earth.* Houghton Mifflin, 2003, 44.

real-life experience to one of the characters. Garth recounts and comments on this character's experience thus:

> 'I felt a curious thrill, as if something had stirred in me, half wakened from sleep. There was something very remote and strange and beautiful behind those words, if I could grasp it, far beyond ancient English...I don't think it is any irreverence to say that it may derive its curiously moving quality from some older world.' [Garth's commentary:] But whose name was Éarendel? The question sparked a lifelong answer.[76]

Much has been written on the meaning of "Earendel" as an angelic messenger in Anglo-Saxon Christianity, even a harbinger of the advent of Christ and symbol of John the Baptist. As a seminal moment in Tolkien's sub-creation of the Middle-earth legendarium, this is a fascinating topic well worth diving into for those who are interested. But for now, we'll leave it at this: Tolkien was so inspired by this Old English name that he wrote a poem about it in late 1914 called "The Voyage of Earendel the Evening Star."

Also around this general time—the mid-1910s—Tolkien was deep into an activity that a lot of people are doing as a hobby now, but was less common then: inventing his own languages. This "secret vice"[77] was something Tolkien had been doing since he was a child, inventing nonsense languages with his cousins. But around 1910, he began work on a new "fairy language" inspired partly by the languages that he enjoyed the most, such as Finnish, Greek, and Latin. He called this language Qenya (the word for "speech" in the language, later spelled Quenya).[78] But as work advanced on this language, Tolkien was

---

76 Ibid.

77 Tolkien himself called inventing languages—most commonly known as "conlanging" today—his "secret vice," and gave a talk about it in 1931 entitled *A Secret Vice*. It is available in publication both in *The Monsters and the Critics and Other Essays* and in a more recent standalone edition edited by Dimitra Fimi and Andrew Higgins.

78 After many years and many changes, Quenya was finally unveiled to the world in *The Lord of the Rings*, where it was the language of the first snippet of Elven speech ever published: Frodo's greeting *"Elen síla lúmenn' omentielvo."* Quenya was one of two primary invented languages of *The Lord of the Rings*: an "Elven Latin," the High-elven language of lore used by scholars and the wise, while the related tongue Sindarin would be used for everyday speech among Elves and closely related people like Aragorn.

also in school learning about philology, and he knew that languages don't just remain static forever. He knew that languages in the real world are constantly changing, and he wanted Qenya to feel like the real-world languages he was spending his school days studying.

But how? How could he—a single person with only one lifetime to work with—introduce the kind of centuries-spanning changes into his invented language that he saw in English or Icelandic? The answer may seem simple now, but at the time, it would have had to have been unthinkable for anyone except him: he needed to invent not just the language itself, but a history for it. And more importantly, a history of the people who spoke it that would explain the changes to which the language would be subjected in the imaginary world of Tolkien's creation. That people would be the Elves, or *Eldar* in Quenya.

Unlike modern-day fantasy writers like George R.R. Martin, Tolkien invented the Elves and their history to provide a world in which his languages could live, rather than inventing languages to add credibility to his fantasy world. The Professor admitted as much himself in a 1955 letter: "The invention of languages is the foundation. The 'stories' were made rather to provide a world for the languages than the reverse."[79]

So that's just what he did. He wrote an entire epic history of the Elves who spoke his languages—Quenya and Gnomish (which would later become Sindarin)—that included the migrations, developments, rivalries, and banishments that would make these languages possible. And in a stroke of genius that he never quite managed to tie off perfectly, he made this history the lost *pre*-history of our own world: starting at the creation of the universe, through centuries of stories that would feel right at home in any Greek or Norse mythology book, and then connecting these ancient places and peoples with modern peoples and places that were important to him in

---

79    Carpenter, *Letters*, No. 165.

the twentieth century, like Warwick, Oxford, and Great Haywood—each of which was said to be a city founded originally by the Elves.

The earliest version of these stories was published after Tolkien's death as *The Book of Lost Tales*, the first two volumes of The History of Middle-earth. But what's important to understand is that Tolkien continued writing and rewriting these stories for his entire life. As the *Lost Tales* developed, the center of gravity of the narrative started coalescing around three stories in particular, which Tolkien would call his "Great Tales" (discussed in detail in a couple of chapters): "The Tale of Tinúviel," "Turambar and the Foalókë," and "The Fall of Gondolin."

After "completing" *The Book of Lost Tales*, Tolkien quickly turned his attention to rewriting some of his Great Tales in fuller detail. The first seems to have been "Turambar," which he started writing an epic poem about sometime between 1918 and 1921 (probably right after the original prose version was finished) called *The Lay of the Children of Húrin*—the "Turambar" of the original title being another name for Túrin,[80] one of the children in question whom the story focused on. Unsurprisingly, Tolkien never finished this lay, but that didn't stop him from trying to share the work-in-progress with a friend in the 1920s. But it turned out that the stories were so intertwined with one another that one could not fully understand one of the Great Tales without a basic understanding of the overall history. One couldn't understand who Túrin was and why he was cursed without knowing how awesome his father was. One couldn't understand how awesome his father was without understanding the relationship between the Edain (or Men) and the Eldar (Elves), and one couldn't understand the relationship between Men and Elves without understanding *basically* the entire history of the world up until the point at which each of these two races was created. "You're welcome," we can hear Tolkien saying.

---

80 We know it's kind of confusing, but get used to it. Túrin Turambar has a lot of names. Like, a *lot* of names.

So when Tolkien tried to share the *Lay* with a friend, he realized he needed to provide that friend with an outline of the entire history of his legendarium up to that point. That outline, called "the Sketch of the Mythology," evolved considerably from *The Book of Lost Tales*, though many of the same concepts were there. And that outline or "Sketch" is also known as the earliest "Silmarillion."

Tolkien kept going back and rewriting the "Silmarillion,"[81] as we discussed in the last chapter, taking breaks occasionally to focus on other works—most notably *The Hobbit* and *The Lord of the Rings*. After *The Lord of the Rings* was completed, Tolkien went back and started rewriting all this stuff again. He really, really wanted to get it published, and to leverage the success of *The Lord of the Rings* as much as possible to make it bankable.

As we noted in the last chapter, Tolkien did end up "mining" the "Silmarillion" material for backstory to make *The Lord of the Rings* better, as Stanley Unwin had recommended. We're glad he did. But he always wanted to see *The Silmarillion* in print, going so far as to risk not publishing *The Lord of the Rings* if he couldn't get them both published together—which, as we discussed last chapter, would have been an awful shame, because there was no way he was going to get them published together. *The Silmarillion* was nowhere near completion, not even when Tolkien died in 1973.

# So How Did It Get Published?

Following Tolkien's passing, Christopher Tolkien was named a director of the Tolkien Estate and its sole *literary executor*—meaning that he was ultimately responsible for preserving his father's literary legacy and managing

---

81    As noted in a footnote in the previous chapter, we will always refer to the protean body of manuscripts covering the stories of the First Age as the "Silmarillion" (in quotation marks) while referring to Christopher Tolkien's 1977 edited-for-publication book as *The Silmarillion* (in italics).

the intellectual property and unpublished manuscripts left behind by his father (and there were a lot of these). Christopher was chosen, no doubt, because he had always taken the greatest interest in his father's work. As we've mentioned previously, young Christopher was already editing his father when he was reading *The Hobbit* to the children at bedtime (and, as fathers ourselves, we know how proud it makes a dad to be corrected by his kid...annoyed, frustrated, sure; but proud). He took after his father, it seems, more than the others: like his father, he also studied English at Oxford (partly under the tutelage of C.S. Lewis), and later lectured in Old and Middle English and Icelandic. He was even a member of the Inklings in his own right for a time. And while Tolkien was writing *The Lord of the Rings*, he wrote to Christopher frequently to pitch ideas and solicit feedback. It's safe to say that Christopher Tolkien was the very first—and always the very biggest—J.R.R. Tolkien fan. So there was no one better who could have been chosen for the task.

Almost immediately after his father's passing, Christopher started working on the publication of his father's unfinished materials. He tested the water early with the 1975 publication of three translations of Middle English poems: *Sir Gawain and the Green Knight, Pearl, and Sir Orfeo* (still available in a single volume today, and a great first step on the road to learning more about Tolkien's academic writings). But by the time *Sir Gawain* was published, Christopher was already hard at work on finishing the task his father never could: publishing *The Silmarillion*. The best introduction to the task at hand comes from Christopher himself, in the foreword to the finished book:

> On my father's death it fell to me to try to bring the work into publishable form. It became clear to me that to attempt to present, within the covers of a single book, the diversity of the materials—to show *The Silmarillion* as in truth a continuing and evolving creation extending over more than half a century—would in fact lead only to confusion and the submerging of what is essential. I set myself therefore to work out a single text,

selecting and arranging in such a way as seemed to me to produce the most coherent and internally self-consistent narrative...[82]

Christopher knew that it wouldn't be feasible to publish everything—all of those lays and lost tales and epic poems—especially because they weren't all finished. What he did instead was attempt to take the loose threads and untied bits of story and put them all together, so that some outline or summary of the history of the First Age could be published as more or less a coherent story, albeit one that takes place over thousands of years and sees main characters come and go more often than Sean Bean dies on screen. He rationalized this, in part, knowing that the basis of *The Silmarillion* was inherently a series of sketches, summaries, annals, and other high-level works, just like the "Sketch" Tolkien had written decades before to provide the context for *The Lay of the Children of Húrin*. Again, Christopher's words from the foreword are illuminating:

> A complete consistency (either within the compass of *The Silmarillion* itself or between *The Silmarillion* and other published writings of my father's) is not to be looked for, and could only be achieved, if at all, at heavy and needless cost. Moreover, my father came to conceive *The Silmarillion* as a compilation, a compendious narrative, made long afterwards from sources of great diversity (poems, and annals, and oral tales) that had survived in agelong tradition; and this conception has indeed its parallel in the actual history of the book, for a great deal of earlier prose and poetry does underlie it, and it is to some extent a compendium in fact and not only in theory. To this may be ascribed the varying speed of the narrative and fullness of detail in different parts, the contrast (for example) of the precise recollections of place and motive in the legend of Túrin Turambar beside the high and remote account of the end of the First Age...[83]

82    Tolkien, *Silmarillion*, 2021, x.
83    Ibid.

While perhaps not a terribly useful example for someone reading the foreword (or this book) who hasn't read *The Silmarillion* yet, we get exactly what Christopher is saying there.

## So Tell Us.

Be patient! We're going to.

For the most part, *The Silmarillion* operates at the proverbial 30,000-foot view of the story: it brushes very quickly past major events at many points, often covering hundreds of years in a couple of pages. There are entire novels' worth of untold material buried in sentences like this: "Fëanor and his sons abode seldom in one place for long, but travelled far and wide upon the confines of Valinor, going even to the borders of the Dark and the cold shores of the Outer Sea, seeking the unknown."[84] Or this: "After many lives of wandering out of the East he had led them at last over the Blue Mountains, the first of the race of Men to enter Beleriand; and they sang because they were glad, and believed that they had escaped from all perils and had come at last to a land without fear."[85] Doesn't it just make you beg for more information?

But you're not going to get it. Much of *The Silmarillion* is like this. It's a bit like flipping through the pages of *Bulfinch's Mythology*, or a classics textbook: high-level summaries of stories when we can get them, and a lot of enticing gee-I-wish-we-knew-more-about-that moments.

But then there are places where the eagle carrying us on its back through the story dips down to near ground level to give us a closer look. Chapter 19, "Of Beren and Lúthien," is like this; so is Chapter 21, "Of Túrin Turambar," which Christopher mentions in the passage we quoted from the foreword.

---

84  Ibid., 52.
85  Ibid., 131.

Not surprisingly, these are two of those Great Tales to which *The Silmarillion* exists primarily to give backstory. In those chapters, the true beauty of the mythology of the First Age is revealed, and shown to be full of great love stories, tragic loss, horrible curses and even more horrible choices, death, un-death, re-death, and more.

Bringing these many stories—some very detailed romantic and epic accounts of the exploits of specific heroes, some mere year-by-year annals of major world-changing events, and all written by another author, no less—into something approaching a coherent narrative would have to have been challenging, even for someone who knew his father's work as well as Christopher did. Keep in mind, it had been challenging for J.R.R. Tolkien himself for decades. Even Christopher needed help to organize and execute the project, and for that help, he turned to a twenty-year-old college student from Canada named Guy Gavriel Kay.[86] Kay moved across the pond to Oxford and worked with Christopher Tolkien on the project for about a year, from 1974 to 1975.

But don't get the wrong idea here. Christopher Tolkien and Guy Gavriel Kay did not write whole new books, or even chapters, from some set of nebulous "notes" left behind by J.R.R. Tolkien.[87] With the exception of one chapter (identified by Douglas Charles Kane in his book *Arda Reconstructed*, which attempts to chronicle Christopher's reconstruction of the published *Silmarillion*), there is very little "editorial invention"; the words are J.R.R. Tolkien's. Christopher and Kay's task was to make sense of the manuscripts and put them together, which they did remarkably well.[88] Kay's work on the project appears to have been limited to just that early stage; he moved

---

86   Kay went on to be an award-winning fantasy writer himself, publishing works like The Fionavar Tapestry trilogy in the 1980s and *Under Heaven* in 2010. Kay originally met Christopher Tolkien through family connections; Christopher's wife Baillie (*née* Klass) was Canadian, and her father taught at the University of Manitoba, where Kay was attending university.

87   At least, apparently not so extensive as (for example) the work of Brian Herbert and Kevin J. Anderson in writing new Dune books from "notes" left behind by Frank Herbert, which has met with mixed reactions from fans and critics.

88   We think so, anyway.

back to Canada in 1975, while *The Silmarillion* took another two years to complete.

In the end, Christopher opted to package the *"Silmarillion* proper" (as he would call it in the foreword) or *Quenta Silmarillion* with four other short works:

- *Ainulindalë*—"the Music of the Ainur," which describes in mythological (virtually biblical) detail the creation of the universe, also known as *Eä*, sung into existence by "big-G God" Eru Ilúvatar and the angelic beings born of his thought, called the Ainur.

- *Valaquenta*—"the account of the Valar and Maiar," a short historical essay identifying the *dramatis personae* of the chapters to come: the Ainur who entered into the universe of Eä to shape and direct it, the great Powers or "little-g gods" called Valar, and their lesser servants the Maiar. If you've read *The Lord of the Rings* and wonder who "A Elbereth Gilthoniel" is a hymn to, or who "Oromë the Great" is (to whom Théoden is compared as he rides to battle at the Pelennor Fields), or even where Balrogs and Sauron come from, pay attention to this chapter.

- *Akallabêth*—"the Downfallen," an account of the rise and fall of the island kingdom of Númenor, also known as Westernesse, the legendary kingdom from which Aragorn's ancestors Elendil and Isildur escaped to Middle-earth to found Arnor and Gondor.

- *Of the Rings of Power and the Third Age*—which tells the story of, uh, the Rings of Power. And how they were made. And then the, uh, stuff that happens after. In the Third, well, Age.

Christopher Tolkien explained that, while these four additions were "wholly separate and independent" from the *Quenta Silmarillion*, they were "included according to [his] father's explicit intention, and by their inclusion the entire history [of the Middle-earth legendarium] is set forth."[89] That's all. Just the entire history of the world (which, we wish to remind you, Tolkien

---

89   Tolkien, *Silmarillion*, 2021, x–xi.

intended to be the forgotten prehistory of our world), from its creation to sometime shortly before the dawn of recorded history.

The story of the *Quenta Silmarillion* itself, episodic as it tends to be, briefly tells the story of the creation of the earth (Arda) by the Valar, before moving on to the "awakening" of the Elves, who, like Men,[90] were not created by the Valar, but were the "Children of Ilúvatar," designed and brought into existence by the big-G God of Tolkien's universe.[91] The Elves awaken in the mysterious land of Cuiviénen under starlight, before the Sun and Moon themselves are in existence, and are soon discovered by the Valar, who take them to the Undying Lands of Valinor in the West to guide and teach them. Of course, not all of the Elves want to go to the Undying Lands, and the decisions and nondecisions, twists, turns, and detours made by various groups of the Elves along the way give rise to the many clans and tribes of Elves that exist in Middle-earth (and, most importantly for Tolkien, that speak the different Elvish languages like Quenya and Sindarin, each of which has a divergent history that made it what it is).

And, wouldn't you know, some of the Elves end up coming *back* to Middle-earth from the Undying Lands, setting up centuries of history of mighty kingdoms, factions, wars against Morgoth (formerly known as Melkor, the fallen Vala and Satan-figure of Tolkien's universe who was the first Dark Lord. He was Sauron's boss and mentor in the First Age), and eventually...alliances, friendships, and even romances with Men, the second-born Children of Ilúvatar. Along the way there are evil dragons, giant spiders, epic battles, star-crossed lovers, intelligent swords, magical artifacts of unspeakable power, betrayal, courage, mourning, wisdom, horrific abominations against nature,

---

90  In almost every instance, Tolkien used the word "Men" to describe the human race, so when we use it here, we mean humans, not males.

91  The origin stories of Dwarves and Ents are also told in the *Quenta Silmarillion*—and are more closely related than you might think. Both of these races were not in origin "Children of Ilúvatar," as each of them owes their creation to one of the Valar, but the Dwarves at least were adopted by Ilúvatar, making them akin to Elves and Men by that action if not explicitly by biology. The origin of Orcs is also discussed, though the version of their origin is only one of many possible ideas Tolkien had, and he wrestled with the origins of Orcs, and especially their apparently irredeemable nature (which he really didn't like or intend), until near the end of his life.

and much more. There's even a whole chapter called "Of Beleriand and its Realms" that literally just describes the map. It's like nothing you've ever read before, and it's mind-boggling that Christopher Tolkien was able to bring it all together into something resembling a single actual book.

Of course, after completing *The Silmarillion*, Christopher's work was done. He commended himself on a job well done, kicked off his shoes, cracked open a cold one, and enjoyed the rest of his life. Right?

## Well...No.

While he certainly seems to have recognized the value in publishing a standalone version of his father's unfinished material as "self-explanatory," Christopher also seems to have almost immediately regretted his decision. After *The Silmarillion* came out in 1977, he spent the next forty years publishing his father's manuscripts in a much less edited, much less polished and "finished" (if you can call it that, which you really can't, and we wouldn't, but we suppose we just did) format: as the *Unfinished Tales of Númenor and Middle-earth* in 1980, and then the twelve-volume History of Middle-earth series published between 1983 and 1996. In these later volumes, Christopher abandoned the idea of trying to present these complex manuscripts with all their drafts and revisions as a single finished project. He instead presented them as drafts with a hefty dose of commentary, analyzing the textual tradition of these manuscripts as the story developed over the course of Tolkien's life.

We'll talk more about those books in the coming chapters. But, although it may be an oversimplification, it's not entirely wrong to say that Christopher Tolkien spent the rest of his life afterwards basically undoing what he'd done: pulling down the curtain to show us the inner workings behind the story, rather than the illusory "finished story" he'd given the world in 1977 as *The Silmarillion*. He even said in the foreword to the first volume of The

History of Middle-earth that he made a significant "error" in one specific way in the way he presented the text: he didn't include a frame narrative, which had been part of his father's wishes (and not surprising, given that Tolkien included frame narrative conceits in his major works like *The Hobbit* and *The Lord of the Rings* as well).

# SO, WHY DO WE LOVE IT?

You might be thinking after all this that we'd say we don't love *The Silmarillion* at all. That we'd say it's better to skip it and go straight to the later "behind the curtain" publications of *Unfinished Tales* and The History of Middle-earth, since those cover more ground. Is that what you're thinking?

[Prince Humperdinck voice] *I would not say such things if I were you!!!* Uh, or if we were us.

*The Silmarillion* is *definitely* where readers should go before embarking on those other works, and it is the one most readers tend to go back to again and again. It's worth reading because, for starters, it's a lot easier to digest than all those other books that Christopher published later. It's good to remember that J.R.R. Tolkien was an Oxford professor of English, and Christopher Tolkien was an Oxford professor of English...and the way they approached the composition (in the case of J.R.R.) and the editing (in the case of Christopher) of all those manuscripts into the *Unfinished Tales* and The History of Middle-earth can be a bit daunting for those of us who aren't... well, Oxford professors of English. Presenting the stories as drafts with commentary provides a fascinating look at the creative process of one of the twentieth century's greatest writers (we'd say the greatest, but we're biased), and it shows how Tolkien was utterly unique among authors of his time, even his mythopoeic[92] peers like C.S. Lewis. The later books are a wonderful look at the development of the story over time, and rich with information that scholars are continually mining for interesting paper topics and conference presentations. And we love reading those papers and listening to those presentations. But it's not exactly page-turning stuff, nor is it necessarily something that a reader new to this material can be expected to be enchanted by in quite the same way as the story of Frodo and Sam climbing up the mountain to throw away the jewelry to defeat the forces of evil.

And it can be mystifying enough for a reader new to the First Age stories to have to remember, for example, the difference between characters with names like Elwë and Olwë and Elmo and Ulmo, let alone the fact that Elwë is also called Thingol—all of which makes *The Silmarillion* challenging enough—without being thrown right into the deep end and also having to remember that in 1917 Tolkien was calling Elwë or Thingol by the name of Linwë Tinto, or sometimes Tinwë Linto, or sometimes Tinwelint.

But it is really important—we can't stress how much—to know this stuff if one wants to get the most out of Tolkien's legendarium. As it turns out, Thingol (whatever we choose to call him) is a really important character in Tolkien's history; his decisions (and his descendants) shape the course of history for many dozens of generations, and we won't fully understand the importance of the actions of those descendants in *The Lord of the Rings* (for they are still around, thousands of years later) without understanding this ancient mythical ancestor. This is the way Tolkien's writing works: the ancient stories are there in the background, "textual ruins" as Michael D.C. Drout calls them, not explained in the pages of *The Hobbit* or *The Lord of the Rings*, but an understanding of them gives a deeper understanding of, and appreciation for, the world. So we always recommend reading *The Silmarillion* after *The Hobbit* and *The Lord of the Rings*, as a gateway into

---

92  Meaning "of, or pertaining to, myth-making," and often applied specifically to the works of J.R.R. Tolkien and other authors like him. Tolkien himself wrote a beautifully insightful poem about his own sub-creative process called "Mythopoeia," and the term has been taken up by many fans and fan organizations, such as the Mythopoeic Society.

these ancient stories—at least, one version of them that's easier to absorb and digest than the complex web of manuscripts and textual history in The History of Middle-earth.

And there's one more important reason we love it: *The Silmarillion* is just really, really good. For all its reputation as an inscrutable, arcane text, there is a great story there that is cut from the same cloth as *The Lord of the Rings*. The same kinds of epic quests, great battles, heartbreaking sacrifices, and earth-shattering tragedies that we see in Tolkien's more well-known work are here, and in fact, for the most part it's all writ much larger (when you get to Húrin's last stand at the Battle of Unnumbered Tears, you'll see why Legolas and Gimli's ongoing competition to see who can slay the most Orcs is child's play). There are artifacts of immeasurable magic power, coveted by a dark lord (who just happens to wear them on his crown—take that, Sauron). There's a ride-or-die romance between a mortal Man and his Elvish girlfriend, where they have to go *literally* to hell and back before they can live happily ever after (that's right, Aragorn and Arwen, we said *literally*). Thought that Balrog under Moria was cool? There are loads of them in the first few chapters of *The Silmarillion* alone. Oh, and did you ever wonder how Gandalf managed to seemingly come back from the dead? You'll find out.

What it lacks in down-to-earth dramatic weight (although it does have heaps of that in a few of those "precise recollection" chapters Christopher Tolkien spoke of) *The Silmarillion* makes up for in sheer epic scale and mythic chutzpah. And it actually delves deeper and more literally into some of Tolkien's favorite themes. In his famous letter to Milton Waldman (mentioned in the last chapter), Tolkien spoke of "Fall, Mortality, and the Machine" as key themes of his legendarium.[93] *The Silmarillion* has multiple Falls: Elves, Men, even one of the Valar (and a second one almost fell). Mortality drips from every page, especially the more we see Men come on the scene in about the second half of the book. And the Machine (by which

---

93    Carpenter, *Letters*, No. 131.

we mean major world-changing artifacts that have the power to cheat death or otherwise change the fabric of the earth, like the Silmarils and of course the One Ring itself) is actually built within its pages.

And there are also other themes that we love from *The Lord of the Rings* that find more room to flex their philosophical muscles in *The Silmarillion*. Hope—the kind that spurs Sam Gamgee on to great feats of valor when the road looks darkest—is an ever more present theme in the story of *The Silmarillion* as Morgoth stretches his dark claw across the lands of Beleriand. Fate and free will—a theme that pops up frequently in the pages of *The Lord of the Rings*—is explored in much greater detail here in *The Silmarillion*, including a bit of metaphysical world-building about what "fate" is and who has true "free will" (not all are equal, according to Tolkien). The fading of the Elves, the nature of evil, the question of redemption for the wickedest creatures of Middle-earth: these are themes explored in *The Lord of the Rings* that are explored even more directly, in many cases, in the pages of *The Silmarillion*.

To be honest, we don't believe it's possible to truly understand the philosophical underpinnings of Tolkien's legendarium without reading *The Silmarillion*. What *The Lord of the Rings* only hints at occasionally through the otherwise gripping and easily accessible story, *The Silmarillion* dares to be much more explicit about. We think that's pretty cool. And we think it's so important to understand the philosophy that drives Tolkien's legendarium that, when we started *The Prancing Pony Podcast* back in 2016, we started—not with the more obviously accessible works like *The Hobbit* or *The Lord of the Rings*—but with *The Silmarillion*.

Give it a try. You may be surprised how much you enjoy it. And if you ever have trouble keeping up, we can recommend a great podcast that can help.

# WHY ALAN LOVES IT

Like I mentioned in the last chapter, I bounced off of *The Silmarillion* every time I tried reading it in high school. Sometimes, I made it past the Ainulindalë, sometimes I didn't. I don't believe I ever made it past "Of the Beginning of Days." The language was archaic, the names unfamiliar, the tone vastly different from the years I'd spent reading *The Hobbit* and *The Lord of the Rings*. By the time I tried again in earnest, I was (if memory serves)[94] twenty years old. I took notes; I read and reread; I drew my own copy of the Elven flow chart keeping track of all the kindreds so I could reference it more easily. There was no internet to ask questions of, no friends at my college (that I knew of) who were deep in Tolkien lore, and certainly no cheerful podcast to welcome me and explain each chapter to me!

Still, weeks later, with pages of notes (that I desperately wish I still had!) and event-tracking outlines, I emerged having successfully completed my first full readthrough of *The Silmarillion*.

It. Changed. *Everything*.

Okay, not my dating life—nothing could fix that. And not my mediocre grades, either. But it changed the way I read and understood *The Lord of the Rings*. I understood—even before I knew the Professor had wanted to publish them together—how intertwined these stories were, how dependent each was upon the other for a fuller understanding. Reading one now always prompted reading the other, sometimes leading to a circle in which one of them was always on my bedside table. Maybe it was that eye-opening nature of my first successful readthrough that led us to tackle *The Silmarillion* in season one of *The Prancing Pony Podcast*: hoping that my experience (and Shawn's, of course) would enable us to do for others what I'd had to do on my own in that college dorm room.

---

94    And, to be clear, as this is a time now more than thirty years in my past, memory does not always serve.

# WHY SHAWN LOVES IT

There is no single book in the history of Western literature that means more to me than *The Silmarillion*.

Immediately after I finished reading *The Lord of the Rings* for the first time, I wanted more Tolkien. I had seen *The Silmarillion* on bookshelves, even heard some kids in class nerdier than me (yes, there were a few) talking about it in hushed tones, so I knew it was the next book to read even though it was a prequel (though I'm not sure I even knew the word *prequel* yet; this was long before *The Phantom Menace*). So I went straight on into *The Silmarillion*, and I was in love with it from the very first sentence: "There was Eru, the One, who in Arda is called Ilúvatar; and he made first the Ainur, the Holy Ones, that were the offspring of his thought, and they were with him before aught else was made." Boom. Mind. Blown.

I can't pretend to have understood every word I read, of course—I was only fifteen. But I had grown up reading classical myths: *Bulfinch's Mythology*, and Edith Hamilton's *Mythology*, and some scattered books of ancient Norse myths and legends; and I was instantly struck by how much Tolkien's *Silmarillion* reminded me of those books: overviews and summaries of expansive bodies of myth to be absorbed, internalized, and retold. A truly *mythopoeic* work, though that was (like *prequel*) a word I didn't know at the time; and unlike those other real-world mythologies, it astonishingly all came from the mind of one single author. I wanted all my friends to read it, just so I'd have someone to talk to about it, so I loaned it to one friend after another, though most of them returned it before getting to the end.[95] I suppose one could say I've been trying to talk people into reading *The Silmarillion* ever since the first time I read *The Silmarillion*.

---

95  I stopped loaning it out after it came back with a name and phone number written inside it; apparently one friend's parents reached for the nearest paper object when trying to jot down someone's contact information. Even in the early 1990s—long before the days when "Shoot me a text so I have your number" was a thing—this was an act of pure chaotic evil. Notepads, people! Come on!

Over the course of six seasons on *The Prancing Pony Podcast*, I made no secret of the fact that *The Silmarillion* is my favorite of Tolkien's works. While *The Hobbit* got me in the door and *The Lord of the Rings* made me a lifelong Tolkien fan, *The Silmarillion* and the deeper body of myth that underlies the Middle-earth legendarium is what's kept me going back. These are stories that have become, for me and for many Tolkien fans, "our mythology": the stories we tell, retell, and receive together, like the ancient Greeks used to do when they gathered at festivals to watch tragic plays of the familiar stories of Theseus or Agamemnon, or the medieval Anglo-Saxons did when they sat in the mead-hall to hear the story of Beowulf fighting Grendel. These stories are a cultural marker for Tolkien fans; we talk about them and make art of them and paint scenes from them on our bodies. For many of us, they are every bit as much a part of our identity as the stories we grew up hearing in church or temple, or told around a campfire by grandparents and uncles. For some of us, they are far more real and personal than those "real world" stories.

Now that I have children of my own, these are stories I tell them,[96] and nothing delights me more than hearing the names of Beren, Lúthien, and Finrod Felagund out of the mouths of my children, though it'll be years before they're ready to read the book themselves. I look forward to the day they do, and hope that someday they'll pass the stories on to their children, remembering how they were first introduced to them by their own father. The stories have grown beyond the pages of the book and become part of our culture (at least, a culture we've borrowed from the generous Professor Tolkien). In this way, Tolkien truly succeeded in creating a mythology that—to me—is every bit as powerful and meaningful as Greek or Roman mythology.

---

96    Maybe not the chapter "Of Túrin Turambar." If you know, you know.

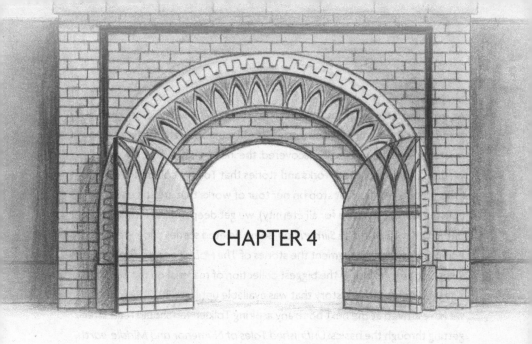

# CHAPTER 4

# FINAL DRAFTS ARE OVERRATED: *UNFINISHED TALES*

*"When the author has ceased to publish his works himself, after subjecting them to his own detailed criticism and comparison, the further knowledge of Middle-earth to be found in his unpublished writings will often conflict with what is already 'known'; and new elements set into the existing edifice will in such cases tend to contribute less to the history of the invented world itself than to the history of its invention."*

—Christopher Tolkien, Unfinished Tales of Númenor and
Middle-earth, *Introduction*[97]

---

97    Tolkien, J.R.R., edited by Christopher Tolkien. *Unfinished Tales of Númenor and Middle-earth.*
      HarperCollins, 2020, 15-16.

As we travel outward through the solar system of Tolkien's works,[98] we gradually come to the edge of the familiar planets and catch a glimpse of mysterious worlds yet to be discovered: the incomplete works, alternate versions of the published works and stories that Tolkien couldn't finish in his lifetime. At this first stop on our tour of works that are still under construction (and will be for all eternity), we get deeper dives into a couple of the Great Tales in *The Silmarillion*, some deleted scenes and extended-edition-type stuff to augment the stories of *The Hobbit* and *The Lord of the Rings*, and (very exciting) the biggest collection of material on the Second Age of Middle-earth's history that was available until late 2022. Readers, we have arrived at the next book any aspiring Tolkien fan should read after getting through the basics: *Unfinished Tales of Númenor and Middle-earth*. In our opinion, it represents a turning point for the new Tolkien fan delving ever deeper: how you react to this book will be a litmus test for how you will receive the rest of the books that are out there. It is a taste of things to come, and a last chance for anything approaching a simple cover-to-cover reading within Tolkien's legendarium.

Like *The Silmarillion*, *Unfinished Tales* was edited by Christopher Tolkien from his father's unpublished manuscripts. It was first published in the autumn of 1980, just three short years after *The Silmarillion*, and the bulk of the volume builds upon the histories of the First and Second Ages of Middle-earth that are covered by its predecessor. But, unlike *The Silmarillion*, the texts collected in *Unfinished Tales* are not presented "as a completed and cohesive entity,"[99] as Christopher states in the introduction. This is the first book in which Christopher adopts the technique of presenting his father's unfinished manuscripts "in the form of an historical study, a complex of divergent texts interlinked by commentary." In some cases, the stories collected in *Unfinished Tales* go on for nearly a hundred pages without a break; in others, narratives stop suddenly between paragraphs, with only

---

98    This sentence works a lot better if you imagine it in the voice of Neil deGrasse Tyson or Carl Sagan. Trust us.

99    Tolkien, *Unfinished Tales*, 2020, 13.

fragments to connect the dots to the next scene. In all cases, Christopher Tolkien preserves the breaks and fragments as they are, not seeking to "finish" anything, but jumping in with his own commentary in the form of footnotes, appendices, and other long-form editorial additions to explain the complex textual history of the many manuscripts his father left behind—some of them actually contradicting each other to offer multiple alternate versions of the same story.

Christopher's own words on the rationale of the book from the introduction are illuminating: "The narratives in this book...constitute no whole, and the book is no more than a collection of writings, disparate in form, intent, finish, and date of composition (and in my own treatment of them), concerned with Númenor and Middle-earth. But the argument for their publication is not different in its nature, though it is of lesser force, from that which I held to justify the publication of *The Silmarillion*."[100]

He says later in the same paragraph that the "imperfections of form in these tales are much outweighed" by what fans have to gain from reading them: breathtaking dramatic moments like the appearance of the Vala of the sea, Ulmo, to a mortal hero, or a classic moment in which Gandalf gets a mic drop in front of Saruman and the White Council when Saruman tries to cut him down for his habit of smoking pipe-weed to clear his mind. These moments are not found in any chapter of *The Silmarillion* or any appendix to *The Lord of the Rings*, as they were mere episodes written down and untethered to any specific point in the broader work. But Christopher presents them to us nonetheless, and our understanding (and enjoyment) of Tolkien's world is much better for it.

---

100    Ibid.

# So Is It Just a Collection of Short Stories?

Not exactly. To call them "short stories" would suggest that they each can stand alone in some sense, telling a complete story. That's not always the case. And then there are some that are not "stories" at all, but more like essays about a particular topic of interest to fans of Middle-earth.

## Tell Us More.

We'd love to!

The first thing you'll notice when looking at the table of contents to *Unfinished Tales* is that it's arranged chronologically, in a very obvious way: its first three major divisions are entitled "The First Age," "The Second Age," and "The Third Age." Don't expect a complete rundown of the history of each of these ages, though, nor a mere replication of material found in *The Silmarillion*. These designations are more like file folders, organizing chapters by the era in which they take place. In reality, you'll get only a glimpse of the broader history from reading *Unfinished Tales* alone; as Christopher himself says in the introduction, he has "throughout assumed on the reader's part a fair knowledge of the published works of my father,"[101] meaning he intends this book for consumption by those who have already read *The Hobbit*, *The Lord of the Rings*, and *The Silmarillion*. Christopher says *The Lord of the Rings* is especially important to have already read, but in our opinion, a first readthrough of all three of the "finished" works is recommended before tackling *Unfinished Tales*. This, after all, is why we put it fourth, after those others.

Part One, "The First Age," contains only two very long chapters. Each of these chapters consists of a long-form telling of one of those Great Tales we

---

101    Tolkien, *Unfinished Tales*, 2020, 17.

talked about last chapter (and will get into more in the next chapter). They are "Of Tuor and His Coming to Gondolin" and *"Narn i Hîn Húrin,"* or "The Tale of the Children of Húrin." While both of these stories are told in *The Silmarillion*, the versions in *Unfinished Tales* are greatly expanded, written in more of a "novel form" than the outline/summary format of the chapters in *The Silmarillion* that tell these stories. For example, this portion of a sentence about Tuor's coming to Gondolin in Chapter 23 of *The Silmarillion*: "Then they were led up the mighty ravine of Orfalch Echor, barred by seven gates, and brought before Ecthelion of the Fountain, the warden of the great gate at the end of the climbing road..."[102] is told over *almost five full pages* in *Unfinished Tales*, with each of these seven gates described in ever-more-stunning detail, with living, breathing characters with whom we experience the sights of the spectacular hidden city of King Turgon of the Noldor.

The problem is that, as the title of the volume indicates, they're not finished. The *Narn* is nearly so, but "Tuor"—a 1951 attempt by Tolkien to rewrite the Great Tale of "The Fall of Gondolin" (first drafted in 1917) as a full *Lord of the Rings*-style narrative—spends over thirty pages just getting that titular hero Tuor *to* Gondolin, and stops there. We never actually get to see the fall that was promised in the original title.

Both of these chapters have been republished in standalone editions since 1980, and we'll talk more about them in the next chapter.

Things really start to get interesting in Part Two, "The Second Age." This is where the "Númenor" reference in the full title of the book (*Unfinished Tales of Númenor and Middle-earth*) comes in, and this is awesome, because Númenor—the mysterious lost island kingdom from whose nobility Aragorn claims descent, and that gave rise to the enlightened kingdoms of Arnor and Gondor in Middle-earth—has really only been hinted at (and received a very short, short summary) in previous books. *Unfinished Tales* Part Two contains

_____

102    Tolkien, *Silmarillion*, 2021, 228.

some of the most detailed and comprehensive material Tolkien ever wrote about Númenor, and if nothing else convinces you to read it, this should.

There's "A Description of the Island of Númenor," which is partly like "Of Beleriand and its Realms" in that it describes the geography of the island and its various administrative divisions; but it goes beyond that and gives us more of a hint of what Númenórean culture was like: pastimes, technology, and even religious observances. There's "The Line of Elros: Kings of Númenor," which is an annal of all of the...well, kings (and queens!) of Númenor. All of them were named in Appendix A to *The Lord of the Rings*, but here we get a paragraph about each of them and their various achievements, struggles, glories, family drama, and crimes and misdemeanors. It's not exactly a fully fleshed-out narrative of palace intrigue and political machinations *à la* George R.R. Martin—and believe us when we say we don't *want* it to be anything like a George R.R. Martin story[103]—but it is a tale told in brief of a nation in gradual decline, and a beautifully sad downward trend of ever more corrupt and wicked rulers whose incompetence and arrogance belie the apparent greatness of their realm and reveal the true rot at the heart of the civilization (and to be honest, despite our protestations, it is at times more like Martin's works than one might expect).

There's even one kinda-sorta "Great Tale" of Númenor in the mix: the story of "Aldarion and Erendis," which tells of the young romance and eventual painfully irreconcilable differences between Aldarion, son of the fifth king (who would go on to become king himself someday), and his wife Erendis. In some ways it's the most human and heartbreaking story Tolkien ever wrote, about a man who, though not necessarily a bad person, simply can't seem to put aside his own selfish interests and give a little bit of his time to the people closest to him: his father, wife, and daughter. His decisions end up having surprisingly profound ramifications for the history of the legendarium

---

103    That is in no way meant to disparage Mr. Martin or the fans of his books, nor the creators and fans of
       the TV series based on his works, which half of the authors of this book have actually watched and read.
       It's just that we want Middle-earth to be Middle-earth and Westeros to be Westeros.

Why We Love Middle-earth

and Númenor's involvement in the affairs of Middle-earth, as well as for the future royal line of Númenor.

However, what's undoubtedly the most talked-about chapter in "The Second Age," and certainly the one that's likely to be of most interest to the average fan—particularly those who have come to Tolkien's books recently from Amazon Prime's *The Rings of Power* series—is "The History of Galadriel and Celeborn." In Christopher Tolkien's own words in the introduction to the chapter: "There is no part of the history of Middle-earth more full of problems than the story of Galadriel and Celeborn, and it must be admitted that there are severe inconsistencies 'embedded in the traditions'; or, to look at the matter from another point of view, that the role and importance of Galadriel only emerged slowly, and that her story underwent continual refashionings."[104]

This chapter, as Christopher's comment suggests, offers multiple conflicting stories of how Galadriel and Celeborn—Elven royalty from two different kindreds—came to be wife and husband, and Lady and Lord of Lothlórien. And when we say "conflicting," we mean it! In *The Silmarillion*, Celeborn is an Elf of the Sindar who never went to the Undying Lands; Galadriel is born in Valinor and meets Celeborn later after she returns to Middle-earth. But in one version captured here, Celeborn was a Telerin Elf of the Undying Lands, and his name wasn't originally Celeborn, which is a Sindarin name.[105] There's a version in which they have a son (which they don't, according to *The Lord of the Rings*). There's an account in which Galadriel is a shining beacon of moral purity, and another in which she comes across as ambitious and unrepentant. It really is a mixed bag of stuff, and as interesting as it all is, it's impossible to accept all of it as canon. And yet, there are so many different possibilities presented here, in Tolkien's own words, that the complaints of *The Rings of Power* critics—including us, at times—about Amazon's Galadriel not being

---

104    Tolkien, *Unfinished Tales*, 2020, 247.

105    The original Telerin name of Celeborn in this particular version is something you have to see to believe. We won't spoil it. Just Google "Celeborn Telerin name," and be careful about what you click and who happens to be nearby when you do.

enough like "Tolkien's Galadriel" (as if there was only one version of her) all seems a little silly when we stop to think about it.[106]

But for all its difficulties, "The History of Galadriel and Celeborn" has some fantastic stuff in it, too. One of the most interesting surprises is a more complete telling of the creation and distribution of the Rings of Power by Celeborn and the "Gwaith-i-Mírdain" Elven-smiths of Eregion, and the subsequent reveal of the One Ring by Sauron and battle with the Dark Lord for control of the Rings (and it must be said here that this is definitely *nothing* like the way it was presented in the first season of *The Rings of Power* on Amazon Prime). Reading it is an incredible experience, and will enrich your understanding of the most important events of the Second Age in Middle-earth. It's just that you'll have to pick and choose which parts of it you want to believe.

The last of the three "Age" sections is "The Third Age," which picks up after the War of the Last Alliance (for those who've seen the Peter Jackson films, this is the climactic battle shown in the Prologue of *The Fellowship of the Ring*, between Sauron and his Orcs on one side, and the Elves led by Gil-galad and Elrond with Men led by Elendil and Isildur on the other side—the battle in which Elendil's sword was broken and Isildur cut the Ring from Sauron's hand). If you've ever wanted to know exactly what happened to Isildur after that battle, you'll find it in "The Disaster of the Gladden Fields" (so, obviously, it doesn't go well—but not quite as badly or as quickly downhill as Peter Jackson suggested in his version of *The Fellowship of the Ring*). There's also "Cirion and Eorl," which tells the story of the founding of Rohan and the history of the ancient alliance between the Kings of Rohan and the Stewards of Gondor.

---

106   Massive hat tip here to Jeff LaSala, author of *The Silmarillion Primer* and numerous other Tolkien articles on Tor.com, who compared "The History of Galadriel and Celeborn" to the classic 1980s movie *Clue* in its many "That's how it could have happened"-type moments, and has done a fantastic job of defending the *Rings of Power* version as simply another alternative version of a character for whom there's simply just not one canon. Some would argue that Tolkien's work even more broadly offers enough alternatives for many stories that there's no such thing as "canon" in Tolkien at all, but that's a conversation we don't have space to get into here.

"The Third Age" finishes with some great supplemental material to *The Hobbit* and *The Lord of the Rings*. "The Quest of Erebor" gives more information about the events leading up to *The Hobbit*, and some of Gandalf's doings when he conveniently left the party in that story—for better or worse, it seems that perhaps Gandalf's selection of Bilbo Baggins for the adventure with the Dwarves may not have been quite so random an occurrence as we were led to believe. "The Hunt for the Ring" gives rare detail on both the White Council of Wizards and Elves, by which Gandalf, Saruman, Elrond, and Galadriel directed their cold war against Sauron for centuries, and the movements of the Black Riders as they searched Middle-earth looking for the One Ring. And "The Battles of the Fords of Isen" shows Tolkien reaching into his medievalist's bag of tricks for inspiration on one of the most important battles of the War of the Ring, which is never shown "on screen" in *The Lord of the Rings*.

Closing out the volume, there's a Part Four containing descriptive and informative essays on some people and objects of Middle-earth that aren't described in great detail elsewhere. The most mind-blowing and essential, we think, is "The Istari," which explains exactly who and what the Wizards of Middle-earth really were, where they came from, and why there are so few of them—we won't spoil the details, but we'll just say that wizardry in Tolkien's legendarium isn't something you can learn simply by studying swish-and-flicks at Hogwarts. A wizard in Middle-earth is a wizard for life... and beyond, as everyone's favorite old greybeard ended up proving.

# But What's It Like Reading It?

A good question. We're glad you asked.

Reading *Unfinished Tales* is...well, it's Tolkien. Clearly. And it feels like Tolkien. But it is very different from everything that you'll have read up to this point (assuming you follow our advice on reading order), because it is all presented as incomplete. There's a lot of great material here, and it is material that we all rely on for a better understanding of Tolkien's world; it is cited in scholarly essays, has been subtly nodded to in adaptations, and yes, has been relied upon and read from by well-meaning podcasters. But it will leave you with questions that will never be answered in any satisfactory way. We're okay with that, but we understand it's not everyone's cup of tea.

Still, we think *every* reader approaching Tolkien's writings for the first time should read *Unfinished Tales*. Based on the conversations we've had, far more people like *Unfinished Tales* than not. The unfinished nature of the stories is rarely a barrier to appreciating them—Tolkien's delightfully archaic prose and his knack for epic world-building shine through, even in these works that don't quite make it to the finish line. And you will learn a lot, including about topics you never realized you were interested in, like the history of the mysterious Woses encountered by the Rohirrim cavalry on the way to the Battle of the Pelennor Fields,[107] and an almost-forgotten (occasionally forgotten by us, until our listeners reminded us of it) fourth marriage between a Man and an Elf. These are the kinds of bits of trivia you'll need to answer nerdy online arguments or impress your friends in Tolkien pub trivia competitions.[108]

The most important reason we can think of for recommending all budding Tolkien fans read *Unfinished Tales*, though, is that it's *the* decision point we use to help newcomers decide what they should read next. After *Unfinished Tales*, the traditional method for continuing on into the deeper levels of the Middle-earth legendarium was the twelve-volume History of Middle-earth series, edited and published by Christopher in the years after this one. That's how we kept going deeper, and it's certainly an option still. But it doesn't get

---

107   Movie fans who haven't read *The Lord of the Rings* yet may be confused by this one. Let's just say there's a lot of stuff that doesn't make it into adaptations of Tolkien's work! See the next section of this book for more.

108   We love pub trivia, and we're surprised it's taken us this long to bring it up in this book. But there you have it. If you don't love pub trivia, come find us and talk to us. We'll make a convert out of you.

any easier from here on out. The "draft plus commentary" approach adopted by Christopher in *Unfinished Tales* is continued through the twelve volumes of The History of Middle-earth, and as you go, the drafts and commentaries become more and more complicated; the book becomes less a chronicle of events and peoples of Middle-earth and more a study of the way Tolkien wrote. Not that there's *anything* wrong with that, and for anyone who is interested in pursuing Tolkien studies even quasi-academically, it's where you're going to end up. But it's not for everyone.

So *Unfinished Tales* is a junction in the road on your journey to Tolkien obsession. If you like the "draft plus commentary" approach presented in this book, and you want more, you'll probably want to go on into The History of Middle-earth. But for others, you may want to turn aside here and check out some of Tolkien's non-legendarium stories that were finished, or biographies, or Tolkien's academic writing and translations. There are lots of options from here, but it's worth reading *Unfinished Tales* to help decide what is going to satisfy your craving for more Tolkien from here on out.

## Has Any of This Stuff Been Published Elsewhere?

Yes, in fact. In recent years, much of the content of *Unfinished Tales* has been republished in standalone editions of Tolkien's Great Tales (more on those next chapter), the very recent *Fall of Númenor*, and elsewhere. But there's a lot that hasn't been published elsewhere and can only be found here, and those tend to be the biggest crowd-pleasers in the volume—like "The History of Galadriel and Celeborn" or the essay on "The Istari."

# So, Why Do We Love It?

This is a tough one. Not because we don't love it, or because we love it less, or anything like that; it's just a different kind of love.

It's hard to imagine any Tolkien fan loving *Unfinished Tales* the way one *loves* a book like *The Lord of the Rings* or *The Silmarillion*.[109] An unfinished story is always going to be *somewhat* unfulfilling. Frequent commentary of the type inserted by Christopher Tolkien (necessary as it is) has a tendency to break immersion and "pull us out of the story" in a way that doesn't happen if you just power through the pages of *The Lord of the Rings*. And though there are many places where the story is dramatic and emotionally powerful, there are also places where you're just...reading annals of kings. So maybe it's not quite as sexy as the other books.

But we *do* love *Unfinished Tales*, and there's a reason it's fourth on our list. For many readers, this book is the first glimpse at the man behind the curtain. It's the first time the editorial point of view of Christopher Tolkien pulls back far enough for us to see not just the words Tolkien wrote, but how he chose them and the challenges he faced getting them on the page. And it's the first time we see *just how much there could have been* to the legendarium if Tolkien had had Elvish immortality (or rather, "serial longevity," in the phrase Tolkien preferred) and unlimited time to write everything that was in his head about this world.

It's also a first glimpse of just how much energy Tolkien spent on making his world as internally consistent as possible. The essays on "The Drúedain" (the aforementioned Woses) and "The Palantíri" go beyond storytelling into questions of genealogy and the physics of the seeing-stones (respectively). Where many fantasy authors would just use devices like the *palantíri* haphazardly to accomplish whatever the story demanded, or explain their powers away vaguely and open-endedly as "magic!" Tolkien puts limitations on the powers of the seeing-stones and describes these limitations in detail here...and much of this stuff seems like it was never even intended for public consumption, but written for his own purposes to remind himself of how his own inventions worked, so he could write them consistently in his stories.

---

109   We're not saying it can't happen, and we see a few of you at the back of the room already standing up
to tell us how wrong we are. Hear us out, and if you still want to comment, send us an email.

So please, do yourself a favor and read *Unfinished Tales*, and if you're not sure where to turn next, check out the chapter after the next one for some suggestions. But before we get there, there are a few more books that we need to talk about as a group in the next chapter. We'll see you there!

# WHY ALAN LOVES IT

The truth is that I can't recall precisely when I first read *Unfinished Tales*, because I didn't read it in its entirety for quite some time after I picked it up. I *think* I bought my first copy of it sometime in the year or two leading up to the release of Jackson's *The Lord of the Rings*, because I wanted to learn more about Isildur and someone had told me about the chapter "The Disaster of the Gladden Fields." I "dabbled" with various stories from *UT* over the years, and quickly discovered how much I admired and enjoyed Tolkien's incredible gift of sub-creation. Here was even *more* on the background of people I always wanted to know more about: Isildur, Gandalf, Tuor, Celebrimbor, Galadriel, and more. We get glimpses of glory: Tuor's approach to Gondolin may be some of Tolkien's most awe-inspiring and evocative prose, and it's stuck here in this book that so few people have taken the opportunity to read. We see a deeply human side of Tolkien's writings in Aldarion and Erendis. And we get to feel like we're in on secrets of Middle-earth throughout!

Just as *The Silmarillion* shines a light on *The Lord of the Rings*, illuminating themes and events in a new way and changing the way the latter is read, *Unfinished Tales* adds texture and detail—even into the smallest corners of Middle-earth. Its impact isn't as widely felt as *The Silmarillion*, but where it comes into play, it brings much-loved detail and richness to the tales of Middle-earth.

# Why Shawn Loves It

Like all the other books we've discussed so far, I first read *Unfinished Tales* in high school on a wild power-tear through Tolkien's major works over the course of several months. Aside from the obvious—that these tales were unfinished; I figured that out from the title—I had no idea what to expect, so I was surprised and mesmerized by this book, which was unlike anything else I'd ever read. If *The Silmarillion* was like reading one of my favorite mythology compilations, *Unfinished Tales* was at times like going straight to Homer or Virgil: there's a breathtaking scene in "Of Tuor and His Coming to Gondolin" in particular that felt like that, a real mortal-man-meets-the-manifestation-of-a-god moment that would be right at home in the *Odyssey*.

I've always been a fan of the Rohirrim (I am, after all, the Lord of the Mark), so "Cirion and Eorl" was always a favorite of mine. It reads a bit more like Appendix A to *The Lord of the Rings* than a lot of what's in this book (and that's all okay with me), but when it does zoom in to the level of dramatic narrative instead of history to show actual human interactions between Cirion, the Steward of Gondor, and Eorl the Young, lord of the Éothéod (that's the Rohirrim before they lived in Rohan), it's pure magic.

Also, "The Istari" was completely mind-blowing for teenage me. The secret origin of Gandalf, Saruman, and the other wizards? Their real names? And, of course, the mystery of the Blue Wizards...oh, this was the stuff that kept me reading deeper into Tolkien even then.

With that said, my appreciation of *Unfinished Tales* has always been more cerebral than my appreciation of *The Lord of the Rings* or *The Silmarillion*. I "love" it with my brain, not so much my heart, which isn't to say that my love of it is less...just different. Reading *Unfinished Tales* was, for me, an early exercise in understanding just how much Tolkien *didn't* write in his lifetime that he wanted to, and that fascinated (and continues to fascinate) me. If it had not been for *Unfinished Tales*, would I still be plumbing the depths of Tolkien's writings? Would I have spent so much of my life in pursuit of a deeper understanding of this amazing author who only just scratched the surface of his own creation? Or would I just be content reading and rereading *The Silmarillion* and the other finished works? I suppose we'll never know, but the what-if is intriguing for me. And I am grateful for *Unfinished Tales* and everything that comes after it, for keeping me on my path of discovery.

CHAPTER 5

# THE GREAT TALES:
# *THE CHILDREN OF HÚRIN,*
# *BEREN AND LÚTHIEN, AND*
# *THE FALL OF GONDOLIN*

*"The chief of the stories of the Silmarillion, and the one most fully treated is the Story of Beren and Lúthien the Elfmaiden. Here we meet, among other things, the first example of the motive (to become dominant in Hobbits) that the great policies of world history, 'the wheels of the world,' are often turned not by the Lords and Governors, even gods, but by the seemingly unknown and weak... As such the story is (I think a beautiful and powerful) heroic-fairy-romance, receivable in itself with only a very general vague knowledge of the background.*

*"There are other stories almost equally full in treatment, and equally independent and yet linked to the general history."*

—J.R.R. Tolkien, 1951 letter to Milton Waldman[110]

---

110   Carpenter, *Letters*, No. 131.

Following the publication of *Unfinished Tales*, Christopher Tolkien edited the "Titles-Not-Appearing-in-This-Book"[111] of The History of Middle-earth, twelve volumes of further unfinished "draft plus commentary" publications, as well as some other academic works of his father's and other manuscripts outside of the Middle-earth legendarium. He completed this flurry of activity in 1996, and as the twentieth century ended, it seemed like that was it. Peter Jackson's *The Lord of the Rings* film trilogy came out between 2001 and 2003, and that was all we got from Middle-earth for a few years. There were Tolkien publications, of course—Tolkien has had more posthumous releases than Tupac—and some incredibly valuable scholarly publications, like *The Annotated Hobbit* edited by Douglas A. Anderson. But nothing new came out from within Middle-earth.

Until 2007. That's when Christopher Tolkien undertook the standalone publication of one of his father's Great Tales, those centers of narrative gravity of the First Age, the stories that the rest of *The Silmarillion* had been sketched around to provide background and context. And the story that Christopher chose to publish in 2007 was *The Children of Húrin*.

Unless you've been skipping around, you've heard us mention this story before in this book. It was previously called the *Narn i Hîn Húrin*, in an unfinished version published in *Unfinished Tales*. It was told in brief as the chapter of *The Silmarillion* called "Of Túrin Turambar," and going back farther than that was called "Turambar and the Foalókë"[112] back in *The Book of Lost Tales*. It was also told in poetry in the unfinished *Lay of the Children of Húrin*, which Tolkien had first put together the "Sketch of the Mythology" for back in the 1920s, and perhaps for that reason alone it would make sense as the first of the Great Tales to publish as a standalone novel.

---

111   We're as surprised as everyone else that there haven't been more Monty Python references in this book.

112   *Foalókë* was an early Elvish word for *dragon*.

# But Why? And Why Now?

Christopher—then in his eighties—explained his rationale for the undertaking in the preface to *The Children of Húrin*:

> It is undeniable that there are a very great many readers of *The Lord of the Rings* for whom the legends of the Elder Days (as previously published in varying forms in *The Silmarillion, Unfinished Tales,* and *The History of Middle-earth*) are altogether unknown... For this reason it has seemed to me for a long time that there was a good case for presenting my father's long version of the legend of the Children of Húrin as an independent work, between its own covers, with a minimum of editorial presence, and above all in continuous narrative without gaps or interruptions...[113]

Going on, Christopher explained how he longed to tell the story in a way that opened it up to new readers, such as those who had only read *The Lord of the Rings* and knew the name of Túrin as a "textual ruin" in that work, and to tell it in a way that both was "vivid and immediate" and also had the feeling of being "handed down from remote ages."[114] He must have known that there were readers out there who knew the story already, but he wanted to open the door wide to a new audience of readers who weren't ready or able to plumb the depths of those unfinished manuscripts, gradually increasing in complexity as we've walked through them even in this book. He wanted the greatest of his father's Great Tales to be accessible to as many fans as possible. It was a wonderfully un-gatekeepery thing to do, and we salute him for it.

Continuing through the preface, we find Christopher asserting that it had always been his father's intention for the three Great Tales to be told in

---

113   Tolkien, J.R.R., edited by Christopher Tolkien. *The Children of Húrin.* Houghton Mifflin, 2007, 7.
114   Ibid., 8. As before, "textual ruin" is not Christopher Tolkien's term, but a coinage by Tolkien scholar Michael D.C. Drout.

Why We Love Middle-earth

fuller form than the rest of the stories of *The Silmarillion*, and that it was "unquestionable" that his father saw the Great Tales as capable of standing on their own without the context of *The Silmarillion*, more than other stories in the cycle. At the same time, however, he recognized that "the tale of the Children of Húrin is integral to the history of Elves and Men in the Elder Days, and there are necessarily a good many references to events and circumstances in that larger story."[115]

So, in other words, he sought to offer the world a standalone version of the story of *The Children of Húrin* that wouldn't require a reader to have read *The Silmarillion*, though there are enough references back to *The Silmarillion* that this new book could conceivably provide a "way in" to *The Silmarillion* for readers who want to keep reading (we still think it's best to read *The Silmarillion* first, but who are we to argue with Christopher's intentions here?).

And what a story it is! Húrin Thalion, Son of Galdor, was a hero of Men in the First Age, who was taken prisoner by the Dark Lord Morgoth after the Battle of Unnumbered Tears (*Nirnaeth Arnoediad* for you Elvish language enthusiasts), after an epic last stand in which he killed *seventy* orcs by his own hand. Morgoth sought information from Húrin about the location of the hidden city of Gondolin, but Húrin defied the Dark Lord, and so Morgoth cursed his family: "...upon all whom you love my thought shall weigh as a cloud of Doom, and it shall bring them down into darkness and despair. Wherever they go, evil shall arise. Whenever they speak, their words shall bring ill counsel. Whatsoever they do shall turn against them. They shall die without hope, cursing both life and death."[116]

The story tells how that curse follows Húrin's children throughout their tragic and unhappy lives: Túrin, a great warrior, general, hero, outlaw, and

---

115 Ibid., 10.
116 Ibid., 64.

dragon-slayer,[117] and Túrin's younger sister Niënor, who manages to get drawn into her brother's bad choices. It's a beautiful but very sad tale of woe, bad luck, loss, grief, accidental murder, mistaken identities, misread portents, and...well, we'll just leave it there. This is the story that Christopher Tolkien brought to life like never before in this edition, where the very human and very painful drama of the family's hardships leaps off the page in a way it never did in the brief outline of the story provided in *The Silmarillion*.

## But Wasn't There Already a Long Prose Version of the Story in *Unfinished Tales*?

Why yes, there was! It's so good to see you've been paying attention!

And in fact, the bulk of the 2007 *The Children of Húrin* is the same text as what's presented in "The First Age" of the *Unfinished Tales* as the *Narn*.[118] They're not entirely the same—and there is an appendix to the 2007 book that details the many differences—but fundamentally, it's reasonable to consider the 2007 *Children* as more or less a "finishing" of the unfinished *Narn*.

But Christopher's whole point now *was to finish it* so that it wouldn't be accessible only to those of us who are willing to read an unfinished manuscript. He wanted to take it out of the textual labyrinth of *Unfinished Tales* and The History of Middle-earth and make it approachable, accessible, fun, sleek, sexy[119] again. Get it out of the minor leagues and out there where *everyone* could see it play. He wanted it without all the commentary and missing pieces; he even said so...back to the preface: "It would be altogether

---

117    Not to mention a god-level man-in-black type, who would make Johnny Cash proud.

118    Whenever we see this word on its own, it's hard not to think of G'Kar from *Babylon 5*. "Your heart is empty, Mollari. Did you know that?"

119    Once you've read it, you'll probably wonder why we chose some of these adjectives. It remains a horribly tragic—beautiful, but tragic—work. Ugh.

contrary to the conception of this book to burden its reading with an abundance of notes giving information..."[120]

So he published it, with some spectacular illustrations by the legendary artist Alan Lee, and it turned out well for all of us. It received positive reviews from the *Independent*, the *Washington Post* (who picked up on its likeness to a Greek tragedy), and many other critics. And though it wasn't universally positively received (*Entertainment Weekly* called it "awkward and immature"), it was a commercial success, exceeding the expectations of both the US and UK publishers of Tolkien's works.

# WHAT ABOUT THE OTHER GREAT TALES?

Ten years later, Christopher decided to do it again. This time, with *Beren and Lúthien*.

The story of the mortal hero Beren and his lover, the Elven princess Lúthien, daughter of Thingol (we mentioned them earlier, you may recall, as well as this story!), was undoubtedly the most personal of all the Great Tales to Tolkien and to his son—seeing as how it was partly inspired by Tolkien's own courtship of his wife Edith.[121] Edith wasn't an eternally youthful and beautiful princess (though it's incredibly sweet that young Ronald wrote her as one), and she wasn't an Elf...but she was a Protestant, and that to the Catholic Tolkien would have seemed nearly as hard a divide to cross back in the early twentieth century—not least of all because his guardian, Father Francis Murray, forbade the relationship when the two were teenagers, forcing Ronald to get back in touch with Edith and court her then, after he had come of age.

---

120    Ibid., 10.

121    One well-known bit of Tolkien lore is that Ronald and Edith Tolkien's grave, in Wolvercote Cemetery in Oxford, bears not only the names of the two people resting there but also the names "Lúthien" and "Beren."

She said yes! But we digress.

Beren and Lúthien meet cute in a forest while she's singing and dancing, making flowers bloom where her feet touch the ground (as one does), and fall instantly in love, sending them eventually on a ride-or-die adventure together just to earn the right to, well, *be together*. Much like Father Francis, Lúthien's father Thingol is none too keen on his immortal baby girl marrying some smelly, hairy mortal—not least because she was not only Elven but also half Maia; her mother Melian was one of the angelic Maiar (see the *Valaquenta* in the *Silmarillion* chapter above) who stayed in Middle-earth to be Thingol's queen *and yes, the hypocrisy of Thingol is thick*. It's a deeply personal story to the Tolkien family, despite its mythic setting and details; we hope that Ronald and Edith never had to fight werewolves or journey into Morgoth's fortress—which is basically literally hell—to make it to their wedding day. And it was a story that Christopher had always wanted to tell properly, as he notes in his preface. Even before embarking on the years-long editorial journey of The History of Middle-earth, back in 1981, he had pitched the idea of a standalone book about Beren and Lúthien: not so much as a finished story, but as "a developing entity." In other words, it would be less of a novel and more of a collection of the many versions of the story Tolkien started work on, to put them all in one place, with a bit of editorial commentary on the textual history in the preface: "I could do 'Beren,' with the original Lost Tale, *The Lay of Leithian*, and an essay on the development of the legend...for the treating of one legend as a developing entity, rather than to give all the Lost Tales at one go..."[122]

But it didn't happen at that time; The History of Middle-earth did. And in publishing those twelve volumes, Christopher managed to publish all the unfinished material from which he would have created that standalone Beren and Lúthien book. But the problem remained that the material scattered across the many volumes of The History of Middle-earth was...well, not the

---

122    Tolkien, J.R.R., edited by Christopher Tolkien. *Beren and Lúthien*. Houghton Mifflin Harcourt, 2017, 10.

easiest thing for readers to parse. The material in History of Middle-earth is presented more or less chronologically, and Christopher was discovering things as he went—his understanding of those manuscripts in 1996, when he finished the long project, was different than it had been in 1983, when he started. And given Professor Tolkien's penchant for writing one version of a story, putting it aside for a few years (or decades), and then picking it up again later after he'd written lots of other stuff, for a reader to get a full picture of the development of a story like the tale of Beren and Lúthien that he worked with on and off for his entire life meant investing the time and money into acquiring and reading all of those (admittedly kind of academic) books. If we may paraphrase his words in the preface, Christopher feared that this was a bit too much to ask of readers, and that coupled with the complexity of the manuscripts themselves presented a "deterrent."[123]

So, with the publication of *Beren and Lúthien* in 2017, Christopher sought to simplify the process. In his own words, he "extract[ed] one narrative element from a vast work of extraordinary richness and complexity," and "tried to separate the story of Beren and Tinúviel (Lúthien) so that it stands alone, so far as that can be done (in my opinion) without distortion,"[124] to bring together many texts to tell the story more or less completely and also give a sense of its development over time.

The finished work is a bit of a hybrid in terms of style and story. It starts with the earliest surviving version of the story from *The Book of Lost Tales*, *The Tale of Tinúviel* (another name for Lúthien, which she bore as a nickname given to her by her lover even in the latest versions of the story). From there, it goes to the later version of the story which aligns with what's told in *The Silmarillion*, but the later version is told in a mixture of poetry and prose: prose excerpts from the manuscripts that formed the basis of *The Silmarillion* alternate with poetic treatments of the story from *The Lay of*

---

123   Ibid., 14.
124   Ibid., 12, 14.

*Leithian.*[125] The prose excerpts are good, but in our opinion, the poetry is where this story really shines. *The Lay of Leithian* is an impressive, expansive work, a modern version of a medieval heroic lay, with fairy-tale magic, ethereal forest dreamscapes, adventure, song battles, and multiple trips into horrific dungeons populated by the most evil and terrifying monsters Tolkien's imagination could devise.

## So Why Didn't Christopher Just Publish *The Lay of Leithian?*

The shortest answer to this question is simply: because it's not finished. *The Lay of Leithian* cuts off suddenly in the middle of Canto (that's like a chapter of a long poetic work) XIV, at a climactic action moment in the story...but nowhere near the end.

A slightly longer answer to this question would reiterate that Christopher Tolkien had already edited and published all the surviving verses of *The Lay of Leithian* in the third volume of The History of Middle-earth, titled *The Lays of Beleriand.* The full available content of the unfinished epic poem is still available in that volume; what's published here is like a highlight reel, a playlist of greatest hits chosen by Christopher Tolkien himself, choosing many of the best moments from the poem to tell the story and filling in other bits with the prose, rather than rehashing the work he'd done previously with *Lays.*

So, while the material was all out there already, this standalone edition of *Beren and Lúthien* is absolutely worth the cover price, for bringing enough of the material together in one place to give a glimpse at the story and its development, especially for newcomers. And, like *The Children of Húrin* published ten years before it, it's also adorned with some spectacular

---

125    Mentioned in Chapter 2. And *Leithian*, despite its similarity to the name *Lúthien*, is not another name
        for the female protagonist; it's an Elvish word meaning "Release from Bondage."

artwork by Alan Lee, whose style lends itself particularly well to the soft-focus faerie-romance story of Tolkien's most famous couple. One particular Lee illustration from the early *Tale of Tinúviel* version is an instant classic, in that it's a rare depiction of a scene involving the infamous Tevildo, Prince of Cats, who serves as an important antagonist in this early version of the story. He's literally just, like, a big black cat. It's phenomenal.[126]

## But I'm a Dog Person.

Then *Beren and Lúthien* has got you covered there, too! Consistent with the "cats are evil" motif of the earliest version of the story, one of the heroes allied to the titular lovers in all versions of the story is... a dog. And not just any dog, but the most loyal, steadfast, protective, brave, strong, who's-a-good-boy talking dog we've ever seen in a fantasy story. His name is Huan, and you're gonna love him. Even the half of the authors of this book who happen to be cat people love Huan.

# SOLD. BUT YOU SAID THERE ARE THREE GREAT TALES?

Well, yes, but there almost weren't three standalone books. Christopher Tolkien closed out the preface to *Beren and Lúthien* by saying: "In my ninety-third year this is (presumptively) my last book in the long series of editions of my father's writings," and explaining how the deeply personal subject matter and relevance to his parents made it the perfect way to close the book (so to speak) on his life of dedication to publishing his father's writings. He goes on for a few more paragraphs, but we cry every time we

---

126   Sadly, Tevildo only appears in this one story of Tolkien's, and only in this earliest version of it. The role played by the Prince of Cats in *The Tale of Tinúviel* is later given to a lieutenant of Morgoth called Thû, later known as Sauron. So in a way, Tevildo is the earliest incarnation of Tolkien's most famous Dark Lord. It's perfectly acceptable to react to this information in whichever way you see fit: mind blown, laugh it off, spend the rest of your life making Sauron lolcat memes, whatever you want.

read it, so you're just going to have to read it yourself. It seemed that after all these years, the world had finally seen its last posthumous publication of Tolkien's work edited by Christopher Tolkien.

But...that's not quite how it turned out. A year later, the then-ninety-four-year-old Christopher Tolkien once again demonstrated his commitment to his father's legacy by editing and publishing one truly final work: the last of the three Great Tales, *The Fall of Gondolin*, published in 2018.

In the preface to *The Fall of Gondolin*, Christopher reveals that he had considered completing this final book even a year before, when he had done *Beren and Lúthien*, but the reason he called that one "presumptively" his last was because he thought it improbable that he could accomplish with *Gondolin* what he had accomplished with *Beren*.[127]

There's a good reason for this. Though it is one of his Great Tales, and ultimately the first tale of the First Age that Tolkien wrote—he wrote it in early 1917, while he was recovering from trench fever in a military hospital in Staffordshire after being shipped back to Britain from France in the Great War—he never really got around to rewriting it, not even to the limited extent he had rewritten the story of Beren and Lúthien or the Children of Húrin. The earliest version of the story, written in 1917, is the only finished version of the story completed by Tolkien, and it's like *nothing else* Tolkien ever wrote. The recent memory of his Great War experience casts a long shadow over this story of a horrific battle between Elves on one side and Orcs and Balrogs on the other, in which a once-beautiful city is destroyed. It's also highly reminiscent of accounts of the fall of Troy, going back to Greek and Roman mythology, so Tolkien's recent time at Oxford as a classics student, before he switched to English (less than five years previously), is also apparent. This makes for a spectacular story in its own right—Balrogs riding atop giant worms of magical flame "like ropes of molten metal" through the

---

127    Tolkien, J.R.R., edited by Christopher Tolkien. *The Fall of Gondolin*. Houghton Mifflin Harcourt, 2018, 9.

broken walls of the hidden city of Gondolin, Orcs hiding in the bellies of massive mechanical iron serpents like WWI-era tanks; blasting fire, epic last stands for the heroes of the Twelve Houses of the Gondothlim—it's truly one of a kind in Tolkien's legendarium; only the Siege of Gondor from *The Lord of the Rings* comes close, and that isn't nearly as brutal (partly because it has a slightly happier ending).

But as great as this story is, the lore underlying it is still embryonic. This tale is from the earliest stage of Tolkien's mythology, the version in *The Book of Lost Tales*, which is so different as to be almost incompatible with the versions developed not long after and immortalized by Christopher in the pages of *The Silmarillion*. Which is not to say that it couldn't be brought into some kind of "harmony" with the later version of the legendarium—and Tolkien did precisely that in the late 1920s, when he wrote a new version of the story that ended up informing the account in *The Silmarillion* when Christopher compiled it, but that ended up just being a compressed outline.

Then there was the beautifully epic version Tolkien began work on in 1951 that made its way into the pages of *Unfinished Tales*, but as we noted in the last chapter, that one didn't get past Tuor's arrival in Gondolin as a wandering hero, and didn't get anywhere near the destruction of the city. As Christopher said in 1980 of this later version: "Deeply changed in style and bearings, yet retaining many of the essentials of the story written in his youth, 'Of Tuor and the Fall of Gondolin' would have given in fine detail the whole legend that constitutes the brief 23rd chapter of the published Silmarillion, but, grievously, he went no further than the coming of Tuor and Voronwë to the last gate and Tuor's sight of Gondolin across the plain of Tumladen. To his reasons for abandoning it there is no clue."[128]

Indeed, not only is there no clue as to *why* Tolkien abandoned the story, but Christopher calls his abandonment of the story "one of the saddest

---

128    Tolkien, *Unfinished Tales*, 2020, 18.

facts in the whole history of incompletion."[129] We couldn't agree more. But regardless, completing *The Fall of Gondolin* in a manner similar to *The Children of Húrin* was out of the question. All Christopher could hope to do was do what he had done with *Beren and Lúthien:* "to follow, using previously published texts, one single particular narrative from its earliest existing form and throughout its later development."[130]

The resulting text is even more fragmentary than *Beren and Lúthien*, and a hodgepodge in its own way: not the mingling of prose and poetry we see in the former book, but a deeply detailed and very odd early story followed by a mix of sketches, summaries, and finally one beautifully, tragically abandoned final story. The many versions of the Gondolin story, from *The Book of Lost Tales* down to "Of Tuor and His Coming to Gondolin," are collected in one place, to tell the "canonical" story of the Fall of Gondolin as much as possible, while also acknowledging the discrepancies in the available material that tells it.

## Sounds Kinda Weird...

It is. But it's not weird in a bad way.

As frustrating as it is, in a way—because we want to know what *the* final version of the story would have been—there's something quite satisfying about this presentation. The different versions—while different in tone and detail and even contradicting each other in places—offer a variety of alternatives, different facets of the same story. A somewhat nuanced and "meta" way of viewing it is to imagine that all of these versions are different accounts of the same event told by different writers (or rewritten later in the many centuries between), and we as readers have to look for the

---

129   Tolkien, J.R.R., edited by Christopher Tolkien. *The Book of Lost Tales Part Two (The History of Middle-earth, Vol. II)*. HarperCollins, 1983, 203.

130   Tolkien, *Fall of Gondolin*, 2018, 13.

"truth" somewhere in between the lines. It's nothing like the way we read modern fantasy, perhaps, but it's very similar to the way we read ancient mythology, or scriptural works: where, for example, the story of the Trojan War is told in slightly differing accounts by authors centuries apart, from Homer to Virgil with Aeschylus and Euripides in between, and readers must synthesize these different stories into one (more or less) consistent account. Considering that Tolkien was at an early point trying to create a "mythology for England" (though he never actually used that phrase himself), it seems fitting that there would be at least one story in the legendarium for which a truly mythological "synthetic" approach is the only way to approach it. That is *The Fall of Gondolin*, and in that case this standalone book offers a great way into the many versions of the story: a "Gondolin Mythology 101" for the newcomer. And yes, there's some great Alan Lee art in it as well.

One more thing that we think is worth noting: at the end of the preface to *The Fall of Gondolin*, Christopher Tolkien makes reference to "all those who generously wrote to me when it appeared that *Beren and Lúthien* was to be my last book."[131] While he doesn't say it explicitly, we like to think that the many letters Christopher received from fans of the Middle-earth legendarium were at least a minor factor in his decision to come out of retirement one last time...and for the last time. We can't prove it, but it's our headcanon. And while we were not among the fans who wrote to Christopher, we kind of wish we had been, and we would like to sincerely thank all the fans who did. So, if you're reading...yeah. Thank you. Consider us inspired.

---

131   Tolkien, *Fall of Gondolin*, 2018, 19.

# Great. So Is There a Particular Order I Should Read Them In?

Once again, the answer is: go not to the podcasters for counsel, for they will say both no and yes.

No, not really, because the three standalone books of the Great Tales are just that: standalone books. None of them requires a deep knowledge of the others in order to make sense of the narrative. We think it's incredibly helpful to have read *The Silmarillion* and thus have a general sense of the history of the First Age and the major players among Elves, Men, and bad guys; but even that isn't explicitly necessary. Christopher Tolkien has included supplemental material with each of these books to give you enough of that background to go on.

But yes, we do have some opinions on how to tackle them. It's just that we would offer options here instead of a single one-size-fits-all approach. So, in the interest of giving you some kind of direction, we'll start by saying that, just like our friends in the fandom of C.S. Lewis's Narnia books, you have two basic choices: chronological order, or publication order.

*Beren and Lúthien* comes first in the chronology of the First Age. Tuor, the hero of the Gondolin story, isn't even born when this story ends. Then comes *The Children of Húrin*, and finally *The Fall of Gondolin*—if you're interested in reading them in chronological order.

However, as we've just discussed in this chapter, Christopher Tolkien published *The Children of Húrin* first, followed by *Beren and Lúthien* and then *The Fall of Gondolin* soon after that. The publication order is actually significant in this case, because part of the reason for publishing *The Children of Húrin* first seems to have been that it was the most complete of the three.

If the fragmentary nature of some of these tales scares you, then publication order is the way to go.

Either way you slice it, *The Fall of Gondolin* should probably be the last one you read, since it is both last in the chronology (and leads directly into events that bring about the end of the First Age) and also the last of the three that was published—and provides a very fitting coda for Christopher Tolkien's lifetime of works in his father's universe. It's also the most fragmentary, so saving it for last will give any new reader a lot of time to get comfortable with the idea of reading Tolkien's unfinished work.

But there's honestly no wrong way, and that seems in keeping with Christopher Tolkien's intentions in publishing these standalone editions: to make them accessible for as many readers as possible, and in the process maybe even entice a few more casual Tolkien fans to tiptoe a little closer to the deep end of the pool.

# So, Why Do We Love Them?

Much like *Unfinished Tales*, the three Great Tales books are an entirely different animal from *The Hobbit*, *The Lord of the Rings*, and even *The Silmarillion*. Though *The Children of Húrin* is at least presented as a finished novel, the other two are not; and the nature of them is about 75 percent narrative fiction and about 25 percent academic study of the textual development of the story. It's hard to compare them with a finished novel, and even harder to get really okay with the notion that, even when at their best—and even recognizing the Entlike effort Christopher Tolkien undertook to bring these books to the public—what we read is ultimately how Christopher saw best to present them to us, not the way J.R.R. Tolkien wanted them presented. We aren't complaining about that. After all, there's no way to know exactly *how* J.R.R. Tolkien would have presented them to us (and, to the extent that we have any idea how he would have, Christopher was the person who knew it best). So we aren't criticizing Christopher's effort; far from it. It's just the reality of the situation we are in as Tolkien fans. These books are not likely to quite touch readers in the same way as the better-known works.

And for the two of us authoring this book, we have a relationship to the Great Tales that's a little different from a lot of Tolkien fans, and certainly different from you, the reader, if you're a new Tolkien fan following our advice in regards to the order in which you make your way through Tolkien's legendarium. By the time these three standalone editions of the Great Tales came out in the early twenty-first century, we had already been Tolkien fans for many years, and had already read much of the material published in these editions, in *Unfinished Tales* and the early volumes of The History of Middle-earth.[132] As we've said, virtually everything in these editions had been published before.

But reading *The Children of Húrin* as a standalone novel makes that story come to life in a way that it simply doesn't do elsewhere, even the version published as the *Narn* in *Unfinished Tales*. Immersed in the story over several hundred pages of Tolkien's rich prose, it's almost impossible not to get swept up in it. As readers, we cheer as Húrin defies Morgoth to his face, earning the ire and curse of the Dark Lord. As the story goes on, we feel the weight of one bad choice after another made by Túrin as he attempts to flee his fate and make his own destiny, and every time someone he loves is hurt by his actions, it's heart-wrenching and poignant. It is truly a masterpiece, combining Tolkien's usual medieval milieu with the best aspects of a modern sensibility and the timelessness of a Greek tragedy, and it's hard to make it to the end with dry eyes. The single chapter devoted to this story in *The Silmarillion*, as good as it is, simply does not have this kind of dramatic power.

---

132   When we talk about reading The History of Middle-earth in our early adulthood, it's hard not to hear the voice of Jamie Lee Curtis speaking to us, paraphrasing one of her classic lines from *A Fish Called Wanda*, the best non-Python Monty Python movie: "Yes, you did. You just didn't understand it."

*Beren and Lúthien* and *The Fall of Gondolin*, presented in their unfinished state, don't have anywhere near the same effect. But with these volumes, the reader is immersed in a different way: by taking the raw materials of each of the Great Tales out of the more-or-less-strictly-chronological presentation of *Unfinished Tales* and The History of Middle-earth and packaging them up in a single place, Christopher takes us on a journey through the disparate versions of the tales, *Rashomon*-ing together a narrative that (though incomplete) comes to life more than accounts presented elsewhere, and contains enough of Tolkien's detailed prose (and significant amounts of very lush, vivid, beautiful, and often terrifying poetry, in the case of *Beren and Lúthien*, which make this story unlike any other that Tolkien wrote in regards to just how many lines of poetry he spilled onto the page over it) for us to get an idea of how Tolkien *might* have finished the story, if only he'd had more time.[133] It's like downloading sample chapters on an e-reader of a book that's out of print, but whose story is summarized elsewhere. Frustrating, yes, but at least you can enjoy what there is of it, and you can go elsewhere to see how the story ends.

All three of the standalone Great Tales editions give a fuller account of the stories within them—in both narrative detail and completeness—than can be found in any other single book, and that alone is worth the price of admission. For those readers who aren't ready (or won't ever be ready) to dig deeply into the Moria-like tunnels of The History of Middle-earth to mine these stories out of the rock themselves, Christopher Tolkien has done it for them. And, as we are big fans of making Tolkien's work more accessible to as many readers as possible—it's the reason we started our podcast in the first place, after all—we are thrilled that Christopher made this effort to democratize these stories, make them even more available and accessible than they already were. Gatekeeping bad; gateways good.

---

133   In some ways, the fact that Tolkien was limited to only one mortal life in which to write his stories and didn't have the "serial longevity" of the Elves is a tragedy as great as Túrin's. How's that for a punch in the gut?

And while we're talking about accessibility, did we mention that each one of the Great Tales books is less than three hundred pages, *and* available in audiobook format? There is no easier way to become an overnight expert in one of Tolkien's Great Tales, the centers of narrative gravity, the nucleation points around which Tolkien's writing accreted over time like bubbles in a glass of beer,[134] than to read these books. This is not a *Star Trek*-sized commitment; we're talking *Firefly* hours invested here.

And yes, Alan Lee's exquisite illustrations are a big plus, too. Not just the one with the giant cat.

Okay, we've got one more. Just stop to think about the fact that, in the last fifteen years of his life, Christopher Tolkien dedicated himself to *finally* publishing his father's three Great Tales as titles in their own right. Forty-five years after J.R.R. Tolkien's passing, the son finally achieved what his father had always wanted to...if not quite how his father would have done it, in the best way he could under the circumstances. There's just no better way to close the book, as it were, on that *two*-lifetime accomplishment of mythmaking.

But of course, the book didn't close there. For, as Samwise Gamgee realized in a moment of epiphany under the shadows of Cirith Ungol: "Why, to think of it, we're in the same tale still! It's going on. Don't the Great Tales never end?"

No, Sam, they never do.

---

134  A strange analogy, perhaps, but we are the two guys who named a Tolkien podcast after a pub.

# WHY ALAN LOVES THEM

By the time *The Children of Húrin* was published in 2007, my place in the Tolkien fandom had shifted a little. Work and family were keeping me busy, and—it embarrasses me to admit this—I'd stopped *reading* Tolkien on a regular basis: those annual readthroughs of *The Lord of the Rings* now belonged to a less busy past. Instead, I'd watch the movies once or twice a year, as it was much easier to commit to three to four hours a week to get through the trilogy than to the time it took to read the books. "Besides," I thought—"I *know* the books."[135] Then I received a copy of the first of the Great Tales for Christmas that year; I recalled having read the *Narn i Hîn Húrin* in *Unfinished Tales*, and the chapter "Of Túrin Turambar" in *The Silmarillion*, but it had been a few years, and the details were murky enough in my recollection that I was immediately interested in reading this new version.[136]

Simply reading Christopher's introduction brought me back to the joy of Tolkien's own words. I devoured the book before the new year began, moved to tears by the tragic story told so beautifully and powerfully. It refreshed my love for Tolkien's books and brought me back to reading them regularly once more.

The story still moves me deeply: it is, in my opinion, the greatest of all Tolkien's stories and yet...and yet it is the one I read the *least* frequently. It is emotionally draining, building sorrow upon sorrow, loss upon loss. Even now, as I consider some of the individual moments—especially the moments of Húrin and Morwen near the end—tears well up in my eyes, unbidden. Pardon me, I need to go read this again now...where are the tissues?

---

135  I laugh at my 2007 self because I learn something new every single time I read Tolkien. I've learned more about the legendarium over the course of this podcast than I knew when I began.

136  The details weren't that murky: I knew it was the darkest and most tragic of all of Tolkien's works, and not a light-hearted romantic comedy about a moody guy who...well, never mind.

# Why Shawn Loves Them

As I've said many times in podcasts, guest appearances, conferences, and elsewhere in this book, I first read Tolkien in 1991. Christopher Tolkien was working through the last few volumes of The History of Middle-earth at that time, and I did read the first five of those in my youngish adult years in Del Rey paperback editions that were affordable on my part-time working student's wages. But once I got through those (not understanding them, really, as noted above), I had reached the end of the Middle-earth writings that were available to me. I didn't notice when *Tales from the Perilous Realm*[137] was first published in 1997. I bought *Roverandom* in 1998, but that children's story about the adventures of an adorable little dog didn't really resonate with a childless (at the time) cat person like myself. And for a long time, there was no new Middle-earth literature on my bookshelf.

The publication of *The Children of Húrin* changed all that for me. This was the first Middle-earth book that I bought in a first edition hardcover and read as soon as it came out. I knew the story already, of course; I'd read the versions that had already been published in *The Silmarillion* and elsewhere, and recognized Tolkien's inspirations in some of my favorite myths: the Norse Sigurd and Greek Oedipus, for starters.[138] I even did a paper on Túrin and Sigurd for finals in a modern epic class I took my freshman year of college (my professor received it lukewarmly at best). So I would say that the story of Túrin and his sister Niënor, the children of Húrin, was one I had spent quite a lot of time with and knew it well. It didn't matter to me one bit that I had read virtually every word of it before; I read *The Children of Húrin* for the first time with a kind of excitement I'd never felt before reading a book of Tolkien's...because this was *new*. In a manner of speaking, of course.

---

137   A collection of non-legendarium works along with some tangentially related poetry called *The Adventures of Tom Bombadil*, though not all of the poems in it are about the titular singing weirdo.

138   Though I didn't know it at the time, Tolkien himself admitted to having based Túrin on Oedipus and Sigurd in the oft-quoted Letter 131 to Milton Waldman in 1951, along with the Finnish tragic hero Kullervo—whom I would never have heard of if not for Tolkien's interest in him.

In 2007, I was still a few years away from jumping onto the social media bandwagon, but there were online message boards and blog posts to read and to comment on, and I did. Buying a new Tolkien book and sharing the experience of it online with other Tolkien fans made me feel like part of a Tolkien fan *community* for the first time in my life. Only a few years later, I would find a huge community of Tolkien fans on Facebook, which led me to my friendship with Alan and eventually the amazing community of people who have come together around *The Prancing Pony Podcast*. It's hard to believe *The Children of Húrin* was only a few short years before all of that.

By the time *Beren and Lúthien* and then *The Fall of Gondolin* came out, *The Prancing Pony Podcast* was growing rapidly, largely through social media outreach and group sharing, and I was deeply embedded in the online Tolkien fan community. My relationship to the community had changed (and to the stories themselves, too, because I had caught up on a lot of Tolkien-related reading in the years between), but that feeling of *newness* was the same. In recent years there has been lots of great new Tolkien material coming out, and it's not hard now to imagine a world in which there *will always be* some new Tolkien material on the way. Of course, that's not really true; eventually, the publishable manuscripts will run out, though that seems to be a long way away still.[139] But if I expand my definition of "Tolkien material" to Tolkien-*related* material, then I can be assured that there will always be something new to discover, and that is what keeps me so excited about this fandom. Indeed, the Great Tales never end...and when we're talking about Tolkien, they're all Great Tales.

---

139    As of writing this, I've just recently received a copy of *The Fall of Númenor*, a "compilation of available material" edition similar to *Beren and Lúthien* and *The Fall of Gondolin* edited by previous guest of *The Prancing Pony Podcast*, Brian Sibley.

# CHAPTER 6

# WHAT SHOULD I READ NEXT?

*"Then all round the Tree, and behind it, through the gaps in the leaves and boughs, a country began to open out; and there were glimpses of a forest marching over the land, and of mountains tipped with snow. Niggle lost interest in his other pictures; or else he took them and tacked them on to the edges of his great picture. Soon the canvas became so large that he had to get a ladder..."*

—J.R.R. Tolkien, "Leaf by Niggle"[140]

*"When he first began to walk far without a guide he thought he would discover the further bounds of the land; but great mountains rose before him, and going by long ways round about them he came at last to a desolate shore. He stood beside the Sea of Windless Storm where the blue waves like snow-clad hills roll silently out of Unlight to the long strand, bearing the white ships that return from battles on the Dark Marches of which men know nothing."*

—J.R.R. Tolkien, Smith of Wootton Major[141]

---

140   Tolkien, J.R.R. "Leaf by Niggle," in *Tales from the Perilous Realm*. Houghton Mifflin Harcourt, 2008, 286.
141   Tolkien, J.R.R. "Smith of Wootton Major," in *Tales from the Perilous Realm*. Houghton Mifflin Harcourt, 2008, 258.

Dear reader, you've arrived at a milestone on your road to Tolkien fandom. You're not at the end; far from it. There are many more books by Tolkien—and about Tolkien—for you to read. But if you've gotten this far, you've pretty much conquered the basics, according to our humble opinion on the matter. Make no mistake: we want you to keep reading. We hope you will keep reading. But from here, you have options, and your road from here on out may not look the same as anyone else's, and will vary depending on your own personal...uh, idiom. We aren't going to tell you what to read next.

But don't fret! We are still here to give you some advice. And we'll start by suggesting some questions to ask yourself, and we'll make some suggestions based on your answers. If this sounds like a fun journey of self-exploration to you, then you should read on. Others may wish to skip on to the next section of the book, which is a good bit and has Elijah Wood in prosthetic feet.

# HOW UNFINISHED IS TOO UNFINISHED?

The first question we suggest you ask yourself is: How unfinished is "too unfinished" a tale for you? In other words, how did you feel about the unfinished drafts and accompanying explanatory commentary in *Unfinished Tales* and parts of the Great Tales standalone books?

If that wasn't too intimidating for you, and you're interested in a deeper dive into the history of Tolkien's composition of the texts that make up the Middle-earth legendarium, then you may enjoy jumping straight into The History of Middle-earth. This maze of manuscripts—ranging in length from lines of verse in collected notebooks to scraps of notes and doodles jotted on the backs of professorial note pages—chronicles the sub-creation of Middle-earth, from Tolkien's earliest poems and mythmaking exercises after the Great War, to philosophical musings on the finer metaphysical points of *The Lord of the Rings* in the months right up until his death in 1973. Not all of the twelve volumes in the collection are created equal, though there is something great to be found in each of them. And though there are benefits to starting at the beginning and reading them in order, you don't really have to do that. You can pick up the series at any point, and in some cases it's not even all that necessary to read an entire book cover to cover.

Interested in seeing the lines of *The Lay of Leithian*, that epic poem about Beren and Lúthien, that didn't make it into the 2017 book? Go straight to Volume Three, *The Lays of Beleriand*. Or maybe you'd like to see the earliest incarnations of the Valar, when they resembled Greek and Norse gods even more than they do in the pages of *The Silmarillion—The Book of Lost Tales* in its two parts (Volumes One and Two) is entertaining, enlightening, and holds a few surprises about where Tolkien might have taken his legendarium if he'd had time to finish it the way he'd wanted to in his youth. Or perhaps you'd just like to learn more about how *The Lord of the Rings* came into being? Check out Volumes Six through Nine.

The History of Middle-earth also has islands of deep study into specific topics that aren't always obvious based on the title of the volume. If learning more about Tolkien's languages is becoming a passion project for you,[142] you may be surprised to find there's a great early dictionary of Elvish word roots in Volume Five, *The Lost Road*, and a good bit on Mannish languages (such as Adûnaic, the language of Númenor) in Volume Nine, *Sauron Defeated*. Or, if you're interested to know how Tolkien's personal theology influenced the ethics and metaphysics of Middle-earth, right down to the nature of evil and his deeply held thoughts about Middle-earth as a "fallen" world, you're going to want to check out Volume Ten, *Morgoth's Ring*. Don't be afraid to do some research online, or ask around, if there's a particular topic you want to find out more about. Chances are there is *something* about it in The History of Middle-earth.

---

142    And who could blame you? Yes, this is Shawn writing this.

Why We Love Middle-earth

And while it may be obvious from the hopefully enticing bits of detail in the paragraphs above, we want to be really clear about one thing: Don't be fooled by the title. The History of Middle-earth is a lot of things, but one thing it is *not* is an "in-universe" continuous history of Middle-earth in chronological order. Okay, to be fair, there are bits of that scattered throughout: annals and histories that can be pieced together to come up with a single contiguous history. But that's not what it's fundamentally about. The History of Middle-earth is (and is called that because it is) a *history* of how Middle-earth came to life, out of Tolkien's mind and onto the many pages of finished and unfinished writing he managed to produce in his lifetime.

One important book whose history is *not* chronicled in The History of Middle-earth is the one we started this book with: *The Hobbit*. The reason for this seems to be because *The Hobbit* wasn't originally intended to be part of the "legendarium," meaning the mythology of the Elves of the First Age as originally envisioned by his father—though *The Hobbit* was eventually "drawn in" to the mythology as we discussed earlier in this book, and today is considered part of it by most fans including us. But regardless of its standing among fans, Christopher did not include the creation of this beloved book in The History of Middle-earth. Not to worry, though; an independent Tolkien scholar named John Rateliff did undertake a very History of Middle-earth-style approach to the *Hobbit* manuscripts in his book *The History of The Hobbit*.[143] If you like what Christopher did in his twelve volumes, Rateliff's similar treatment of *The Hobbit* is sure to please as well.

And in recent years, there's been another addition: *The Nature of Middle-earth*, edited by Carl F. Hostetter and published in 2021, again from unfinished manuscripts (and largely unpublished manuscripts, though some sections of the book are expansions of material previously edited and

---

143   Originally a collaboration between Rateliff and his friend Taum Santoski, who passed away in 1991. Rateliff continued the work, "rel[ying] upon Taum's pioneering work at establishing the correct manuscript sequence," though "all the text and commentary are [Rateliff's] own," as noted in the Acknowledgements to *The History of The Hobbit*, which was finally published in 2007.

published) left behind by Tolkien. Many fans view *Nature* as the unofficial thirteenth volume to The History of Middle-earth, and it is without a doubt a crucial entry in the collection of Tolkien's unfinished works.

# Actually, I'm Ready to Go Back to Reading Some "Finished Tales"...

If this is the case, we can't really blame you. The draft-plus-commentary style of the last few books we've introduced you to is great for some, but we certainly understand the desire to just read some actual finished *stories* again. That's okay! There are plenty of other writings out there by Tolkien to choose from; we just will have to reach outside the Middle-earth legendarium to find them. In these books, you won't find hobbits[144] or rings or Silmarils, but you will certainly find a lot of things and ideas that remind you of the Middle-earth legendarium, like greedy dragons and glowing stars, deep meditations on mortality, and slightly goofy wizards. We hereby present to you...the non-legendarium fiction works of J.R.R. Tolkien.

If you're looking for a gateway from Tolkien's legendarium to his other works, and one that just happens to have virtually all of Tolkien's most popular and well-loved non-legendarium works in it (convenient, isn't it?), you can't do better than *Tales from the Perilous Realm*. Originally published in 1997, *Tales* is a compilation of short stories and poems that had been published earlier in the twentieth century in various standalone, double-header, and smaller compilation editions. The expanded edition of *Tales* published in 2008 (and most commonly available now) contains a veritable who's who—or what's what—of stories, including:

---

144    With one exception we'll mention in a moment.

- *The Adventures of Tom Bombadil*—this misleadingly titled entry is not, as you might think, a series of episodes chronicling the Indiana Jones-esque exploits of everyone's favorite Middle-earth weirdo, nor a buddy cop procedural in which Tom and Farmer Maggot solve crimes in the Old Forest, nor even a will-they-won't-they romantic screwball comedy showing how Tom met and fell in love with his wife, the River-daughter Goldberry. It's actually a collection of sixteen poems, loosely linked to the legendarium only by a meta-narrative that says they're Hobbit poems documented in the *Red Book of Westmarch*. The first two poems in the collection actually do involve the titular Tom (and, to be fair, one of them does tell the story of how he met Goldberry), but the others are all over the place: there are alternate versions of poems that ended up in the pages of *The Lord of the Rings*, rollicking singalongs, spooky mood pieces, sad ruminations on mortality, and silly verses about trolls, cats, giant turtles...and oliphaunts, of course.

- *Farmer Giles of Ham*—a clever yarn about an unlikely hero of a farmer and a devious dragon with the tongue-twisting name of Chrysophylax Dives. Like most of Tolkien's written works, it's full of philological references; but rarely has Tolkien been so *funny* about it, filling the pages of *Farmer Giles* with elaborate puns and false etymologies about well-known place-names in England to tickle the funny bones of word-nerds everywhere (at least, those who are lucky enough to be familiar with those place-names). According to Tom Shippey, writing in the introduction to the current edition of *Tales*, *Farmer Giles* was partly inspired by Tolkien's "urge to 'make sense' of the local Buckinghamshire place names"[145] he was surrounded by. Still, while a little bit of critical help may aid even the most provincial American reader[146] in understanding Tolkien's references, the story remains quite funny even without.

- *Roverandom*—a charming bedtime story originally written for Michael, the second-oldest of the Tolkien children, after he lost his favorite toy. It tells of the adventures of a dog who is turned into a toy by a spiteful wizard, and must travel far and wide to undo the spell. This one tops the list of fan favorites for many Tolkien fans,[147]

---

145   Tolkien, *Tales from the Perilous Realm*, 2008, xviii.
146   We know what you're thinking: "Like Alan and Shawn."
147   Particularly those fans who root for Team Huan rather than Team Tevildo. Woof.

and even contains some *Giles*-like puns and linguistic jokes along with a few surprising nods to the legendarium, which is cited by the luminary Tolkien scholars Christina Scull and Wayne G. Hammond as evidence of how the *legendarium* impacted Tolkien's other stories, and conversely how *Roverandom* itself may have influenced Tolkien's later legendarium writings, such as *The Hobbit*. It also describes a trip to the dark side of the moon. (Stoner voice: *Floyd, dude!*)

- *Smith of Wootton Major*—Shawn's favorite of the Professor's non-legendarium works, this story started out as an introduction for a new edition of *The Golden Key*, a book by the Victorian author George MacDonald,[148] and ended up taking on a life of its own as a fairy tale about a village smith gifted with a special passport to the land of Faery, and the inspiration he brings back home from his journeys there. The key to the collection in a way—Faery is *the* "perilous realm," after all—*Smith* also offers readers a window into Tolkien's (possibly allegorical, according to some readings) thoughts on his own inspiration, near the end of his life, in this story he called in a 1967 letter (299 in Carpenter's collection) "an old man's book, already weighted with the passage of bereavement," but that manages to be more uplifting than sad with its poignant reflection.

- *Leaf by Niggle*—Alan's favorite non-legendarium work, this short story about an artist diligently painting an awe-inspiring tree, each leaf painstakingly and obsessively detailed, while unavoidable human commitments seek to draw him away from his work, offers another angle of self-reflection by Tolkien on his own creative process. Almost certainly allegorical and certainly deeply spiritual, *Leaf* is almost universally loved by Tolkien's fans who have read it, as it is as full of antitheses as Tolkien himself was: charming in its simple accessibility but layered with complex symbolism, heartwarming but at times frustrating in the best possible way, foreboding but full of hope. Tolkien's Niggle is much like Tolkien himself; in fact, Priscilla Tolkien, writing in a blog post on the Tolkien Estate website, called *Leaf* her father's "most directly autobiographical" work, "in that it concerns the life of an artist and how an artist is to respond both to the pressures

---

148  When asked to do the preface to a new edition of MacDonald's work by Pantheon Books, Tolkien agreed, even though he wrote back (in Letter 262 in the Carpenter collection) that he was "not as warm an admirer of George MacDonald as C. S. Lewis was." In any event, the preface was never finished, and the world got this lovely story instead.

of his absorption in his creative ideas and to the demands of living an ordinary life in the ordinary world."

- "On Fairy-stories"—the eye-opening (and, dare we say, essential) essay/lecture on the nature of fantasy and fairy-stories we've previously mentioned in this book. It's a short read, and while it's not exactly light fare, it's approachable enough and gives fans of Middle-earth an indispensable lexicon for talking about Tolkien's work. And it is conveniently included in the most recent editions of *Tales from the Perilous Realm*.

Not that "On Fairy-stories" is hard to find by any stretch of the imagination. Apparently knowing just how darned important it is to understanding Tolkien's fantasy, Tolkien's publishers at HarperCollins and Houghton Mifflin Harcourt have included it in many other collections besides *Tales*. Another such volume that's certainly worth a look by any reader interested in reading more fictional material by Tolkien is *Tree and Leaf*. Originally published in 1964, containing only "On Fairy-stories" and *Leaf by Niggle*, current editions also include the lovely poem "Mythopoeia"—a verse exploration dedicated to C. S. Lewis on the spiritual nature of sub-creation, which was defined and described more academically in "On Fairy-stories"—and also *The Homecoming of Beorhtnoth Beorhthelm's Son*, a short dramatic work based on the historical Battle of Maldon[149] and also containing some brief academic reflections by Tolkien on the historical battle and the fragmentary medieval poem (also called *The Battle of Maldon*) which preserves the historical account of the battle.

Making a complete 180 from *Homecoming*, there are some surprisingly light, kid-oriented fiction works in Tolkien's back catalog, too. *Mr. Bliss* is a single-sitting picture book written and illustrated by Tolkien for his own children, and published posthumously. It tells the story of a gentleman taking his first drive in a motorcar, complete with misadventures, angry neighbors, bears (again—remember how much the Tolkien kids loved bears?), and a sprinkling

---

149    Fought in the year 991 in Essex, between an English army led by the titular Beorhtnoth (or Byrhtnoth) and a force of invading Vikings.

of lightly anti-automobile propaganda inspired by the real experiences of the Professor himself, who often spoke of his dislike for the "infernal combustion engine" (not a typo). If your favorite Disneyland ride is Mr. Toad's Wild Ride,[150] or at least if your favorite Rush song is "Red Barchetta,"[151] you will want to check this one out. There's also *The Father Christmas Letters*, a collection of letters written by Father Christmas to the Tolkien children every year, in response to their annual letters to the North Pole. Saint Nick's writing style is curiously similar to Professor Tolkien's in a way that must have made the kids suspicious about the whole thing at a young age,[152] and over the years the letters evolve past the standard "Happy Christmas, kids, I'm bringing you some toys" kind of fare and turn into an annual news digest of an epic-fantasy world not unlike the legendarium itself, with an epic war taking place between the elves and goblins of the North Pole (it's like *The Silmarillion* for tots), goofy adventures of the North Pole staff that make Will Ferrell's antics as Buddy the Elf seem tame, and of course, bears. It's definitely highly recommended by both of the authors of this book, though it may be best to wait until the kids are over the whole Santa Claus thing; otherwise you may have some explaining to do about why Tolkien's name is on the book spine—and about why your own kids don't get such awesome letters from Santa.

# COOL, BUT WASN'T TOLKIEN A COLLEGE PROFESSOR? DIDN'T HE EVER DO ANY WORK FOR HIS DAY JOB?

Yes, he did. He was actually *very* busy in his day job, and did a fair bit of academic publishing as well, which is another area ripe for exploration...

---

150 Shawn's is.

151 Alan's is.

152 Oh, what a laugh it would have been if Ronald had only seen Edith kissing Santa Claus last night!

particularly for any reader whose encounters with Middle-earth have inspired them to learn more about medieval literature and philology.

*The Monsters and the Critics and Other Essays* is a great place to start on Tolkien's scholarly work. It contains not only "On Fairy-stories" and "*Beowulf*: The Monsters and the Critics," both of which we've discussed in this book already, but it also includes additional (and reasonably accessible) essays on medieval poems, on linguistics, and even an essay on language invention called "A Secret Vice." And if language invention (or "conlanging") is something you're interested in, don't miss out on the standalone critical edition of *A Secret Vice*, published not long ago with additional early drafts and supplemental materials: a word-nerd's dream.

There are also several books (most published after Tolkien's death, and many of them within the twenty-first century) of Tolkien's translations and adaptations of stories and poems from the Middle Ages. Perhaps the best known of these is *Sir Gawain and the Green Knight, Pearl, and Sir Orfeo*, three poems translated by Tolkien from Middle English, edited by Christopher Tolkien and first published in a single volume in 1975. Tolkien's translation of these poems was truly a byproduct of his day job. *Sir Gawain* and *Pearl* are fourteenth-century poems exemplary of what medievalists call the "Alliterative Revival" in England, a shift away from explicitly rhyming poetry and trending toward more alliterative[153] poetic forms, which had been popular in England many years before. While Tolkien is primarily remembered for his academic work in Old English, he did a not-insignificant amount of work on Middle English poems as well, and had a particular affinity

---

153 Unlike more traditional forms of poetry, which rely on rhyming the ends of words (usually at the ends of lines) for their poetic effect, medieval Old English poetry—like the poetry of other Germanic-speaking peoples, including the Norse—relied on *alliteration*, which is the repetition of initial consonant sounds. Following the conquest of English by the French-speaking Normans in 1066, French-style rhyming became popular among poets, but a number of poems from England in the thirteenth and fourteenth centuries show a return to the alliterative style for a brief period. Compare the first two lines of *Sir Gawain and the Green Knight*: "**S**ithen the **s**ege and the **as**saut was **s**esed at Troye/the **b**orgh **br**ittened and **br**ent to **br**ondez and a**s**kez" ("When the siege and the assault had ceased at Troy/the fortress destroyed and burned to embers and ashes") with its many initial S and B sounds, to the rhyme in the first two lines of Chaucer's *Canterbury Tales*: " Whan that Aprille with his shoures **soote**/The droghte of March hath perced to the **roote**."

for the West Midlands dialect of Middle English—i.e., the dialect spoken in the regions of England Tolkien himself had grown up in, including the areas around Birmingham and Warwickshire—which *Sir Gawain* and *Pearl* are written in. These poems are believed to have been written by the same author; both are highly allegorical works, filled with Christian symbolism and spiritual lessons, and Tolkien's translations of them are lush and vivid, retaining much of the alliteration of the originals. They are both highly worth reading, even if only one of them has a jolly green giant with an axe to grind against the neck of a knight of King Arthur's Round Table. The third poem in the collection, *Sir Orfeo*, was written roughly around the same time or a little earlier than the other two, and retells the ancient Greek myth of Orpheus and Eurydice as a modern (well, modern for the thirteenth or fourteenth century) Breton-style "lai"—a tale of romance and chivalry—full of fairies in a forest that would make Bilbo Baggins scared to go to sleep.

Then there's also Tolkien's own translation of *Beowulf*, the Old English epic poem that needs no introduction. Though it deviates from the poetic meter of the original, in that Tolkien's translation is written in prose, there's tons of great alliteration to be found, and it's a delight to read aloud. For the Tolkien fan looking to read this classic of English literature for the first time, we can't think of a better translation to start with than Tolkien's own. How else can one best understand how Tolkien saw this critically important text—the text that inspired all the wonderful dragon-stuff in *The Hobbit*, the text that comes to life for modern readers as an influence on the very language and culture of the Riders of Rohan, the text that Tolkien built an academic reputation upon with his seminal essay "Beowulf: The Monsters and the Critics"—but to read Tolkien's translation of it in his own words? Plus, in addition to the translation, there's some very enlightening commentary on the poem, and original short story by Tolkien based on an Old Norse saga.

Somewhat lesser known—and perhaps a bit more niche than these crowd-pleasers—are Tolkien's adaptations of medieval mythology, including the recently published *The Lay of Aotrou and Itroun*, another "Breton lai" of

Tolkien's own invention about a Breton lord and lady and a Celtic witch whom some have seen as an early archetype of Galadriel. Another is *The Story of Kullervo*, Tolkien's retelling (written very early, in his twenties) of a story from the Finnish mythic cycle *Kalevala*, about an ill-fated young man whose story was admittedly a major inspiration for the story of the Children of Húrin, one of Tolkien's Great Tales. Both of these early works by Tolkien are available in recently published editions edited by the esteemed Tolkien scholar Verlyn Flieger, whose commentary helps unlock the gift of comprehension for even the newbiest of newbie readers of this stuff.

# I REALLY LIKE THE ILLUSTRATIONS TOLKIEN DID FOR HIS OWN BOOKS. WHERE CAN I FIND OUT MORE ABOUT THOSE?

Dear reader, you are in luck!

Of course, there are many excellent books of art inspired by Tolkien's works by well-known artists—including Alan Lee (who was one of the conceptual artists for Peter Jackson's *Lord of the Rings* and *Hobbit* films), John Howe (who has been not only a conceptual artist for Peter Jackson's films, but also *The Rings of Power* on Amazon), Ted Nasmith (whose work on *The Silmarillion* is spectacular), and many others. As it turns out, however, Tolkien himself was a talented illustrator as well, and did illustrations for many of his written works, though he seems to have always been quite humble about his talents with regard to the visual arts. His illustrations had appeared in publications of his own work going all the way back to the first edition of *The Hobbit* in 1937, which was printed with ten of Tolkien's own illustrations (not to mention the charmingly epic blue, black, and green dust jacket, and of course the famous maps). But aside from that, collections of Tolkien's artwork were sparse until after his death, when his publishers (first Ballantine Books in the United States, then Allen & Unwin in the United Kingdom) started publishing Tolkien's art in calendars in the 1970s. In 1979, after the last calendar in the series was published—*The J.R.R. Tolkien Calendar 1979*—the pictures were collected into a single volume, some additional illustrations[154] and text by Christopher Tolkien were added to the collection, and it was published as *Pictures by J.R.R. Tolkien* in 1979. Most recently in 2021, the book was reissued in a hardback edition with a beautiful slipcase adorned with (what else?) one of Tolkien's illustrations, featuring Glaurung, the Father of Dragons from the First Age of Middle-earth.

An even broader survey of Tolkien's illustrative art can be found in 1995's *J.R.R. Tolkien: Artist and Illustrator*. Edited and with commentary by the husband-and-wife team of Wayne G. Hammond and Christina Scull (the latter of whom has a background in art history, and brings a wealth of experience to the study of Tolkien's art),[155] this collection explores Tolkien's art diachronically over the course of his life, not just the illustrations he did for the books in the Middle-earth legendarium, but also artworks he did for other stories and poems, and standalone curiosities that showcase the very real artistic talent of our favorite author. Hammond and Scull later followed up this collection with *The Art of* The Lord of the Rings *by J.R.R. Tolkien* and *The Art of* The Hobbit *by J.R.R. Tolkien*, which take a similar diachronic look— from early drafts to finished products—of artworks created by Tolkien in conjunction with the composition of these books. And once you've made your way through all of these books, there's also *Tolkien: Maker of Middle-earth*, a collection of artworks, facsimiles of letters, and manuscripts (many of which are works of art themselves, between Tolkien's lush calligraphy and

---

154   Among the added illustrations were a series of delightful, colorful patterns—flowers, paisley-like swirls, and more—done in ballpoint pen on newspaper while the Professor was doing his crossword puzzles. Alan and Shawn were treated to an amazing story about these patterns by Simon Tolkien, the Professor's grandson, when interviewing him for Episode 37 of *The Prancing Pony Podcast*.

155   We had the pleasure of speaking to Hammond and Scull about the genesis of this book in another episode of the podcast: Episode 135.

his penchant for doodling in the margins) originally published in conjunction with a 2018 exhibition of artworks that appeared at the Bodleian Library in Oxford, and later at the Morgan Library and Museum in New York. While all of the books mentioned in this paragraph are worth reading for the words, not just the pictures, the words in *Maker of Middle-earth* boast an especially impressive pedigree, as the essays within the volume were contributed by seven of the world's leading Tolkien scholars and biographers, and serve as a great introduction to their bodies of work as well.

# SCHOLARS AND BIOGRAPHERS, YOU SAY...?

Oh, yeah. *Maker of Middle-earth* is just scratching the surface. There are bookshelves and bookshelves of stuff written *about* Tolkien that we could spend an entire book talking about—and maybe we will someday, if our publishers let us. But for now, we'll just whet your appetite with some brief remarks on the essentials.

If you want to learn about Tolkien's life, there really is only one place to start: Humphrey Carpenter's *J.R.R. Tolkien: A Biography*, which we've already mentioned several times in this book. Carpenter—a writer and radio producer who actually met Tolkien in his lifetime[156]—was the only authorized biographer of the Professor, and had access to friends and family and unpublished papers to complete what is widely regarded as the authoritative account of Tolkien's life. From Tolkien's birth in Bloemfontein in the nineteenth century, through the tragic deaths of both his parents, through

---

156  In the 1960s, Carpenter and a friend named Paul Drayton collaborated on a musical stage production of *The Hobbit* for New College School, a prep school for boys in Oxford. Unwilling to undertake the production without Tolkien's blessing, Carpenter worked some family connections to get a private meeting with the Professor, who (to Carpenter's surprise) gave his permission...and even went to see the show with Edith. Carpenter would later recall: "He sat near the front... I was able to watch his reactions. These were very simple: he had a broad smile on his face whenever the narration and dialogue stuck to his own words, which was replaced by a frown the moment there was the slightest departure from the book." Ouch.

Oxford to the Somme and back to Oxford and the Inklings, all the way to Tolkien's twilight years: Carpenter's biography is the best way to understand the Professor's life in broad strokes, which can be filled in through later reading elsewhere. Though it has been criticized by some for being a bit too effusive in its praise, not to mention for brief fictional interludes such as imagining what a typical day in the life of the Professor would have been like, these have never been problems for us. The facts are there, with seemingly minimal embellishment, and so for that reason Carpenter's *Biography* is essential reading, even if one wishes to dig deeper into specific periods of Tolkien's life through other sources where possible.

Not long after the *Biography*, Carpenter went on to edit and publish the authoritative collection of Tolkien's letters, aptly titled *The Letters of J.R.R. Tolkien* and mentioned several times already in this book. If you've listened to an episode of *The Prancing Pony Podcast*, read a critical essay, or, like, read a paragraph of this book that mentions a letter by number, that number comes from here and from Carpenter's chronologically ordered numbering system. All of the important ones are here: the linguistics-heavy No. 144 to Naomi Mitchison of 1954, the highly theological No. 156 to Father Robert Murray in 1954, letters to other writers like W.H. Auden and (of course) C.S. Lewis, numerous letters to Sir Stanley Unwin, Rayner Unwin, and other employees of Tolkien's publishers, and of course, the incomparable (in content, but also incomparably long) No. 131 to Milton Waldman in 1951, which covers more or less the entirety of the history of *The Silmarillion* in just a few pages. There's also the infamous (and hilarious) No. 210, to the legendary science fiction editor Forrest J. Ackerman, in which Tolkien critically shreds an ill-conceived, and thankfully ill-fated, attempt to turn *The Lord of the Rings* into a film in the 1950s.[157] But the letters aren't all full of shop-talk; there are personal and heartfelt letters to his children as well; the ones written to Christopher in the 1940s, while he was away in South Africa with the Royal Air Force in World War II, are especially poignant, and offer

---

157   For more, see Part II of this book, in which we discuss adaptations of Tolkien's works into other media.

Why We Love Middle-earth

not only Professor Tolkien's innermost thoughts on topics like the war he fought in, politics, and racism; they also include a great deal of content about the developing work-in-progress that *The Lord of the Rings* was during that decade. There are even early letters written to Edith, before the two were married. The letters are not only interesting for historical and biographical information; for an author who famously wished for his written output to stand on its own two colossal feet and left behind very little formal commentary on "what it all means," the letters are Tolkien fans' single best resource for insight into Tolkien's own thoughts on and interpretation of his written works. Ever wonder how Tolkien nerds like us can say with such certainty that Gandalf really died and came back to life, that the whole Moria thing wasn't just a long con to mess with the forces of Sauron? It's in the *Letters*. Whom did Tolkien consider to be the true hero of *The Lord of the Rings*? You'll find an answer in the *Letters* (with some ambiguity, admittedly). What did Sauron do with the Ring when his physical body was destroyed and he had to slowly rebuild it over centuries? You'll find out in the *Letters*.

There are two important caveats to keep in mind when reading the *Letters*, though. First of all, and this should hopefully be obvious, Carpenter's collection doesn't include *every* letter Tolkien wrote—and we don't just mean that the letters from Father Christmas that he wrote to his kids every year, and any super-special love letters to Edith, are left out (though they are, thankfully—even our literary hero deserves some privacy). According to Hammond and Scull, writing on their blog,[158] "there was an 'agenda' in the editing" of the *Letters*, namely that priority was given to "letters in which Tolkien discussed his Middle-earth stories, with the result that other subjects were given less attention than many of us would like, such as Tolkien's family life, his academic career, and his dealings with publishers." Seeing as how the Middle-earth stories are the primary focus of interest for just about anyone reading the *Letters*, this certainly isn't a major problem.

---

158    Hammond and Scull, "Tolkien's Modern Reading," *Tolkien Gateway*. May 25, 2021.

The other caveat that's important to keep in mind—and we have the great Verlyn Flieger to thank for this insight[159]—is that one should always pay attention to who the audience is when reading Tolkien's letters. In an essay appropriately entitled "But What Did He Really Mean?"[160] Flieger points out that "Tolkien tailored his letters to their particular addressees, although... he went farther in this than do many letter-writers." So it's no accident that Tolkien leans into his Catholic influences when writing a letter to a Jesuit priest friend, but calls out the similarity of his Valar to the little-g gods of pagan mythologies in a letter to another recipient. Flieger observes that, taken together, Tolkien's letters can appear to "make ambiguous and even contradictory statements,"[161] and that this has the effect of "permitting advocates with opposite views to cherry-pick the statements that best support their positions." In other words, it's all too easy to cite one letter as evidence for Tolkien having held a particular position or interpretation about his work, while ignoring other letters that refute that same position or interpretation. But, with a careful approach and an understanding of these possible pitfalls, the *Letters* have always been a priceless resource for understanding Tolkien's interpretation of his own world...at least on a particular day and year, which are usually conveniently recorded for historical reference.

Carpenter also published a historical/biographical book on Tolkien's friends, *The Inklings*. Full of great information about the group of writers as a whole, and offering quite a bit of insight into C.S. Lewis and Charles Williams (at least for Tolkien fans interested in how these men knew each other and influenced each other; serious fans of Lewis and Williams will want to delve deeper into other books to learn more about them as individuals), it's an excellent companion piece to the *Biography* that goes a little further to

---

159   See Episode 90 of *The Prancing Pony Podcast*, in which we interviewed Verlyn Flieger, who discussed this concept
with us.

160   Flieger, Verlyn. "But What Did He Really Mean?" *There Would Always Be a Fairy Tale*. Kent State University Press, 2017, 17-31.

161   Ibid 17.

show Tolkien in context with the friends and colleagues with whom he spent his free time, and who were the first people in the world to hear excerpts from *The Lord of the Rings* while it was being written.

After Carpenter, the best place to go for a deeper understanding of Tolkien's life is definitely the work of John Garth. For years, Garth has brought an investigative journalist-style approach to the study of Tolkien's early life, namely his years as a student in Birmingham and Oxford, and his time in France during World War I. Garth's award-winning 2003 book *Tolkien and the Great War* is the definitive exploration of Tolkien's early life, and succeeds at bringing to life not only the young Ronald Tolkien himself, but also his friends from King Edward's School, the "Tea Club and Barrovian Society" or TCBS. This was the first of the informal "clubs," groups of friends that Tolkien would find himself involved in throughout his life—the most famous, of course, being the Inklings much later on—comprising the "immortal four" of the TCBS, the core group that continued to be friends after graduation, meeting in person when they could during their college years and writing to each other in 1916, when all four of them were serving in the military during the war. Though two of the "immortal four"—Robert Quilter Gilson and Geoffrey Bache Smith—were killed in action that year, Garth explores how the influence and inspiration they lent to Tolkien clearly was a fuel on the fire of his creativity as a young man, and how the experiences of the war, horrific as they were, had a notable influence on Tolkien's writing: his early writings, like *The Book of Lost Tales* and the Great Tales particularly, which were largely written while Tolkien was still in an army hospital and these experiences were fresh in his mind; but even *The Lord of the Rings*, particularly Frodo and Sam's journey "behind enemy lines" into Mordor, owes a great debt to Tolkien's wartime experience in the depths of horror it depicts. In addition to *Tolkien and the Great War*, Garth has also written and published a shorter work dedicated to Tolkien's time at Oxford, titled *Tolkien at Exeter College*. Though this period of Tolkien's life isn't covered in the same detail that his King Edward's School and wartime life is in *Great War*, *Exeter College* is nevertheless an enlightening look at Tolkien's surprisingly rowdy college years, and an interesting companion to bring along on one's first Tolkien tour of Oxford.

John Garth's work on Tolkien's early life is so rich and enlightening that it makes one sad that there isn't anything like it for Tolkien's later life. However, Christina Scull and Wayne G. Hammond (whom we've mentioned several times already in this book) have done work to help fill that void with their *Chronology*. Available as one of the volumes in the three-volume *The J.R.R. Tolkien Companion and Guide*, the *Chronology* isn't exactly a biography in the traditional sense—it doesn't tell a continuous narrative. But what it is is something impressive indeed: a hundreds-of-pages-long timeline of events in Tolkien's life, arranged chronologically, ranging in importance from the births of his children and the publications of his books to routine faculty meetings at the colleges where he worked. According to Scull and Hammond, the decision to compile this information as a chronology rather than a traditional biography was intentional: "This has allowed us reasonably to assemble—as a biographical essay would not have done, demanding more selection and brevity—many of the miscellaneous details about Tolkien we have gathered in the course of research, details which individual may be of little moment, but in relation to one another can be illuminating."[162]

Indeed, the course of the research they must have done to come up with the material in the *Chronology* is truly mind-boggling. Some of the information presented is available in other sources: the dates of important letters that appear in Carpenter's *Letters* collection, for example, or information about significant media interviews Tolkien gave in his later life. But we can't imagine the painstaking effort that must have gone into sorting through files and files of Tolkien family materials in the Bodleian Library at Oxford University, the Raynor Library at Marquette University in Milwaukee,[163] and elsewhere to discover the dates, agendas, and minutes of faculty committee meetings

---

162   Scull & Hammond, *The J.R.R. Tolkien Companion and Guide: Chronology*, 2017, ix.

163   Home to the largest collection of Tolkien manuscripts and materials in North America, including the original manuscripts to *The Hobbit* and *The Lord of the Rings*. It is truly the heart of Tolkien fandom in America.

Tolkien attended at Merton College, or exactly when Tolkien popped over to the pub for a beer with his friends. The considerable skill Scull and Hammond have at organizing, categorizing, and chronicling this vast wealth of information is impressive on its own, even if the information wasn't absolutely jaw-droppingly wonderful at opening one's eyes to the very busy and productive day-to-day life Tolkien had as, like, just a guy with a job and a family...who also just somehow managed to find time to write some of the most beloved books ever written. Sometimes it's a mystery how he managed to find the time at all, but we're certainly happy that he did.

# What about, y'know, Books about his Books?

Well, this is going to be tough...because there has been so much incredible critical work done on Tolkien's works as literature that we couldn't possibly give a comprehensive overview here, and we're very worried about offending someone by leaving them out. So let's just apologize in advance: to you, the reader, for not being able to cover everything here; and to the many brilliant scholars in the Tolkien fandom and critical community worldwide— many of whom we are lucky to count among our friends, colleagues, and supporters—for the possibility that we may leave someone out.

Critical analysis of Tolkien's work has been around since almost the initial publication of *The Lord of the Rings*, but one of the interesting side effects of so much material being published after Tolkien's lifetime (like *The Silmarillion*, The History of Middle-earth, and numerous linguistic and philosophical essays about Middle-earth by Tolkien published in journals) is that sometimes, early criticism doesn't hold up to what we know now. Speculation or interpretation by a well-meaning scholar in the 1970s is all too often blown out of the water by something Tolkien himself said in an essay that wasn't published until twenty years later, which is a tough break for those early commentators who deserve more credit than they get for helping to pave the way for modern Tolkien studies. But some of the early works are still very much worth your time, even if some of their points have been refuted since publication. A couple of our favorites in this category are Jane Chance's *Tolkien's Art: A Mythology for England* and Paul Kocher's *Master of Middle-earth: The Fiction of J.R.R. Tolkien*.

No survey of literary criticism about Tolkien would be complete without first mentioning the two elder statespersons of scholars still working in the field: Verlyn Flieger and T.A. ("Tom") Shippey. Shippey, a self-described "Tolkien polemicist," has been fighting for years for Tolkien's right to be recognized as a writer of serious literary merit, in the face of blinkered takes by academics and critics who deride Tolkien's fiction as childish or old-fashioned, and demand everyone accept James Joyce[164] and other modernists as their literary saviors. Shippey's two most significant books are *The Road to Middle-earth* and *J.R.R. Tolkien: Author of the Century*, and both are essential reading for those embarking on the road of Tolkien studies. Shippey's career as a medievalist has mirrored Tolkien's in many ways, including actually teaching Old English at Oxford from essentially the same syllabus that Tolkien created decades before. Shippey brings a wealth of medieval and philological knowledge to the study of Tolkien's works that highlights the Professor's influences and wordplay in a way that no one else likely *could* do, except perhaps for Tolkien himself, and Shippey's writing wanders from point to point, taking the reader on a journey through these little epiphanies that leaves one feeling fulfilled and enlightened. *Road* is the earlier and perhaps more mind-blowing of the two volumes, but *Author* is a bit more accessible to those unaccustomed to Shippey's style. In our opinion, you can start with either one.

Verlyn Flieger's style as a scholar and writer could not be more different from Shippey's. Where Shippey takes the reader on a journey, Flieger writes

---

164  We mean no offense to James Joyce or his many appreciators. One of the authors of this book actually considers himself a Joyce fan and has even done a Joyce-themed tour of Dublin, though we haven't yet told Tom Shippey that.

with the clarity and precision of the best college professor you ever had, expounding on complex interpretations the average person would never think of in a million life-ages of the earth, with a simple directness that makes it all seem so obvious and may just make you wonder why you never thought of it before. Much like Tolkien himself, who often spoke of his process of composition as a process of "discovering" a story rather than inventing it—remember, this is the man who hit upon the idea of his art as "sub-creation," not "creation"—Flieger's writing has a way of making readers feel they've discovered some exciting new interpretation, rather than having been taught it by her writing. Flieger is best known for *Splintered Light: Logos and Language in Tolkien's World*, a book tying together such various threads as the mythology of *The Silmarillion*, Tolkien's Catholicism, and Frodo's quest in *The Lord of the Rings* into a single strand of awareness of Tolkien's expert use of light and darkness as motifs in his storytelling. It's one that definitely should not be missed, and probably the best place to start with Flieger, but she has written many other eye-opening books as well, including multiple collections of essays and a few other monographs, including our second favorite (or at least the one that has been second-most useful to us and frequently referenced by us on *The Prancing Pony Podcast*), *A Question of Time*, which is *not* about a song off Depeche Mode's fifth album, but rather about Tolkien's use of time in his writings—for example, as a construct in showcasing the distance between the experiences of Elves and Men in *The Lord of the Rings*, or quite literally looking at Tolkien's experiments with time travel in some of his unfinished works.

There are so many more we could mention. Fans of *The Hobbit* will likely be interested in the work of "Tolkien Professor" Corey Olsen, the author, academic, and podcast personality who paved the way for the rest of us—much as Bandobras "Bullroarer" Took's intrepid exploits paved the way for the not entirely respectable adventures of Bilbo and Frodo Baggins. In addition to his work in a variety of media, he has published one of the few books dedicated to scholarly analysis of *The Hobbit*, fittingly titled *Exploring J.R.R. Tolkien's* The Hobbit. Those interested in race theory and Tolkien's relationship to the often-concerning social mores of the times in which he lived will want to look at Dimitra Fimi's *Tolkien, Race, and Cultural History*. There are books about Tolkien and language, Tolkien and geography (real-world and imaginary), and Tolkien and religion. There are books exploring women's studies, queer studies, philosophy, and science in the works of J.R.R. Tolkien. There are even whole books about plants in Middle-earth.[165] There are books about ancient myths, legends, and epic poems that influenced Tolkien, and there are books about modern books that influenced Tolkien. There's even a book that's just a catalog of *other books* that we know Tolkien owned,[166] because he talked about them in a letter, essay, or elsewhere. Honestly, if there's an angle you're interested in approaching Tolkien from, chances are someone's written a book about it.

And if not a book, then there's probably an article about it somewhere. There are many peer-reviewed academic journals currently publishing shorter-form scholarship on Tolkien, from the aptly named *Tolkien Studies* to *Mallorn* (the journal of the Tolkien Society), to *Mythlore* (the journal of the Mythopoeic Society, focusing not exclusively on Tolkien but also the other Inklings and fantasy literature in general), not to mention journals published in languages other than English. And there are journals dedicated to publication of material focused on Tolkien's languages, such as *Vinyar Tengwar* and *Parma Eldalamberon*—both of which, and especially the latter, have published vast quantities of Tolkien's own linguistic manuscripts.

There's so much more we could write about, but that should be enough to get you started down the road with reading more *by*, and *about*, Tolkien. We hope it's obvious by now that a lifelong love of Tolkien discovery doesn't end with the last page of *The Silmarillion*, or even *The Fall of Gondolin*. To be honest, we've been immersing ourselves in this stuff for decades, and we haven't come anywhere near the end of the road; there is still so

---

165   Our favorite is *Flora of Middle-earth* by Walter S. Judd and Graham A. Judd.

166   The surprisingly exciting *Tolkien's Library* by Oronzo Cilli. Curious whether Tolkien had heard of your favorite book? You'll find out here!

much we have to discover—we're both pretty sure that there will *always* be something new to discover, because there are already so many books, articles, and blog posts out there to spend nearly a lifetime exploring, and there is new stuff coming out all the time. And we must point out that everything we've talked about so far in this book has been *books*. There's an entire world of Tolkien media and fandom out there to discover, which we haven't even talked about yet. But we will, very soon.

So dive in, curl up with a favorite book (or a stack of them), and get yourself reading. And when you're ready to start exploring Tolkien's work beyond the printed page,[167] come back here. We'll join you for more in Part II.

# WHAT ALAN LOVES, AND WHY

If Tolkien's Middle-earth legendarium is the main course, his other works represent one of the most delicious dessert menus you will ever find. Feeling in the mood for something charming and heartwarming? *The Father Christmas Letters* will do just nicely.[168] Feeling really smart, but also a bit snarky? Well then, let me introduce you to *Farmer Giles of Ham*. Maybe the ordinary day-to-day of this world is grinding your soul into dust: read *Smith of Wootton Major* and travel to Faerie for the day. I could go on—though I'll let Shawn do that, as he stretches the word limit with his take on this chapter! Simply put, Tolkien's non-legendarium works are home to some of the richest treasures he's shared with us, and your experience of Tolkien will be greater for having read them.

---

167    Yes, we're singing "beyond the printed page" to the tune of the line "beyond the gilded cage" from Rush's "Limelight." Aren't you?

168    Fair warning to other fathers: this book *will* make you feel like a failure as a father. Not only have you not held a chair at Oxford, written a genre-defining work, *and* sent the finest illustrated letters to your children, you've certainly not done them all at the same time.

As the footnote in the chapter suggested, it is *Leaf by Niggle* that is my favorite of these works: for a man who claims to "cordially dislike allegory in all its forms," Tolkien certainly has proven to be the master of it. Another story that never fails to move me, it can be read in a couple of hours—and pondered for a couple of weeks.

Like Shawn, I find Carpenter's biography to be an absolute must-read. Despite some of its shortcomings, it is the starting point for learning more about the Professor. I always recommend following that up with John Garth's *Tolkien and the Great War*, and then Tom Shippey's *Author of the Century*. After that, pick up books on topics you like: botany, philology, maps, theology, ecology—whatever subject intrigues you, someone has likely written a very good book on it. And if you want your mind blown, follow our advice and read Verlyn Flieger.

# WHAT SHAWN LOVES, AND WHY

After blazing through all the books mentioned in the first few chapters which you've already read about (not the Great Tales; those came out later) teenage me went straight on into The History of Middle-earth. I was enchanted by the raw, unfiltered mythic awesomeness of both volumes of *The Book of Lost Tales;* while it was certainly very different from the version of the legendarium I had fallen in love with in *The Silmarillion*, I was a big fan of ancient stories of gods and monsters, and so Tolkien's earliest attempts at writing his mythology pulled me in quickly. I even enjoyed the poetry in *The Lays of Beleriand*, though ultimately the epic lays in question were unfinished. After that point, though, I didn't go on with The History of Middle-earth for a long time; the material got a lot denser in very short order, and, as a young adult now heading out of high school into the choppy waters of my college studies (not to mention the always-challenging social pressures of these times in our lives), I just didn't have the mental bandwidth for it. So

I took a break from this gradual course of "delving greedily and deep" into Tolkien's unfinished works,[169] and contented myself with rereading the basics every year or two...for a long time.

It was several years later, when I read Carpenter's *Biography* for the first time, that I realized just how many doors of Tolkien study had suddenly opened before me. The next biography to catch my eye was Garth's *Tolkien and the Great War*, which was (and remains, for me) unlike any other book about Tolkien's life I've ever read. The depth of investigation Garth brings to that early period of Tolkien's life, combined with a gift for making it all come to life in such vivid color; not to mention a very deep understanding of the early works of the legendarium like *The Book of Lost Tales* that were taking shape during that period of Tolkien's life: for these reasons, Garth's *Great War* is uncontested as the single greatest biographical work on Tolkien's life. But Carpenter was the genesis of a great deal of Tolkien exploration for me, and for that it will always have a special place in my heart.

In the course of becoming a frothing-at-the-mouth rabid Tolkien fan, podcaster, writer, and commentator, I've come across some scholarly works that really speak to me and my personal hobbyhorses in the world of Tolkien fandom. *The Ring of Words: Tolkien and the Oxford English Dictionary* is one that I always find myself recommending to nascent word-nerds, as it offers not only a brief biography of Tolkien's time working for the *Oxford English Dictionary*—where he researched and wrote definitions and etymologies primarily for English words derived from Germanic roots and

---

169 This anecdotal information is offered as a confession, not a recommendation. Young Shawn's decision to take a break from the middle and later volumes of The History of Middle-earth as a college freshman was right for him at the time, but there's nothing that says you can't go straight on if you have the time and the inclination. For what it's worth, when I did finally go back to these volumes, I found a lot to love, from the linguistic delights of *The Lost Road* (Vol. V) to the deep and rich philosophical musings of *Morgoth's Ring* (Vol. IX). Now I wish I had read them much earlier.

beginning with the letter W[170]—but also a glossary of rare, resurrected, or otherwise just plain interesting English words that appear in Tolkien's writing. *Flora of Middle-earth*, the aforementioned exploration of plants in Tolkien's works, made me far more of a plant-nerd than I ever thought I'd be.

But without a doubt, the single work of Tolkien scholarship that changed my understanding of Tolkien (and, dare I say without coming across as too dramatic, my life) was Verlyn Flieger's *Splintered Light*. Her unimaginably profound thesis about the interplay of opposites in Tolkien's work—light and dark, good and evil, hope and despair—breathed such life into my interpretation, my awareness, and just how I sit down and read Tolkien's books. Flieger calls attention to the balance of opposites in Tolkien's work, while crafting a work of scholarship that balances opposites just as skillfully. Profound but simply so, mind-blowing but welcomingly obvious in hindsight, spiritually uplifting without demanding any particular religious or philosophical worldview from the reader to give it meaning: Flieger's work is, to me, the absolute pinnacle of Tolkien scholarship.

But enough about writers who aren't Tolkien. As people who have listened to *The Prancing Pony Podcast* know (because I've said it many, many times), my favorite non-legendarium work of Tolkien's is unquestionably *Smith of Wootton Major*. And yes, this is partly because the titular character Smith bears a more-than-passing resemblance to my favorite *in*-legendarium character, Eärendil the Mariner, with the shining star on his brow that might as well be a Silmaril, and his journeys to the immortal land of Faery that bring boons to the people back home. But there's a lot more to *Smith* than this. Written, as we mentioned earlier, near the end of his life, *Smith* gives us a chance to sit beside Tolkien as he reflects back on his long career of sub-creation, and the crafting of a beautiful literary artifact which has brought

---

170  This might sound like a weirdly specific assignment, but it was actually quite straightforward. The development of the *Oxford English Dictionary* had been underway for over sixty years when Tolkien joined the team, so the lexicographers working on it were near the end of the alphabet. Tolkien was a gifted scholar of Germanic philology, so he was tasked with writing entries for words with particularly challenging Germanic etymologies; the letter which happened to appear at the beginning of the most challenging entries left to be written was W.

inspiration, hope, and joy to millions around the world; but which he knew, with sad resignation, he would never finish to his own satisfaction before he died. It is poignant, inspiring, awakening, and mournful at the same time; and I defy anyone to get through it without shedding a tear.

This short reflection on non-Tolkien and non-legendarium works that move me has gone on for far longer than I intended it to, but understand, I could have gone on a *lot* longer. There are simply so many astoundingly brilliant books written by and about Tolkien beyond the books of the legendarium, and I hope that I've encouraged you to crack one or two of them open.

E.Austin

# PART II

# OTHER MINDS AND HANDS: MIDDLE-EARTH IN ADAPTATION

# CHAPTER 7

# CH-CH-CH-CHANGES: TOLKIEN ON ADAPTATION

*"I would draw some of the great tales in fullness, and leave many only placed in the scheme, and sketched. The cycles should be linked to a majestic whole, and yet leave scope for other minds and hands..."*

—*J.R.R. Tolkien, from a 1951 letter to Milton Waldman*[171]

There may not be a Tolkien quote more frequently taken out of context than this line, often used to support the argument that Tolkien himself intended for others to write new stories set in the vast world of Middle-earth that he created, with his characters and languages taking center stage. Oft-ignored are the two thoughts expressed in the remaining portion of the paragraph: "...wielding paint and music and drama," and Tolkien's abrupt dismissal, "Absurd." The former defines the limits of Tolkien's original vision with its notable absence of "literature," while the latter evidences Tolkien's

---

171   Carpenter, *Letters*, No. 131.

recognition that such a plan—or, as he calls it, "such an overweening purpose"—was unreasonable at best, if not outright farcical.

In fact, a 1966 letter to his publisher's secretary[172] reveals that Tolkien was strongly opposed to others writing stories set in Middle-earth. In the letter, we are treated to Tolkien's biting response to a proposed "sequel" that a fan was planning to write: "I send you the enclosed impertinent contribution to my troubles.... I suppose...that there is no legal obstacle to this young ass publishing his sequel, if he could find any publisher, either respectable or disreputable, who would accept such tripe."[173] So clearly, even if one chooses to accept a much more liberal interpretation than what we think is appropriate, "other minds and hands" didn't include people who write as badly as this poor guy.

But *adaptations* are a different thing from the creation of entirely new tales, and—as Tolkien apparently hoped to "leave scope for other minds and hands wielding...drama"—it could only be expected that adaptations of Tolkien's work would come. And come they did! Beginning with an adaptation that not many readers will know about, and even fewer will have heard.

The very first adaptation of Tolkien's works was, in fact, a twelve-episode dramatization on BBC Radio's Third Programme in 1955–56. This was the only adaptation of Tolkien's work that was released during his lifetime; you'd be correct in supposing that he had opinions about it:

> I think poorly of the broadcast adaptations. Except for a few details I think they are not well done, even granted the script and the legitimacy of the enterprise (which I do not grant).[174]

---

172  Carpenter, *Letters*, No. 292 to Joy Hill, the secretary at his publisher, Allen & Unwin.

173  In case you're wondering, both of the authors of this book were born *after* 1966, so neither of us was the "young ass" in question here. Notably, this does not preclude us from being labeled as such later on.

174  Carpenter, *Letters*, No. 176 to Naomi Mitchison, 1955. Also...ouch!

> Here is a book very unsuitable for dramatic or semi-dramatic representation. If that is attempted, it needs more space, a lot of space. [...] I feel you have had a very hard task.[175]

> I think the book quite unsuitable for "dramatization," and have not enjoyed the broadcasts....[176]

Tolkien said each of these things *despite* being involved in the creation of the scripts for the dramatization! Catherine McIlwaine, Tolkien archivist at the Bodleian Libraries, says, "Not only did [Tolkien] agree to the adaptation of his book soon after publication, but he was willing to work with the scriptwriters, to abridge the text and adjust the balance of narration and dialogue, so that it fitted the requirements of radio and the limited time available."[177]

Soon, Tolkien—together with his publisher, Stanley Unwin—developed a very simple policy when it came to possible adaptations: "*Art or Cash*. Either very profitable terms indeed; or absolute author's veto on objectionable features or alterations."[178] So, in 1969, Tolkien sold the film rights to *The Lord of the Rings* and *The Hobbit* to United Artists for an amount reported to be a little over £100,000. That's an amount roughly equivalent to £5 million today, not including the 7.5 percent royalty interest in all future adaptations (a right held by the Tolkien Estate today). Tolkien chose cash, and the rest is adaptation history.

Before we move into individual chapters on some of the more well-known adaptations, we want to take a high-level look at the timeline of the

---

175  Carpenter, *Letters*, No. 194 to Terence Tiller, 1956.

176  Carpenter, *Letters*, No. 175 to Mrs. Molly Waldron, 1955.

177  Alberge, Dalya. "Hoard of the rings: 'lost' scripts for BBC Tolkien drama discovered." *The Guardian*, March 12, 2022. www.theguardian.com/film/2022/mar/12/hoard-of-the-rings-lost-scripts-for-bbc-tolkien-drama-discovered.

178  Carpenter, *Letters*, No. 202 to Christopher and Faith Tolkien, 1957.

adaptations, as we believe this is key to understanding the current Tolkien fandom and the direction the fandom is going:

- 1977: *The Hobbit*, an animated made-for-television film produced by Rankin/Bass

- 1978: *The Lord of the Rings*, an animated theatrical film directed by Ralph Bakshi and produced by Saul Zaentz

- 1979: the NPR dramatization of *The Lord of the Rings*, produced by The Mind's Eye

- 1980: *The Return of the King*, another made-for-TV animated special from Rankin/Bass

- 1981: the BBC Radio dramatization of *The Lord of the Rings*, written by Brian Sibley and Michael Bakewell

- 2001 to 2003: New Line Cinema's *The Lord of the Rings* film trilogy, directed by Peter Jackson

- 2012 to 2014: Warner Brother's *The Hobbit* film trilogy, directed by Peter Jackson

- 2022 and continuing: Amazon Prime Video's *The Lord of the Rings: The Rings of Power* television series

Looking closely at these dates, we see an interesting pattern emerge. For the first twenty-two years after the first volume of *The Lord of the Rings* was published, there were virtually no adaptations.[179] Then, in a short four-year span starting in 1977, there were two made-for-TV animated shows, a theatrical animated film, and two radio dramatizations. Yet it was a full twenty years after the BBC Radio production—and forty-five years after the publication of the full *The Lord of the Rings*—before the Jackson films brought the masses to Middle-earth.

---

179   Only the 1955–56 BBC radio dramatization, but that (a) was only available in the UK, and (b) could only have been experienced "live," and not listened to at a later date.

Even after that award-winning series of films, it would be nearly another decade before an attempt was made at adapting *The Hobbit*, and nearly a decade after that before the current spate of adaptations: Amazon's *The Rings of Power*, the slated-for-2024 anime take on *The War of the Rohirrim*, and whatever films New Line Cinema and Warner Brothers will develop in partnership with Embracer Group.[180]

For Tolkien fans in the Boomer Generation (1946–64) and before, the books were the only available entry into Middle-earth for decades. But for Tolkien fans in Generation X (1965–79), the sheer number of adaptations made between 1977 and 1981 mean that some came into Middle-earth through the Rankin/Bass productions or Bakshi's *Rings*. And for Millennials (1980–94), their first experience of Tolkien's works will likely have come through the far more successful and critically-acclaimed Jackson trilogy.[181] Similarly, the Tolkien fandom will soon be joined by folks from Generation Z (1995–2012) and later, whose first experience in Middle-earth may very well be Amazon's *The Rings of Power*.

In other words, if you were to graph the percentage of Tolkien fans whose first exposure to Middle-earth came through the *books* compared to those fans whose first exposure came through *adaptations*, you'd see a fairly obvious curve—something like this entirely made-up chart, which we made up entirely:

---

180   Middle-earth Enterprises, the entity that holds the film rights, was recently sold by The Saul Zaentz Company to Embracer Group. The new owners have recently agreed to license the film rights to New Line and WB, who have stated their intent to make a Marvel- or Star Wars-type movie "universe.'"

181   Bakshi's *The Lord of the Rings* grossed $30.5 million while Jackson's trilogy grossed nearly $3 *billion*. Even when adjusting for inflation, Jackson's films were nearly *thirty-five times* as financially successful.

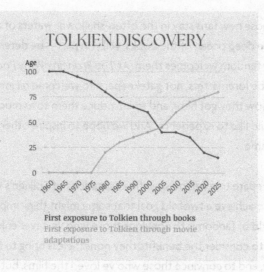

**TOLKIEN DISCOVERY**

Age

First exposure to Tolkien through books
First exposure to Tolkien through movie adaptations

With the help of social media, we surveyed over a thousand members of the Tolkien Society and found that the percentage of members whose first exposure was to the books was 68 percent, while 10 percent came to Middle-earth through the film adaptations between 1977–80, and 18 percent through Jackson's film trilogy. Notably, this fan group skews older than our podcast's average listenership.

When we polled over a thousand members of our podcast's Facebook group with the same question, first exposure to the books dropped to 56 percent, while Jackson's film trilogy was the point of entry for 29 percent. Our group skews a bit younger than the Tolkien Society, so we weren't shocked by this result. Finally, when we surveyed nearly eight hundred followers of the podcast on TikTok (a platform that skews significantly younger than Facebook), we found that only 46 percent of followers were first introduced to Tolkien through the books, with 54 percent coming to Middle-earth via adaptations. Yes, these were informal polls—no, we are not social scientists—yes, the results of these polls are of questionable scientific use. But the anecdotal evidence—and a bit of common sense—suggests that, as time goes on, more and more people will find their way into the Tolkien fandom through adaptations of one kind or another.

Whether those new fans stay in the often-shallower waters of adaptation, or dive into the deep ocean of the books, will—in part—be determined by how the existing fandom welcomes them. At *The Prancing Pony Podcast*, our intent is to be loremasters, not gatekeepers: to welcome *all* into the fandom, no matter how they got here, and to introduce them to as much of the text as they would like to experience. And we hope to inspire other Tolkien fans to do the same.

So, as we prepare to examine specific adaptations of Tolkien's works, it's our intent to achieve a twofold goal that some might think impossible in today's world of fandoms: to convince those who've never enjoyed a single adaptation to consider the benefits they nonetheless bring to the Tolkien community, and to convince those who've loved the films, but could never be bothered to crack open a book, to sit down and actually read the books—perhaps with the company of a certain podcast!

With that in mind, any discussion of Tolkien adaptations has to begin with the recognition that, anytime a beloved work is brought to life in a different medium, there will be changes to the material. Tolkien himself acknowledged as much in his 1958 letter to Forrest J. Ackerman: "The canons of narrative art in any medium cannot be wholly different"[182] They can be different, perhaps even *substantially* different; they just can't be *wholly* different. But let's set the stage for this comment before going any further.

Ackerman, a literary agent for sci-fi authors including Isaac Asimov and Ray Bradbury, was known as "the godfather of geek" and had approached Tolkien and his publisher with a film proposal for *The Lord of the Rings* in 1957. The screenplay was being written by Morton Grady Zimmerman and, *boy*, did Tolkien have thoughts. And while those specific comments are *very* entertaining—unless you're Mr. Zimmerman, we suppose—it is Tolkien's all-

---

182    Carpenter, *Letters*, No. 210.

too-brief discussion about "the canons of narrative art" that we want to take a look at. In whole, the paragraph reads:

> The canons of narrative art in any medium cannot be wholly different; and the failure of poor films is often precisely in exaggeration, and in the intrusion of unwarranted matter owing to not perceiving where the core of the original lies.

Noted Tolkien scholar Tom Shippey used this phrase of Tolkien's to build a simple, two-question framework for discussing changes made in adaptations:[183]

- Was the change inevitable as a result of the change in medium? In other words, is the change needed in order to tell the story cinematically?

- Does it create a different result from the book? That is, does it change or miss the "core of the original"?

It is this framework—what we've often referred to on the podcast as "the Shippey Test"—that we will use as we take a closer look at many of the attempts to adapt Middle-earth.

We'll start with the three animated films: Rankin/Bass's *The Hobbit* (1977), Ralph Bakshi's *The Lord of the Rings* (1978), and Rankin/Bass's *The Return of the King* (1980), before we discuss Peter Jackson's film trilogies, *The Lord of the Rings* (2001–03) and *The Hobbit* (2012–14). While we'll present them in chronological order, we'll make the assumption that most of you have seen at least the Jackson *Rings* films, and will often reference them during our discussions. With Jackson's enormously successful films—by all standards: awards, box office, and pop culture awareness—as a measuring standard, how will these three animated films stand up? What are their strengths and

---

183    Shippey, T. A., "Another Road to Middle-earth: Peter Jackson's Movie Trilogy," in *Roots and Branches: Selected Papers on Tolkien*, Walking Tree Publishers, 2007, 368.

weaknesses? And what's the unusual story linking them together? What do we, as Tolkien fans, think of these oft-nostalgic films?

In a follow-up volume to this book, we plan on also talking about the BBC Radio dramatization (1981), and maybe even briefly mentioning the NPR dramatization (1979). Along those same audio-oriented lines, our next book will talk about the audiobooks: you might not think of an audiobook as an "adaptation," but there are reasons you might prefer one more than another: the way the narrator pronounces a name, or emphasizes a piece of dialogue, the music he's chosen to sing for one of Tolkien's poems, or the way he voices your favorite hobbit or dragon. These choices make audiobooks adaptations of a kind, even if the range of choices is smaller than the one that a filmmaker employs.

And in that eventual sequel, we'll spend time talking about the massive world of video game adaptations set in Middle-earth. While we can't talk about every Middle-earth game ever made, we'll spend some time covering the history of these adaptations before talking about some of the bigger games in the space, including *The Lord of the Rings Online*, *Middle-earth: Shadow of Mordor*, and more, including titles that have not yet been released as of the date of this book's completion.

We understand that Amazon's *The Lord of the Rings: The Rings of Power* is conspicuous in its absence from this book, given its current status as adaptation *du jour*, but we don't believe we can provide a fair discussion of the television series until we've seen more than 20 percent of it. So you can expect the same in-depth discussion and analysis of *The Rings of Power* in our next book. Similarly, *The War of the Rohirrim*, the animated film slated to adapt a piece of the history of Rohan, will release in 2024, and we'll take a look at that. All that is to say: buy this book, so we can write another one!

We might as well warn you now that we may not love every adaptation you love. We may criticize, and even make fun of, a work that you deeply appreciate—and that's okay! Because if *you* love it, don't take our criticisms to mean that you shouldn't. Love what you love; the fandom is big enough for all of us. The books remain precisely what they were before any of the adaptations, and will always remain so. Don't listen to the sky-is-falling naysayers who say, "It's ruining Tolkien's legacy!" or "That's destroying the lore!" Many of the folks who claim that "Tolkien is rolling in his grave because of this!" haven't even been to Wolvercote Cemetery. We can tell you if we think an adaptation is missing the core of Tolkien's original; we can offer you our opinion on the particular qualities of an adaptation. But it's not our place to tell you what you can enjoy; in fact, that's *nobody*'s place but your own. Welcome to the Tolkien fandom!

# CHAPTER 8

# TRA-LA-LA-LALLY: RANKIN/BASS'S *THE HOBBIT*

*"Oh, Bilbo Baggins, if you really understood that ring, as someday
members of your family not yet born will, then you'd realize that this
story has not ended...but is only beginning."*

—*Gandalf, to Bilbo, at the end of Rankin/Bass's* The Hobbit

*"Whaaaaaaat?"*

—*Alan and Shawn, after the end of Rankin/Bass's* The Hobbit

For Tolkien fans of a certain age—particularly those in America, where it was
first aired—the animated version of *The Hobbit*, produced by Rankin/Bass
and originally broadcast in November of 1977, carries with it a high degree
of nostalgia. The cartoon art style, the use of so many of Tolkien's own song

lyrics, and Glenn Yarbrough's folksy rendition of "The Greatest Adventure"[184] often bring warm memories to the hearts of fans who experienced this very first on-screen adaptation of Middle-earth. As it turns out, nostalgia isn't what it used to be.

By 1972, the film rights to *The Hobbit* and *The Lord of the Rings* had been "out there" for a few years; as we talked about in the last chapter, Tolkien had sold those rights in 1969 for what would now be considered a bargain price. And before that sale, Tolkien had rejected a number of potential adaptations. The most famous, or infamous, of these was a treatment of *The Lord of the Rings* that is often referred to as "the Zimmerman script," and that was the subject of a *scathing* letter from Tolkien in 1958.[185] And while other attempts at creating a film version of *The Lord of the Rings* were begun, but never completed,[186] *The Hobbit* had not yet had any takers.[187] But in 1972, animators Arthur Rankin, Jr. and Jules Bass decided they wanted to make animated television specials based on the works of Tolkien. In a 2003 interview, Rankin said that he thought trying to adapt the entirety of *The Lord of the Rings* was "impossible" and that people "wouldn't sit still for it."[188] Instead, Rankin opted to adapt *The Hobbit* first, with an eye toward adapting *The Return of the King* at a later date.

On November 27, 1977, the animated *Hobbit* was broadcast on NBC television. Earlier that day, the New York Times wrote about the film, saying

---

184  We should note, *not* one of Tolkien's own songs, though quotes from the song's lyrics have occasionally been mistakenly attributed to Tolkien.

185  Carpenter, *Letters*, No. 210, mentioned in the previous chapter, is well worth the read, even if the proposed adaptation was never made.

186  Including a script by John Boorman that saw Frodo having sex with Galadriel (more on that in the next chapter), and a potential project starring The Beatles to be directed by Stanley Kubrick. The world is a better place for neither of these seeing production. As is this book.

187  No *real* takers. There was an attempt by William L. Snyder to adapt *The Hobbit* for his production company, Rembrandt Films. While he leased the rights for five years in 1962, it didn't go very far. Only when the rights were about to expire in 1967 did he put out a twelve-minute short that was nothing more than narration over still images; he showed it in a New York theater to a dozen spectators pulled in off the street, in a failed attempt to extend his control over the rights.

188  "The Enchanted World of Rankin-Bass: Arthur Rankin Jr., Interview at the Museum of Television & Radio (2003)—Part 2," https://www.youtube.com/watch?v=AZe6OhmPnx8, starting at 12:26.

that "the $3-million[189] cost of *The Hobbit* makes it the most expensive animated television show in history."[190] Even then, the Tolkien fandom had a reputation for exacting standards (or pedantic nerdiness, depending on your perspective), as the *Times* points out: "Tolkien's legions of fans have very precise ideas about how Middle-earth and its inhabitants should look and sound…"

That was true forty-six years ago, and it's true now; and while the two of us aren't "legions" of fans, we have at least some *vague* ideas about how Middle-earth and its inhabitants should look and sound, and—well, let's just say that this adaptation made some…interesting choices. Elrond with a beard. Trolls with tusks. Gollum is what we can only describe as a stoned frog. Properly ugly Orcs. Wood-elves that are even uglier than the Orcs. Men of Dale wearing skirts and Burt Reynolds mustaches. A furry American dragon. But it's still *The Hobbit*, right?

This is the point in our discussion when we would normally talk about the "Shippey Test" that we *just* painstakingly introduced in the last chapter: are the changes simply the necessary result of a change in medium? Or do the changes come from the filmmaker's failure to perceive the core of the original? And, to expand on the Shippey Test a bit by going back to Tolkien's own words, are there exaggerations and intrusions that demonstrate this failure to perceive the core of the original? It was certainly our plan to apply that structure here, at any rate. Instead, this is the point in our discussion where we have to acknowledge that our preferred method of analyzing adaptations doesn't work well here, because the biggest problem with Rankin/Bass's *The Hobbit* is that they didn't so much make substantive changes to the story as, instead, drastically *cut* so many crucial events and themes from the story. In fact, the only "intrusion" here is the intrusion of a

---

189  Approximately fifteen million dollars in 2023.

190  Culhane, John. "Will the Video Version of Tolkien Be Hobbit Forming?" *The New York Times*, November 27, 1977. https://web.archive.org/web/20160110060623/http://www.nytimes.com/1977/11/27/books/tolkien-hobbitani.html.

limited run time that allowed no more than about seventy-five minutes to tell the entire story.

By cutting the length of the tale to fit broadcast television requirements, the filmmakers (in our humble opinion) missed just about everything related to the core of the original: from Bilbo's internal Took/Baggins debate to the role of fate and luck, from Thorin's greed to the importance of pity. And while those cuts are certainly related to the change in medium, they're pervasive and result in a severely weakened story. So while the movie receives a grade of "mostly harmless" from us, it's also "mostly not *The Hobbit*."

Rankin/Bass's adaptation does have a certain charm to some of the character designs: Gandalf is faithfully represented as "an old man with a staff...a tall pointed blue hat,[191] a long grey cloak, a silver scarf over which his long white beard hung down below his waist and immense black boots," while Bilbo is drawn in a comfortable style that certainly seems to fit his hobbity nature: short, beardless, plump, smoking a pipe, and wearing bright clothing.[192] The actors who voiced these two beloved characters (John Huston as Gandalf and Orson Bean as Bilbo) did a wonderful job of conveying their temperaments: Bilbo initially is portrayed as fussy and proper, but becomes more comfortable in his own skin over the course of his adventures, while Gandalf is, more often than not, the right blend of grumpy and kind.

The same *cannot* be said for Rankin/Bass's other casting choices. Hans Conried, the actor who voiced Captain Hook in Disney's *Peter Pan*, has such a distinctly recognizable voice as Thorin Oakenshield that we kept expecting one of the dwarves to be introduced as Smee, and for Smaug to be a fire-breathing version of Tick-Tock the Crocodile. Don't get us started on the

---

191  Okay, the film gives him a *hood* instead of a hat, but everything else is there.

192  The eagle-eyed among us will note that they have drawn Bilbo with ordinary round ears, not pointed ears. Believe it or not, though, the only mention of the shape of hobbit ears is in a 1938 letter Tolkien wrote to his American publisher (No. 27), in which he describes hobbits as having "ears only slightly pointed and 'elvish.' "

casting of the Elvenking in Mirkwood:[193] Otto Preminger's heavy Austrian accent has modern viewers imagining him to tell the Dwarves to "get to da choppah."[194] And casting Smaug with the American actor Richard Boone, who was most known for his role as Paladin in the Western *Have Gun—Will Travel*, had us looking over Smaug's armor for a holster and six-shooter instead of a weak spot. "You have nice manners for a thief and a liar. Yeeeehaw!"

But it isn't the voice acting or character design that's the real problem here—even if Smaug looks vaguely like a bobcat, complete with fur. The problem is how much they had to cut. For example, Gandalf first arrives at the 1:07 mark—without so much as a "Good morning"—and the dwarves show up at 1:53. The entire scene that establishes who Gandalf is, his connection with hobbits in general, and Bilbo in particular, along with Bilbo's general disdain of adventure, is over in well under a single minute. And it's less than sixteen minutes later when we meet Elrond in Rivendell in this Cliff's Notes version of the story! There's simply not enough time for characters to be developed, or for them to grow. The entire sequence with the Wood-elves—from their capture in Mirkwood, to their escape in the barrels—lasts less than two minutes, with the Elvenking on screen for twenty seconds.[195] We don't get to know Thorin well enough for him to be distinct from the other dwarves, the rest of whom are entirely interchangeable anyway. So, while we'll have some things to say later about Peter Jackson's trilogy of *The Hobbit* films and their unnecessary length (nearly nine hours), it turns out that covering the book in only seventy-seven minutes results in something that bears only superficial resemblance to the actual story.

Sometimes, a dim light flickering in darkness seems like a bright light. "Riddles in the Dark" is that dim light in the Rankin/Bass *Hobbit*; it's the scene closest

---

193  Thranduil, though he's never named as such in *The Hobbit* itself.

194  In a footnote utterly irrelevant to all things Tolkien, Preminger is better-known (and properly so) for directing and producing dozens of films, including *Anatomy of a Murder*, nominated for Best Picture of 1959. Starring Jimmy Stewart, one of the smaller parts in the film was played by Orson Bean, the actor who played Bilbo in *The Hobbit*. Small world.

195  Though this is a blessing in disguise, given the orc-like appearance of the Wood-elves, and the inexplicable Austrian accent of their king.

to the book, and the actor portraying Gollum, Brother Theodore, brings a wonderfully inhuman creepiness to the role. Unfortunately, the scene is hampered by the film's decision to eliminate one of the most important moments in the legendarium: "[Bilbo] must fight. He must stab the foul thing, put its eyes out, kill it. It meant to kill him. No, not a fair fight. He was invisible now. Gollum had no sword. Gollum had not actually threatened to kill him, or tried to yet. And he was miserable, alone, lost. A sudden understanding, a pity mixed with horror, welled up in Bilbo's heart: a glimpse of endless unmarked days without light or hope of betterment, hard stone, cold fish, sneaking and whispering" is replaced with a mocking "Ta-ta!" as Bilbo escapes Gollum's cave. The moment of Bilbo's pity, so central to the rest of the story of the Ring and of the Third Age, is simply absent.

The other major theme of *The Hobbit*—Thorin's descent into madness and greed, driven by desire for the Arkenstone, and his repentance before his death—is also completely absent. There is no Arkenstone at all; Bilbo doesn't steal it, nor does he offer it to Thranduil and Bard as a bargaining chip, nor does Thorin try to throw Bilbo from the wall for his theft. Yes, there's a scene in which Thorin dies after saying kind things to Bilbo, but it's ultimately hollow because there's nothing for him to repent *of*, aside from a bit of name-calling, and viewers are left watching it and wondering if we should care. The film even kills off more dwarves than the book, but doesn't bother to name any of them aside from Bombur: we never learn that Kili and Fili are dead, let alone that they are Thorin's kin and that his entire kingly line is gone.

And while there are other missing elements—the eagles take the group from the burning fir trees straight to the edge of Mirkwood, bypassing Beorn altogether, and Thorin gives Bilbo a suit of armor, not a coat of *mithril*—it's the absence of thematic material that a viewer can't help but notice most.

At the very end of the film, after Bilbo has returned safely home, we are introduced to the one "intrusion" into the story: Gandalf telling Bilbo, and us as the unfortunate viewers, that the "souvenir ring" Bilbo acquired on his adventures was something far more than he might think. Gandalf says, "...

if you really understood that ring, as someday members of your family not yet born will, then you'd realize that this story has not ended...but is only beginning." This blatant sequel hook raises so many questions: how does Gandalf know that this is the One Ring already? Why is he okay leaving it in Bilbo's custody without any warning to never use it at all? Why will he wait sixty years before he investigates the matter?

# SO WHY DO WE LOVE IT? OR DO WE?

And yet...while the film disappoints in a hundred different ways, we nevertheless recommend everyone experience it at least once. Probably only once, actually. Its place in Tolkien history as the very first on-screen adaptation of Middle-earth tends to make us want to forgive some of its more egregious offenses, and its folksy charm allows us to overlook a few of the lesser ones. If only Rankin/Bass had stopped while they were ahead—but we'll get to their take on *The Return of the King* soon enough.

# WHY ALAN LOVES IT

There's always a place in your heart for your very first, and Rankin/Bass's *The Hobbit* was my first experience of Middle-earth. Yes, I was nine years old; no, I didn't understand that it was an adaptation that failed in so many ways. All that nine-year-old me knew in 1977 was that I was fascinated by this story, and I couldn't wait to read the book and find out more about hobbits, dwarves, dragons, and that Gandalf fella. And when I was gifted that book a few months later, it was an illustrated edition using still images from the Rankin/Bass special. It didn't take me long to imagine Orcs as something much different from the renditions shown in the film and my book; it took no time at all to imagine Elves as something far less orc-like. I confess, however, that it took a long time for me to stop imagining Gollum as a stoned frog.

# WHY SHAWN LOVES IT

I remember being aware that there was a cartoon called *The Hobbit* long before I knew what it was or was about, let alone saw it. My first introduction to Rankin/Bass's adaptation came through a dimly remembered TV advertisement with a 1-800 number, probably for mail-ordering a copy of the film on VHS (or maybe even Betamax); it was so long ago that I don't clearly remember. But for a long time, when I heard people talk about Tolkien's "Middle-earth" (which I imagined as literally in the *middle* of the *earth*, on account of scenes from the caves of "Riddles in the Dark" in that same commercial), it was flashes of this cartoon commercial that I got in my head. I didn't actually watch the cartoon until many, *many* years later, as an adult; sadly I can't recall the year, but it was several years after reading the books for the first time, but before Peter Jackson's *The Lord of the Rings* came out.

With all that said, I don't hold an abundance of nostalgia for this particular adaptation, and while I recognize its well-earned place in the annals of Tolkien fandom, and the special place it holds in the hearts of many fans, it's not one that I find myself going back to again and again. The last time I watched it was during the COVID-19 pandemic, when I showed it to my kids.

To be completely fair, it's not bad. I mean, I don't care for the character designs overmuch, particularly that of Bilbo—whose haircut I can only describe as "Endor-era Princess Leia drawn by generative AI," and who looks one quadruple espresso away from having his eyes popping out of his head like Disney's Mr. Toad—not to mention the Elves and Gollum (which we've already mentioned). But it's a sweet and earnest little children's cartoon, and most of the "core of the original" stuff that it's missing is stuff that even I didn't pick up on when I first read the book as a younger reader. And it does a decent job of capturing the childlike wonder of some of the book's best moments, and all with a folksy quality that should do hobbits proud... Though, thanks to the largely American voice cast and choice of an American folk singer to compose the music, it lacks an essential *Englishness* needed to properly capture hobbits or Tolkien's vision.

But there's still a lot to enjoy here, particularly for newer fans or fans introducing the story to younger viewers. And frankly, I'd rather watch it than sit through all three episodes of Peter Jackson's *Hobbit* attempt...but that's a topic for a later chapter.

Why We Love Middle-earth

# CHAPTER 9

# THE COINCIDENTAL CLIFFHANGER: RALPH BAKSHI'S *THE LORD OF THE RINGS*

*"The forces of darkness were driven forever from the face of Middle-Earth by the valiant friends of Frodo. As their gallant battle ended, so too ends the first great tale of The Lord of the Rings!"*

—Narration at the conclusion of Bakshi's The Lord of the Rings

*"We've had one great tale, yes.*
*But what about a second great tale?"*

*"I don't think the studio knows about that."*

—Alan and Shawn, after the end of Bakshi's The Lord of the Rings

It is entirely reasonable to wonder why more than a decade passed between Tolkien's 1967 sale of the film rights to *The Lord of the Rings* and the release of the first cinematic adaptation, Ralph Bakshi's *The Lord of the Rings*, in 1978. After all, the books were selling in vast numbers: over three million copies worldwide by 1968. Yet it is this very delay that led to the existence of the Bakshi adaptation, since it could only have happened at the end of a very long chain of events. Just chance...if chance you call it.

Shortly after United Artists purchased the filmmaking rights from Tolkien, they were approached by John Boorman, the English director of *Point Blank* and *Hell in the Pacific*, who wanted to create an epic based on King Arthur and the Grail. They offered him *The Lord of the Rings* instead. He took it and, along with cowriter Rospo Pallenberg, handed UA a script that was nearly unrecognizable: the Council of Elrond as a circus theater, psychedelic mushrooms, a "sparsely-clad" Galadriel who sleeps with Frodo, thus disappointing everyone else in the Fellowship, and Gimli opening the doors to Moria by dancing a jig, to name some of the changes. Even though the script cost UA three million dollars to produce, they—quite understandably, we might add—rejected the project in 1970.[196]

Enter Ralph Bakshi. The maverick animator was the creative force behind countercultural and controversial films in the 1970s, including America's first X-rated cartoon, 1972's *Fritz the Cat*. Bakshi was a longtime fan of fantasy and science fiction and had wanted to turn *The Lord of the Rings* into an animated film since reading the books shortly after they were published. When he found out that Boorman's project was dead, he approached UA and, in 1975, convinced them to allow him to shop the project around to see if someone would be willing to pay back the three million dollars UA had spent on Boorman's script. Bakshi was able to convince the president of MGM, Dan Melnick (who Bakshi knew had read *The Lord of the Rings*)

---

196   Ultimately the story ended well for all concerned. Not only was the world spared the sight of Boorman's adaptation of *The Lord of the Rings* on screen, but Boorman ended up getting the King Arthur project he wanted all along: 1981's *Excalibur*, also a collaboration with Pallenberg.

Why We Love Middle-earth

to do exactly that, and work began on what was to be two animated films. Just months later, however, Melnick was fired from the studio, and the new studio head informed Bakshi that his project was dead in the water.

And now we get to a name in the story that many of you might recognize: Saul Zaentz. An investor in Bakshi's *Fritz the Cat*, which had gone on to make ninety million dollars worldwide, Zaentz had generated quite a return for himself. With an eye for wise investments, he'd put some of those returns into *One Flew Over the Cuckoo's Nest*, a successful and Oscar-winning film.[197] So when Bakshi approached Zaentz to ask him to finance his vision for *The Lord of the Rings*, Zaentz—sensing opportunity—agreed. Zaentz approached UA in 1976, and the studio—desperate for cash, as it was pouring millions into the production of *Heaven's Gate*[198]—sold the filmmaking rights to Tolkien's stories for three million dollars. Zaentz created Middle-earth Enterprises as the rights-holding entity that still exists today, though it was sold to Embracer Group in 2022.

Back to Bakshi, though. After obtaining Zaentz's financial backing, Bakshi met with Priscilla Tolkien, the author's daughter, who showed him the room where Tolkien did his writing and drawing. Bakshi says that he promised her that he would "be pure to the book." His job, he said, wasn't to make changes, but "to say 'This is what the genius said.'" Later, he would say that the important thing about the adaptation was not necessarily what hobbits look like, but that "the energy of Tolkien survives." And he confessed, "The biggest challenge was to be true to the book." How did he fare?

When you first watch this adaptation, one of the things that stands out is some of the unique animation techniques that Bakshi employs. The

---

197  By "successful," we mean a box office of over $160 million on a budget of a little over $4 million. And by "Oscar-winning," we mean it won all five major Academy Awards for 1975: Best Picture, Actor, Actress, Director, and Screenplay. Providing evidence of the small world of cinema, Brad Dourif was nominated for Best Supporting Actor in *Cuckoo's Nest*, and would go on to play Gríma Wormtongue in Jackson's adaptations more than twenty-five years later.

198  One of the biggest box-office bombs of all time, it eventually led to UA being sold to MGM and ceasing to exist as an independent studio.

prologue is silhouetted live action, viewed through a red filter so we only see the shapes of the characters. There are other times when he utilizes colored overlays of live-action footage (the Men of Bree, for example), or solarized scenes (the Battle at Helm's Deep). And then there's the famous rotoscoping used throughout (although inconsistently): this is when scenes are first shot in live action and afterward traced onto animation cels; by using real-life movement as the base, the animation displays more realistic character movement. But animation techniques aren't going to make up for "not perceiving where the core of the original lies," so let's take a look at the story itself.

The film starts with a prologue set in the Second Age, with the Elven-smiths forging Rings of Power: nine for Men, seven for the Dwarf-lords, and three for Elven kings. Sauron then learns the art of ring-making and crafts the Master Ring: the One Ring to rule them all. This ring is so powerful that all of Middle-earth is his, and he cannot be defeated. The Last Alliance of Men and Elves is defeated, but during the battle, Sauron doesn't notice "the heroic shadow who slipped in": Isildur—or IZZ-ill-dur, as they call him—hacks away, and the Ring falls off, free for him to pick it up. He refuses to destroy it and is killed, losing the Ring in the river Anduin. While the Ring is lost, Sauron is said to "capture" the nine rings, turning their bearers into the Ringwraiths. We come back to the Ring for the now-familiar story of Déagol and Sméagol, Sméagol's descent into madness and transition to Gollum, Bilbo's finding of the Ring, and his escape from Gollum.

The existence of the prologue itself, along with the way it is structured, foreshadows the beginning of the Jackson films more than twenty years in the future. In fact, as we watch the Bakshi film today—in light of the overwhelming shadow the Jackson films have cast on all Tolkien adaptations, before or after—it's almost impossible not to see the moments in *this* film that inspired Jackson in the creation of *his* films: the prologue is simply the first of many. And while you should get used to us saying, "Yes, but Jackson did it better," the fact that Bakshi did it *at all* deserves at least some credit.

Beginning the story as the book does, with preparations for Bilbo's 111th birthday party, sounds like a wonderful idea—right up until you have to spend all your time doing exposition in The Shadow of the Past. Moving some of that exposition to the introduction certainly seems to be a prime example of how "the canons of narrative art" genuinely differ between a book and a film.

Having said that, the lore that the prologue attempts to convey is filled with errors that appear to be due to a simple lack of attention, and not to the change in medium. Why show Sauron learning the "craft of ring-making" only *after* the Elves made the Nine, the Seven, and the Three?[199] Why make the Last Alliance face imminent and inevitable defeat? Why have Isildur "slip in" and hack off the Ring? And while these arguably don't cut to the "core of the original," these are sloppy lore errors that simply set the tone for more sloppy lore errors throughout Bakshi's film.

After the prologue, the story itself opens years later, with Gandalf arriving in the Shire in time for Bilbo's 111th birthday party.[200] Bilbo delivers some of his famous lines from the book, including the roster of family names, culminating in "Proudfoots" being corrected to "Proudfeet" by one of that family whose large feet are on the table, a shot that admittedly inspired Jackson, even down to the camera angle.[201] On goes the Ring, and—after a superfluous sparkle, musical chime, and flash of lights—Bilbo disappears, only to reappear in his home, where he puts the Ring in an envelope, has a brief confrontation with Gandalf, and finally departs.

---

199   And, we might add, why have Sauron look like one of The Knights Who Say 'Ni'?

200   We have to compliment Bakshi here on the Shire: it's seen as a town populated with many hobbit holes, whereas Bag End in the Rankin/Bass *Hobbit* may as well have been the only hobbit hole for miles around.

201   In the audio commentary on Jackson's *The Fellowship of the Ring*, he says this was an intentional homage to Bakshi's film and expressed his opinion that this was "a brilliant angle."

To his credit, Bakshi says that seventeen years pass between Bilbo's departure and Gandalf knocking on what is now Frodo's door at Bag End.[202] Frodo is genuinely thrilled to see Gandalf for the first time since Bilbo's party, and the two immediately start talking about "Bilbo's funny ring" before Gandalf tosses it into the fire.[203] Gandalf—quite theatrically[204]—explains that the Ring is "altogether evil," and describes the corruption that happens to anyone who possesses the Ring—until they come under the power of SORE-on, the poorly-pronounced Dark Lord of Mordor.[205] And when Frodo expresses his wish that this need not have happened in his time, Gandalf's brief retort, "So do I," seems woefully inadequate. As does his altogether too-brief mention of Bilbo's pity. Both of these matters are central themes of *The Lord of the Rings*, very close to "the core of the original," especially the latter, and their near-elimination here is an oversight that is hard to ignore. One could argue the need to save time, but Bakshi spends *six minutes* on the Black Riders' chase of Frodo to the Ford of Bruinen later, so an extra thirty seconds here would not have made a difference.

When Gandalf—in a seemingly random act of grabbing—pulls Sam out of a nearby shrub,[206] we begin to discover that Bakshi is relying on the viewers' *knowledge* of the story, rather than on *telling* the story. We are not introduced to who Sam is, nor what his relationship is to Frodo. And—spoilers—we're *never* given those rather important details. And in another "we are relying on the fact that you know what we're talking about" moment, Bakshi's Sam lists the things he's heard Gandalf talking about, including Elves—and how much he'd "dearly love to see Elves." But there's one

---

202  *How* he showed this—with a rapid-fire transition between all four seasons in a sequence that might trigger seizures in sensitive persons—leaves room for improvement.

203  The terrified look on Frodo's face when Gandalf throws the Ring into the fire is worth the price of admission alone; his face *morphs* into sheer terror in a way no human face ever could.

204  Gandalf's total inability to simply sit down and *talk* to Frodo is telling, while his wildly gesticulating hands bring to mind the film trope of "Milking the Giant Cow."

205  It's worth noting for those who haven't read the books yet that Tolkien makes it very clear that Sauron's name is pronounced SOW-ron. Why this detail—very clearly presented in Appendix E—was unknown to Bakshi is a mystery. Perhaps he just stopped at "Well, I'm back."

206  In the book, pulling Sam from under the verge makes sense; here, pulling him from a random bush by the river where Frodo and Gandalf have been walking leads to some *very* uncomfortable questions about Sam.

unfortunate detail: Gandalf and Frodo never spoke about Elves near Sam! Or at all, even. Not once. The only time that Elves are mentioned in the film up to this point is in the prologue—which we can only assume Sam has *not* been forced to watch. This assumption—that the viewer will fill in the blanks—is evidenced throughout the film, so get used to it. You'll also need to get used to this juvenile and pathetic Sam: far and away the worst characterization of the film.

Eventually, we come to the scene that was either Jackson's biggest homage, or biggest theft, depending on your perspective: the encounter that Frodo and the hobbits have with the first of the Black Riders. The tension builds wonderfully as the Black Rider approaches and the hobbits all hide under the tree, though the tension is almost broken by the zombie shuffle that the Black Rider employs when he gets off the horse. The camera angle, and the wordless way that Frodo is tempted to put on the Ring, not only make for good cinema here, in one of the film's strongest moments, but also made for similarly good cinema twenty-three years later in Jackson's version.

The Bakshi version skips quite a bit after this: the encounter with Gildor and the Elves in the Woody End, Farmer Maggot, Bucklebury Ferry, Crickhollow, the Old Forest, Tom Bombadil,[207] and the Barrow-downs, as the hobbits decide to stop at Bree for a bath and a night's sleep. Once at The Prancing Pony,[208] the hobbits watch the locals party for a bit before Merry steps out for some fresh air, where he encounters two Black Riders and succumbs to the Black Breath. Back at the inn, Frodo sings, dances, and disappears, causing quite the stir and frustrating poor old Butterbur, just as in the book. And when they get back to their room, they encounter Strider (voiced by John Hurt, in perhaps the best performance of the film). The meme is correct: Gondor has no pants, Gondor needs no pants. But it *does* apparently need the largest belt buckle in all of Middle-earth.

---

207    Known in some circles as "Sir-not-appearing-in-any-film."

208    Do you know how hard it is to *not* type 'Podcast' after those two words now?

Bakshi then spends nearly two minutes building tension for the Black Riders' attack on the hobbits' beds; after they discover their mistake, they shriek and engage in some unexpected dancing while we cut to Aragorn and the hobbits safely in another room. This was yet another scene that clearly inspired Jackson—it certainly wasn't inspired by the book, because this doesn't actually happen! Yes, the hobbits discover that their room was attacked during the night, but it was clearly townspeople, most likely led by Bill Ferny, who were the culprits—not a set of incompetent Black Riders. But let's chalk this up to the difference in narrative arts: show the action and build up the danger of the Black Riders.

After the journey to, and fight on, Weathertop, they quickly encounter Glorfindel Legolas on the road,[209] much to Sam's delight, who informs them that there has been no news of Gandalf in Rivendell. We should mention here that Legolas is voiced by Anthony Daniels; I keep wanting him to tell Sam off like he's R2-D2.

Now we reach the Black Riders' chase and attack at the Ford, and it feels like this is really a turning point in the film. Up to this point, the pacing has been decent—a bit off in spots, but to be expected when telling the story in a little over two hours—but this scene drags on and on. And on. And when you think it might be done, it drags on some more. For nearly six interminable minutes, it drags before Frodo wakes in Rivendell.[210]

And it is in Rivendell that the film changes gears and accelerates: the entirety of the Council of Elrond is over in three minutes: *half* the time that the Black Riders spent chasing Frodo. It's as though Bakshi has decided that we've been given enough exposition, and now it's time to just do a highlight reel.

---

209   Just as in Jackson's version, replacing Glorfindel with another character makes cinematic sense: Glorfindel never appears in the books after the Council, so we're introduced to another major character at this point instead. Still, Glorfindel and Tom Bombadil should start a club.

210   Which, if Bakshi's art design is anything to go by, was inspired by Tibetan monasteries high in the Himalayas.

Why We Love Middle-earth

As a result, the film becomes a bit more incoherent and disjointed from Rivendell onwards.

At the Council, though, we are introduced to a few new characters: an aloof Elrond, who appears to have better things to do than provide more exposition to us; Boromir, who looks like a bad cosplay Viking; and Gimli the Dwarf, who sometimes appears as tall as Legolas. And very few pants all around. To the scene's credit, in the short time it is given, the dialogue is mostly faithful to the text—although, because it is so truncated, it doesn't give the viewers the same sense of weightiness, significance, and courage on Frodo's part. Or even context. Aragorn says he is the descendant of Elendil and that he holds the Sword that was Broken. But the film has never told us who Elendil is (only IZZ-ildehr), or even how the sword got broken in the first place. Similarly, Boromir stomps around, asking, "Why do you speak of hiding and destroying?" when, in fact, no one has said anything about hiding or destroying: Elrond has said we aren't able to do either one. Get used to this reliance on the audience to fill in the gaps: it only grows from here.

When we get to the Doors of Moria, Gandalf struggles with the password: apparently, it's *meklon* because *mellon* would be too confusing? The Watcher in the Water attacks almost immediately, and we are treated to an extended fight sequence, with Boromir hacking tentacles as the Company make their way inside. And, for some reason, Bakshi leaves us with a last vision of Bill the Pony about to be grabbed by the Watcher, perhaps as a snack. Poor Bill, indeed.

Their journey through Moria begins, complete with all the highlights and none of the cumbersome character development. The Orcs attack—yes, with a cave troll—and the Company run, after a brief battle in which Frodo appears to have been killed by a spear wielded by an Orc moving with the speed of a glacier. Speaking of Orcs, the first thing we thought of when we saw Bakshi's Orcs was Star Wars. They have the red eyes of the Jawas, but look, act, and even *sound* like the Sandpeople of Tatooine. With the massive success of *Star Wars* just one year before, in 1977, this perhaps should come as little surprise.

As the Company flee the ~~Sandpeople~~ Orcs, we bear witness to the moment in the film when both character design *and* common sense fail: the arrival of the Balrog. You've heard of the mythological chimera: a creature with the body of a lion, the head of a goat, and the tail of a snake. Or the manticore: a beast with the body of a lion, the wings of a dragon, the tail of a scorpion, and a vaguely human head. We have searched through the works of classical mythology, and have not found a creature like this Balrog: the body of a retired weightlifter, the head of a gorilla-lion, the wings of a red moth, and the bedroom slippers of Sasquatch. If you have a name for this monstrosity, please let us know.

It is hard to take the film seriously at this point, despite the film's attempt to remain accurate to the dialogue of the scene. This becomes doubly true when the Balrog literally *flies*, utilizing its metaphorical wings of shadow. What hope we might have had for this movie fades as rapidly as Gandalf falling down the chasm.

The remaining hour of this film moves at an absurd pace: when you realize the first half has gotten us to the fall of Gandalf, and the second half is supposed to complete the *entirety* of The Lord of the Rings, what else can it do? We meet the Lady Galadriel and her husband, Sell-a-born.[211] The Elves— or their children's choir, to be specific—sing a truly cringey song about Gandalf's death. An oddly blue Galadriel shows Sam and Frodo her Mirror and reveals her Ring to Frodo as it shoots out laser beams and sparkles— because "magic"—before Frodo offers her the One Ring. She passes the test, and the Company are immediately on the Anduin: no gifts, no farewell, no

---

211   Much like Sauron's name, the proper pronunciation of Celeborn's name is very clear from the most cursory reading of Appendix E. In Tolkien's own words, "C has always the value of *k* even before *e* and *i*." Honestly, Mr. Bakshi, it's on the first page of the appendix. (*The Return of the King*, 1087)

explanation. In fact, only two minutes pass between the Mirror and Boromir's attempt to persuade Frodo to lend him the Ring![212]

The scene between Frodo and Boromir *almost* works, aside from Boromir's gesticulation, which is clearly inspired by Gandalf's grand gesturing. The Breaking of the Fellowship happens quickly, with Aragorn really laying into Boromir and Sam going after Frodo. Merry and Pippin quite literally run into their would-be captors and Boromir comes to their rescue, until he is brutally killed—we counted at least seven arrows. The last of these finally stops him blowing his horn, but not before it has alerted Aragorn, Legolas, and Gimli. Aragorn recognizes the horn blast as Boromir's, which is interesting, as it sounded precisely like the Orc horn in Moria. And will sound exactly the same as the horns of the Riders of Rohan. And the horn of Helm Hammerhand. The budget allowed for only one horn call, apparently.

From here, Bakshi's adaptation sacrifices screen time for the story in order to give screen time to battle. Yes, Merry and Pippin meet Treebeard: but to what end? The Ents never attack Isengard and don't appear at Helm's Deep, so he's just another "highlight"—just another moment of Bakshi relying on preexisting audience knowledge.

We do, however, finally get to meet Gollum, encountered by Frodo and Sam in the Emyn Muil. In a pre-Andy Serkis world, it must be said that the voicing (by Peter Woodthorpe) qualifies as another of the film's strengths. It is unfortunate that we only get a couple more scenes with Frodo, Sam, and Gollum—as Bakshi spends most of the last twenty minutes of the film in the Battle of Helm's Deep.

Before we get there, however, we do get to meet the resurrected Gandalf, and then go with him, Aragorn, Legolas, and Gimli to Edoras: where GRY-muh Wormtongue pets the king, Éowyn says and does nothing at all, and we

---

212    In order to protect Minus Tirith; we prefer Plus Tirith.

meet THEE-oh-den King. The rest of the film is taken up by singing Orcs and solarized actors, as well as (S)aruman's[213] long-range Magic Missiles that fill in as "the fire of Isengard" in place of, say, a gunpowder equivalent. Tolkien's Saruman is known for his honeyed and persuasive voice; an entire chapter is named after it. In contrast, Bakshi's (S)aruman lacks vocal presence and relies on flashing lights and other visual "magic" to convey his wizard-ness.

The film reaches its climax, if you want to call it that, when Gandalf arrives at Helm's Deep, with Éomer and his Riders,[214] and begins to slaughter orcs in rather bloody detail. The narrator tells us that "The forces of darkness were driven forever from the face of Middle-earth by the valiant friends of Frodo. As their gallant battle ended, so too ends the first great tale of *The Lord of the Rings*!" This would have come as a very confusing surprise to anyone watching this film in theaters: it had been marketed as the complete *Lord of the Rings* and not Part One, as Bakshi had intended. The studio believed that no one would willingly go see only the *first* part of a story, so they marketed it as the entire tale, and the existence of Part Two would have to rely on the success of the stealthy Part One. Unfortunately,[215] despite the film being a modest box office success (thirty-eight million dollars worldwide on a reported budget of eight million), Part Two never happened.

At the end of the day, this is an example of a film that, although it avoided the "intrusion of unwarranted matter," failed primarily due to what Tolkien called "exaggeration" (over-emphasizing battle sequences, resulting in poor pacing and a confusing narrative). Given the missing thematic material, this would seem due to a failure to understand "where the core of the original lies." Many of the overarching themes of *The Lord of the Rings*: hope and despair, fate and free will, the burden of the Ring, and more, are either entirely absent or barely touched upon.

---

213   Bakshi's film occasionally omits the S from Saruman's name and calls him Aruman, apparently because test audiences confused him with Sauron. Not all the audio got changed, so he is inconsistently referred to by his correct name as well.

214   Poor Erkenbrand; he should join that club that Tom Bombadil and Glorfindel started.

215   Or, perhaps, fortunately.

# So Why Do We Love It? Or Do We?

Spoiler: we don't love it. But it's fair to say we love *moments* of it. It is evident that, in many parts of the film, Bakshi was striving to be "pure to the book"—and we really want to cheer for that. But the film's many failings—inconsistent pacing, disjointed storytelling, careless mispronunciations and historical references, the elimination of crucial characters (Frodo and Sam never encounter Faramir, and Arwen is never mentioned; Éowyn might as well have been eliminated, as she never spoke or did anything), the lack of vital thematic content, inconsistent and often simply ugly animation, truly awful characters like the Balrog, (S)aruman, and even Sam, along with a heavy reliance on fight scenes in the second half—doom the effort. Should you still see it? Perhaps, but only as a piece of adaptation history and because of the influence it had on Peter Jackson in the creation of his retelling of *The Lord of the Rings*. Just don't go into it expecting it to be anything better than "merely decent in moments."

# Why Alan Loves It

I will always be grateful that this rather unusual film exists if, for no other reason, than that it served as inspiration for Peter Jackson in creating his film trilogy. Though we'll point this out again in the chapter on Jackson's *The Lord of the Rings*, it's worth teasing now: a seventeen-year-old Peter Jackson saw Bakshi's film and was at the Wellington train station when he saw a paperback set of the books with Bakshi's Ringwraiths on the cover. He bought those books and later said, "In some respects if I hadn't seen his movie I might not have read the book, and may or may not have made the film...."[216]

---

216    Ian Nathan, *Anything You Can Imagine: Peter Jackson and the Making of Middle-earth*. HarperCollins, 2018, 18.

On its own merit, however, I can't say I love Bakshi's adaptation to any degree at all, really. I suppose I can love the stated intent to be faithful to Tolkien's text—and in the moments where that goal is met, which are unfortunately few and far between, I find some satisfaction. But, to me, this fails as both a good movie *and* a good adaptation. As a movie, the pacing is truly awful, with some scenes dragged out to interminable lengths—the Ringwraiths chasing Frodo at the Ford of Bruinen[217]—and others compressed to the point of meaninglessness. The animation—while groundbreaking in spots—is inconsistent and often distracting. Bakshi constantly relies on the preexisting knowledge of the viewers, which might be okay if it weren't for the fact that he was also exceedingly lazy in paying attention to relevant details: like the *names and pronunciations of several characters*. The fact that the film ends abruptly is the insulting icing on the really awful cake: that the responsibility for this is not Bakshi's is of no consequence to the viewer.

# Why Shawn Loves It

Unlike Rankin/Bass's *The Hobbit*—which I saw late in life, as discussed in the previous chapter—I *did* see Bakshi's *The Lord of the Rings* when I was a teenager, less than two years after reading Tolkien's books for the first time. I was still very much in the honeymoon stage of my Tolkien fandom, and so excited when I discovered that there was an animated film of it from the 1970s.[218] Even some fifteen years later, on home video, there was nothing about the marketing language on the package to suggest that it was anything less than a complete adaptation of *The Lord of the Rings* (except for the just-over-two-hour runtime, if I had been paying attention to that, which I hadn't). So when I got to the "end" at Helm's Deep, I was...well..."annoyed" is a nice word for it.

---

217  "Come on down to Ford of Bruinen and get your next 4x4—perfect for escaping from enemies on horseback!" Listeners of the podcast will know we had to get that in here.

218  Am I dating myself if I reveal that I discovered Bakshi's *The Lord of the Rings* on the shelf of my local Blockbuster Video? Don't answer that.

Why We Love Middle-earth

Feel free to file this next comment in a drawer labeled "One Man's Opinion" in some locked cabinet in a dusty basement storage room, and never look at it again. But, as someone who is not only a Tolkien fan, but also a moderately well-versed fan of movies, it occurs to me that one of the most common traits of disappointing movie adaptations is that it's not entirely clear whom they're made for. This is 100 percent the case with Ralph Bakshi's *The Lord of the Rings*. As we've noted above, the breakneck pace leaves little room for exposition, and so the film relies heavily on viewers already knowing this story, why plot points matter, who the characters are, and why we should care about them. Without some existing knowledge of Tolkien's story, I can't see this film working on any level for a casual viewer. And yet the lack of attention to detail and sloppy errors made with regard to lore (not to mention simple consistency, let alone Tolkien's "inner consistency of reality") and languages (in a story which Tolkien himself said was based on a "foundation" of languages, in Letter 165) are very hard for someone with knowledge and interest in Tolkien's works to forgive. The film seems based upon—and best appreciated with only—a superficial understanding of the story, like something you read a long time ago and only dimly remember.

And so I'm left with the impression that that's "the answer to all the riddles," as Faramir might say.[219] That is, the answer to the question "Who was this movie made for?" is: people who casually read the books in the 1960s— probably because they were in college and it was the cool thing to do—but never became fans. People whose "minds were, like, totally blown, man" that the *Fritz the Cat* guy was making a movie of a book they all read in their youth nearly a decade ago. It feels like pure nostalgia, like Michael Bay's Transformers movies or the latest iteration of Mighty Morphin Power Rangers to people from my generation; only made in the 1970s, before people had the benefit of heaps of streaming content and online fan wikis to help them actually remember what the thing they were nostalgic about was actually about. In such an environment, I can certainly imagine many a former

---

219   At least, he might say that if Bakshi had bothered to include him.

hippie clinging to fond memories of hobbits and elves watching Bakshi's film, seeing Samwise Gamgee show up criminally unintroduced, saying "I remember that guy!" and laughing at Sam's corniness for the rest of the film, never concerned about whether he comes across as the "chief hero" of the story, as Tolkien said he was.

I suppose what I'm saying, rather harshly, is that, with all due respect to the many people who must have worked very hard behind the scenes to make it, I find Ralph Bakshi's *The Lord of the Rings* to be—*by far*—the most disappointing of the many (legitimate) adaptations of Tolkien's work to hit the screen. Which is not to say that it has no redeeming qualities. It's got some great visuals (some of which inspired Peter Jackson, clearly), and the animation is often darkly beautiful. And, as a fantasy movie released just a couple of years before the start of a real golden age for sword-and-sorcery cinema—with movies like *Conan the Barbarian*, *Dragonslayer*, *The Beastmaster*, and yes, *Excalibur* coming out in the first years of the 1980s—it's a cool harbinger of a coming zeitgeist that I was really steeped in as a child. But it doesn't feel like Tolkien, and it doesn't even feel like it was made by *people who understood Tolkien*. As much as it hurts me to say it, it fails to represent the book in any meaningful way—I'm not even sure it knows what ZIP code the core of the original is in. So it's hard to recommend it to anyone—especially new fans just exploring Tolkien's works for the first time.

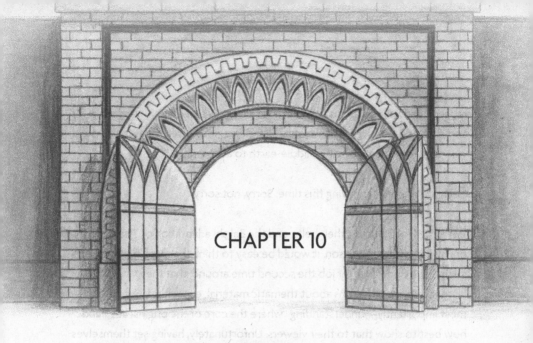

# CHAPTER 10

# WHERE THERE'S A WHIP: RANKIN/BASS'S *THE RETURN OF THE KING*

*"It's so easy not to try; let the world go drifting by."*

—Lyrics from Rankin/Bass's The Return of the King

*"Sounds like the filmmakers took their own advice."*

—Alan and Shawn, after watching Rankin/Bass's The Return of the King

Just a couple of chapters ago, we acknowledged the "certain charm" that Rankin/Bass's adaptation of *The Hobbit* possessed: some of the character designs were faithful, and a few of the voice actors (Orson Bean as Bilbo, John Huston as Gandalf, and Brother Theodore as Gollum) did a great job with their portrayals. In the end, was it a great film? No; it cut too much and missed nearly all the thematic material of Tolkien's story. But it was folksy and cute, and we forgave some of its more egregious offenses, as it was the very first attempt at bringing Middle-earth to a screen.

Yeah, we're not as forgiving this time. Sorry, not sorry.

With *The Hobbit* under their belts, and the Bakshi adaptation of *The Lord of the Rings* for comparison, it would be easy to think that Rankin/Bass might have done a better job the second time around; that they would have learned important lessons about thematic material, exposition, pacing, and—most importantly—understanding "where the core of the original lies," and how best to show that to their viewers. Unfortunately, having set themselves the nearly impossible task of adapting the final one-third of a complex, thematically rich, multi-threaded epic into a ninety-minute TV musical cartoon, it comes as little surprise that they struggled.

When Rankin/Bass adapted *The Hobbit*, they were taking a children's story and adapting it to a children's medium: a cutely drawn, musical cartoon. Sure, they missed nearly everything that made that story important, but at least it didn't create the sort of cognitive dissonance that is immediately present in their adaptation of *The Return of the King*. There's so much of a split personality, it's almost as though there were two films being made. The first film, made by the same people who made the stop-action *Rudolph the Red-Nosed Reindeer*, was intended to be a children's musical cartoon, fitting somewhere between Saturday morning TV and a Disney movie. The second film was the Tolkien adaptation, written by (apparently) knowledgeable fans who seemed determined to squeeze in as many of Tolkien's actual words as possible. Unfortunately, the two films work together about as well as Denethor and a family therapist: resulting in a movie that doesn't even reach the low bar set by *The Hobbit*, just three years earlier.

Being *The Return of the King*, the film obviously skips the events of *The Fellowship of the Ring* and *The Two Towers*. And, while the awful framing device of the Minstrel of Gondor, singing at Bilbo's 129th birthday party in Rivendell, briefly recaps the events of *The Hobbit*, the viewer gets almost no exposition, no explanation of the events between then and where the movie proper begins. Here, dear reader, is the entirety of that explanation, in song!

> The power of the Ring, it grew, and Gandalf sat in thought.
> He knew that it must be destroyed in fires where it was wrought.
> For if into evil hands it fell, the earth would know its end.
> No force of arms would win the day. No army could contend.

Gandalf narrates a bit more exposition: "For evil flourished everywhere, and lay on the land like a festering malignancy. There was one hope, though: in a distant land, the noble Aragorn, heir to the empty throne of Gondor, awaited with a small band to return and become king. But he could not triumph until the Ring was destroyed: so went the prophecy." Then we return to the musical version:

> Frodo of the nine fingers, and the Ring of Doom,
> accepted a heavy burden, for the fires to consume.

Finally, Gandalf tells the incredibly long story of the first two books of *The Lord of the Rings*. Grab a cuppa and a cozy blanket, and get ready for this page-turning epic: "Frodo and his gallant companion, Samwise, had many brave adventures until finally they reached the rocky border of Mordor, domain of the Black Lord Sore-on. There, Frodo was captured and imprisoned in the tower of See-reth Ungol. Samwise vowed to enter the orc-infested tower alone to save him." We understand if you need to take a break before we move on with the actual story; that was really draining.

As a result of this minimal—let's be frank, almost nonexistent—exposition, Rankin/Bass do the same thing that Bakshi did, only to a much more extreme degree: rely on the viewer's preexisting knowledge to fill in the gaps. So when they end up using Tolkien's dialogue—and they do use a *lot* of straight-out-of-the-book text, which should be refreshing—it usually lands completely flat, because we don't have any context or an understanding of who the characters are, or why we should care.

The film alternates between two storylines: Frodo, Sam, and eventually Gollum in Mordor, and the Battle of the Pelennor Fields. We spend the majority of our time in the first storyline, and that's where we open as well: with Sam trying to get into the tower of Cirith Ungol to rescue Frodo. Conveniently, he finds the Ring on the ground outside the tower, and has a bit of internal monologue about it.[220,221] Sam puts the Ring's chain around his neck, then stumbles upon Frodo's cloak and sword, Sting—which not only glows when Orcs are around, but makes an annoying ringing sound as well! He makes his way through Shelob's Lair—unnamed and with no spiders about—and declares that he has crossed into Mordor.

Stunningly, he decides to forego rescuing Frodo, declares that he "must be the Ringbearer now," and leaves to go destroy the Ring, abandoning his dear friend and master to the torment of the Orcs—instead of reluctantly choosing to carry on the quest believing Frodo to be dead, as Sam does in the books. We spend the next five minutes of the film enduring a cringey song, and Sam's vision of himself as Samwise the Strong: leading an army of Men against Barad-dûr,[222] turning the plateau of Gorgoroth into a garden,[223] and turning Orcs into opossums, lemurs, and other wild animals. Yes, Sam does have a similar vision—minus the Orcs' bizarre metamorphosis—in the books, as he approaches the Tower of Cirith Ungol wearing the Ring, but

---

220   Here, Sam pronounces Sauron as "Soren"; in an interesting twist, the actor voicing Sam—Roddy McDowall—would end up playing the antagonist in the 1994 film *Star Trek: Generations*, a character named...Soren.

221   The best out-of-context quote in the film comes in Sam's internal chat: "I can feel you throbbing with excitement." This is where we'd make an inappropriate joke if we weren't family-friendly podcast hosts writing a family-friendly book.

222   Here pronounced "BEAR-uh-dehr," leading me to conclude that Rankin/Bass followed Bakshi's example by simply not bothering with Appendix C.

223   Or the new and improved version, now with extra syllables: "Gor-uh-gor-uth."

it lasts *one paragraph* and is but a brief moment. And it is, thankfully, *not* followed by another cringey song, as it is in the film.

Sam eventually rescues Frodo from the tower,[224] after using a heretofore unknown, and never actually explained Phial of Galadriel to get past the Watchers, but not before the film segues to Minas Tirith.[225] To its credit, the film gets the visuals right: rolling farmlands, the Rammas Echor, the ruins of Osgiliath on either side of the Anduin, a seven-level city with the Citadel and tower on the top level, gates in the right places, and the plain white flag of the Stewards. Even the outer wall is black, as described in the book. It's another example of fidelity to detail that often goes for naught in terms of the story, thanks to the lack of context, inexplicable voice acting, erroneous pronunciations, confusing timelines, and distracting songs.

But the beautiful Minas Tirith of Gandalf's narration is replaced with the one under siege: fires burning on the Pelennor, siege engines hurling projectiles, Orcs feasting and heading toward an inevitable victory, backed by...several Skeletors atop black Pegasi?[226] We briefly meet Denethor, who, we are told by the narrating Gandalf, has "succumbed to an eerie fire of the brain" and has ordered his own execution. But why? There's no mention of Boromir or his death; no mention of Faramir and his wounding by the Nazgûl. Pippin, in an example of dialogue *not* from the book, tells Gandalf that Denethor has "gone looney, I tell you." When the cackling-mad Denethor foretells the failing of the West, he says he's looked in his *palantír*, which Gandalf describes as "a crystal ball to see the future."[227] Again, Denethor speaks dialogue directly from the book—but because his despair makes no sense, the monologue has no emotional impact at all. And his suicide by fire—

---

224    In narration, Gandalf tells us that Seereth Ungol is "an ancient world of towered fortress cities." It's a good thing they're not talking about Cirith Ungol, since that's simply a mountain pass, guarded by a single tower. <end sarcasm>

225    Credit where credit is due: at least the incorrect Rankin/Bass pronunciations are consistent, including the capital of Gondor being called "MINE-us teereth." We'll have none of that "(S)aruman" confusion here!

226    Or, instead of Skeletors, maybe liches from *Dungeons & Dragons*; we've yet to reach a conclusion.

227    No, we're not kidding. We wish we were.

without an attempt made to stop it—simply pushes an unnecessary and unhelpful character off the stage. Then, in a moment that shows a total lack of understanding "the core of the original," Gandalf loses all hope. Gondor is done; its days are over. The Ring is lost, all is gone.

After Sam's rescue of Frodo—which includes a Ring-powered interrogation of a magical expository Orc, and another musical dream sequence—the hobbits dress as Orcs to make their way toward Mount Doom, but are stopped at the Watchers again. The Phial—which apparently only works because Frodo hasn't revealed the magic, like a sleight-of-hand magician—doesn't have any effect until a "Wonder Twin powers, activate!" moment when Frodo and Sam hold it together, resulting in the complete and total destruction of the entire tower. An arriving ~~Skeletor~~ Nazgûl causes Frodo and Sam to seek a quick escape into the plains of Gorgoroth, where Frodo eventually discards his armor—despite Sam's worry about Gollum: a character about whom we've heard *nothing*, outside the frame narrative at the beginning. After they collapse from exhaustion, we're introduced to the song that, for many, is the nostalgic reason why they still love this movie: "Where There's a Whip, There's a Way."[228] Frodo and Sam are discovered and forced to march with the Orcs until they goad the Orcs into fighting a unit of Men encountered later, allowing them to get away, exhausted, when Frodo falls into a pit.

We come back to Minas Tirith, and one of the best sequences in the film, relatively speaking: the arrival of Grond and the breaking of the Great Gate. It begins poorly, though, with Gandalf making it clear that he views his task of standing in the breach as a suicide mission: "Then we'll leave this life together," he tells Pippin, before allowing the hobbit to accompany him to certain death. Ooookay. But Grond itself is properly terrifying: glowing red eyes, fiery drool pouring from its snarling mouth. The Witch-king, instead of looking like Skeletor as the other Nazgûl do, has his own deathly appearance

---

228    Anything we can say about this song may prove divisive, so...enjoy it if you do, and skip it if you don't.

shrouded beneath his hooded cloak: a crown on an invisible head, above glowing red eyes. Grond batters the door as the Witch-king cries out, until the gate bursts—leaving Gandalf, atop the majestically calm Shadowfax, to deny the Witch-king entry, in dialogue taken straight from the text. Unfortunately, the laughable robotic voice filter that was applied to the Witch-king immediately renders the scene comedic rather than tense.

Fortunately, a cock crows and horns blow, so we don't have to be subjected to the Witch-king's Saturday morning cartoon voice anymore. "Rohan had come at last," which I'm sure would be moving if we knew the slightest thing about the nation of Rohan, their king Théoden, their relationship to Gondor, or why Merry was chosen to be dispatched with the Red Arrow to obtain their help.[229] This army of total strangers turns the tides of battle and we return to Frodo and Sam—in the first big clue that something is not quite right with the timeline. Frodo has a particularly odd, and musically disturbing, dream—including a vision of himself and Sam having a smoke and a snack in the Shire and waving at a couple of passing Orcs as though they're friendly strangers, as well as a vision of Frodo casually tossing the Ring into the fire. If only. Finally, dream-Sam and dream-Gandalf turn into Orcs, just not the friendly ones from the Shire. All so we have something to look at to distract us from the song.

As they near the Cracks of Doom, it's time for another song, and philosophical musings from Gandalf on the nature of the Dark Lord. Finally, more than an hour into *The Return of the King*, we meet ~~the frog-creature~~ Gollum, who promptly hurls a large boulder toward our heroes before attempting to take the Ring. Frodo, with the power of the Ring, drives Gollum back long enough to continue the quest while Sam confronts the wretched creature. In a moment that even Jackson didn't try to adapt, Gollum pleads to be allowed to live: the destruction of the Ring will destroy him, too. This would have been a perfect moment to demonstrate an understanding of the

---

229    Or why the nation is pronounced ROW-uhn and its king's name THEE-oh-den.

role of pity in the core of the original, but Sam's disgust is the only reason he allows Gollum to live. We should take a moment here to say that Brother Theodore as Gollum turns in the film's best performance, by far.

Sam makes his way into the mountain as we return to the Pelennor Fields, as the battle for Minas Tirith continues and we witness the reunion of Merry and Pippin. You'd be forgiven for imagining Merry as Shaggy from the Scooby-Doo cartoons, as he's voiced by Casey Kasem. As for Pippin, well... let's just say Scooby would have been an improvement. An inexplicable shadow arrives over the battlefield, causing Théoden's horse, Snowmane, to toss the King, killing him instantly. Merry swears vengeance: Zoinks! Gandalf wonders aloud what could have caused this darkness, and we segue back to Frodo in the Cracks of Doom, who cackles like a cartoon villain before claiming the Ring for himself and disappearing.

Cut back to the other "this could have been great" scene, as the Witch-king arrives on the Pelennor—this time on a proper fell beast! Then a rider approaches and starts saying Éowyn's lines from the text, including "dwimmerlaik": oh wait, it *is* Éowyn! Only we don't know that, nor do we know who Éowyn is, or how she's connected to Théoden. Merry and Pippin appear in order to provide a minimal amount of character exposition before she wields some magic in striking down the fell beast. The actual confrontation is mercifully short, as Merry stabs the Witch-king in the back, Éowyn strikes, and the Lord of the Nazgûl audibly deflates like a balloon. Éowyn tearfully speaks about having avenged her uncle, in a moment that could actually have been moving if we had the slightest idea who any of these people are. The Orcs are driven in retreat to the River, where they find new hope in the arrival of the Black Fleet; that hope is temporary, of course, as Aragorn reveals his standard and ends the battle.

The council held after Aragorn's arrival reveals the new king is...less wise than we might have hoped. He decides to chase Sauron's army down across the plains of Gorgoroth, to Barad-dûr itself—and no mention is made of this being a ploy to distract Sauron from Frodo. Of course not, because

Frodo has already claimed the Ring! It takes Aragorn and his army "days and nights" to march to the Black Gate; one can't help wondering what Frodo is doing to pass the time. The Army of the West arrives to a properly Orc-ish song and the confrontation with the Mouth of Sauron ends quickly: after all, he doesn't have Sam's sword, an Elven brooch, and Frodo's mithril coat as leverage!

We come back to Sam, who has been searching for Frodo inside Mount Doom "for these many days." Apparently, Sauron has been out of the office. Sam watches Gollum dancing with himself before coming to the realization that it must be Frodo, bearing the Ring and invisible. The struggle plays out as we might expect—but to a song about Frodo of the Nine Fingers. Gollum bites off Frodo's finger, celebrates his victory, and dances his way off the precipice, finally destroying the Ring and triggering the eruption of Mount Doom. Frodo and Sam flee while Barad-dûr and the Towers of the Teeth collapse, the Nazgûl's Pegasi fall out of the sky, and the Eye of Sauron explodes. The Eagles arrive—not to fight the Nazgûl, and not to save Frodo and Sam—but to act as personnel carriers for Aragorn's forces, carrying them to safety as the hobbits continue to flee the eruption. Gwaihir and a friend do, in fact, make it back just in time to save Frodo and Sam and bring them to safety.

Months pass—months?—before Aragorn enters Minas Tirith and is crowned king. For a moment, we see Éowyn astride her horse, next to a man on his own steed: one can only assume that it's Faramir, but how would we know?[230] The hobbits and Gandalf watch from above as the people of Minas Tirith celebrate their new king—and, quite possibly, the end of this film. But alas, we must still hear the Minstrel of Gondor conclude the tale before Bilbo explains that he will be leaving with Gandalf and Elrond to the Grey Havens the next day. Gandalf explains why he's leaving: "We are old," among others. Frodo makes a snap decision to ask for a seat on the next day's boat, but the other hobbits will stay and Sam will finish the book.

---

230  If it is Faramir, then he's done something that Legolas, Gimli, Éomer, Beregond, and several others haven't managed: to appear in this film.

Sam provides some incorrect exposition: "The orcs and trolls are gone to dust. The Elves are slowly departing. Dwarves have disappeared into their misty mountains. And there have been no dragons for ages." Doubtful. True. Nope. And seventy-eight years is not "ages," but fine. Then the movie decides to end on a truly silly note, as Sam expresses concern that there will be no room for hobbits in the coming age of Man. Gandalf comforts him: first, by implying that hobbits will *grow into* Men. That's right: "Frodo is a bit larger than Bilbo just as you are larger than Frodo, and younger still than you—and larger—are Merry and Pippin." He even tells Sam that, someday, humans will wonder, "Is there hobbit in me?" before breaking the fourth wall and actually asking all the unfortunate children still awake and watching this, "Is there?"[231] Just...wow. Still, at least the film has the decency to end with Bilbo, Frodo, Elrond, and Gandalf departing the Grey Havens while Sam, Merry, and Pippin watch. The seagulls were a nice touch.

Were the changes in this film necessary because of the change in medium? Maybe some of them, if we're generous. But, as with the Rankin/Bass adaptation of *The Hobbit*, the result shows a total lack of understanding when it comes to "the core of the original": the big themes of *The Lord of the Rings* are either entirely absent or nearly unrecognizable.

# So Why Do We Love It? Or Do We?

We wanted desperately to love this; as with the Rankin/Bass adaptation of *The Hobbit*, nostalgia is a powerful thing. Memories of "Where There's a Whip, There's a Way," Éowyn's confrontation with the Witch-king, and Gandalf's narration gave us hope that this would be better than either the Rankin/Bass adaptation of *The Hobbit* or Bakshi's *The Lord of the Rings*.

---

231  This Gandalf moment reminds us of nothing so much as Dr. Hibbert's "I couldn't possibly solve this mystery...can you?" comment at the end of the first half of "Who Shot Mr. Burns?" from season six of *The Simpsons*, which appears to be breaking the fourth wall until the "camera" pulls out to reveal he's talking to Chief Wiggum.

Sadly, reality is more powerful than nostalgia. No, we don't love it—but we love the spirit behind it. We love the intent to be faithful to the text. We love the desire to bring an amazing story to the screen. Despite the effort having failed, we can still love the attempt. Should you watch it? We suppose that depends on your threshold for cringe. If you are able to bring your expectations in line with 1980 low-budget cartoons, *The Return of the King* actually becomes quite the accomplishment!

## WHY ALAN LOVES IT

I have fond memories of "Where There's a Whip..." but now I can't get the song out of my head and I'm no longer as big a fan as I once was. This was a rough one to watch, truly. As we said earlier in this chapter, *The Hobbit* may have been imperfect, but at least it tried to adapt a story suitable for children into a children's medium. Here, they tried to shoehorn one of the world's most epic stories—and one that is *not* particularly kid-friendly—into a children's medium. The sheer quantity of songs became a problem as well, as at least two of them seemed to be written for dream sequences that destroyed what little pacing the film managed to provide. I commend Rankin/Bass for spending more time on Sam and Frodo, and for making that relationship significantly better than the version we saw in Bakshi's adaptation. And I absolutely loved their frequent reliance on the text for dialogue. But, as a whole, this may be the weakest of the three films in the unofficial animated "trilogy," and I'm glad I don't have to watch it again.

## WHY SHAWN LOVES IT

Readers familiar with *The Prancing Pony Podcast* will know that Alan and I rarely disagree on *anything*, but in this case I'll go on record saying that I don't think Rankin/Bass's *Return of the King* is the weakest of the three animated adaptations, simply because I don't dislike it as much as I do

Bakshi's *Lord of the Rings*. To be fair, Bakshi's film is probably objectively better: it at least starts out somewhat coherently, has some solid visuals, and is no less incomplete than many movie and TV franchises that promised sequels that were never produced. But because—just like their *Hobbit*—I watched Rankin/Bass's *Return of the King* later in life and had lower expectations, it didn't annoy me nearly as much as Bakshi's *Lord of the Rings* did...and at least Rankin/Bass's *Return of the King* didn't market itself as something it's not (i.e., a complete adaptation of *The Lord of the Rings*).

To be honest, Rankin/Bass's *Return of the King* suffers from many of the same problems as Bakshi's effort. Notably, it struggles with pronunciation (if not quite as inconsistently as to "only occasionally" drop an S from the beginning of the name of a major antagonist), and relies too heavily on viewers having existing knowledge of the story, so that the film feels more like an exercise in reminding than in storytelling. And its heavy borrowing of details of the book (such as Tolkien's dialogue) without establishing a more properly Tolkienesque context is a very similar missing-the-forest-for-the-trees approach to Bakshi's work.

However, there's a whole other set of problems with *The Return of the King*: the cutesy character designs. The folksy hobbit *everything*. The notorious fourth-wall break by Gandalf to make each child watching at home think *they too* might have some hobbit in them. And the songs. Oh my goodness, all the songs. This is precisely the kind of stuff that makes Rankin/Bass's *The Hobbit* actually kind of work despite its flaws, and one can imagine the filmmakers patting themselves on the back for putting so much of that winning stuff into *The Lord of the Rings*. The problem, of course, is *The Lord of the Rings* is emphatically *not* a children's story, even if *The Hobbit* is, and these cloying family-friendly additions are utterly out of place in an adaptation of Tolkien's more complex, epic, and adult sequel—particularly the final third of it.

But I do think they were *trying* to be faithful to the source material, and I give *The Return of the King* some credit for that. They seem to have at least picked up a copy of Tolkien's book in the months prior to filming, and that's not nothing considering how bad things could be. Still, I consider this one for completionists only, and unlike Rankin/Bass's *The Hobbit* and even Bakshi's *The Lord of the Rings* (which does have its fans), I don't know many Tolkien fans who feel strongly the other way. And yes, it being "for completionists only" means I *do* have a copy of it on DVD. I just don't watch it.

# CHAPTER 11

# BIG BUDGET BOOM: PETER JACKSON'S *THE LORD OF THE RINGS*

*"A day may come when the courage of men fails, but it is not this day!"*

—*Aragorn at the Black Gate, in Peter Jackson's* The Return of the King

In the spring of 1997, Peter Jackson purchased his second copy of *The Lord of the Rings*: a box set of three large, Alan Lee-illustrated paperbacks, in downtown Wellington. The motivation? A phone call from Miramax Films confirming that he would be directing a two-film adaptation of the Tolkien story. And if you've seen some of the making-of documentaries, you've likely seen Jackson scribbling notes in the margin of this very set. His first set of books? Nearly twenty years earlier, the seventeen-year-old was at the Wellington train station, ready to board for a trip to Auckland. He'd just seen Ralph Bakshi's *The Lord of the Rings* at a Wellington theater; while he admits he was a bit confused at the disjointed storytelling, he became interested in reading the books. So when he saw a paperback set of the books with

Bakshi's Ringwraiths on the cover, he knew he had some reading for the twelve-hour journey. Jackson would later say, "In some respects if I hadn't seen his movie I might not have read the book, and may or may not have made the film...."[232]

But a year after Jackson purchased that second set of books, relations with Miramax were deteriorating. The studio, run by Harvey and Bob Weinstein, had limited the two-film epic to a budget of only seventy-five million dollars, and it had become abundantly clear that this was woefully inadequate.[233] Even after an experienced producer had come on board to more carefully consider costs, the estimate was $130–135 million. Something had to give. Jackson and his partner Fran Walsh were summoned to Miramax's New York office and the infamous "sweatbox": "a small unventilated room walled in frosted glass," given its moniker by independent filmmakers subjected to the mercurial tempers of the Weinstein brothers.[234] Harvey was angry and delivered an ultimatum to Jackson and Walsh: cut *The Lord of the Rings* down to a single, two-hour film for no more than seventy-five million dollars, or you're out and Quentin Tarantino will do it.[235]

Jackson and Walsh, under immense pressure to capitulate, called their manager Ken Kamins to have him tell Weinstein that they were out. But Kamins had one more card to play: on his own initiative, their manager went back to Harvey and asked for the chance to shop the project elsewhere. Weinstein said yes, but attached truly outrageous conditions, including a four-week turnaround in an industry more accustomed to a six-month to one-year timeline. They had less than a month to find a studio willing to finance this huge, risky project.

---

232  Nathan, *Anything You Can Imagine*, 2018, 18.

233  Consider that *Independence Day*, a summer blockbuster released two years earlier, had a seventy-five million dollar budget on its own.

234  Nathan, *Anything You Can Imagine*, 2018, 63.

235  Pause to reflect and to thank Eru and all the Valar that a Tarantino-helmed *Lord of the Rings* never came to pass, with Galadriel slicing up Orcs in blood-spattered *Kill Bill*-style shots.

Kamins shopped it everywhere: Paramount said no, as they were working on C.S. Lewis's *The Lion, the Witch, and the Wardrobe*. Fox considered it, until they found out Saul Zaentz would get a fee.[236] Sony didn't like the scripts. Universal wasn't buying. PolyGram was interested, but didn't have the budget. Kamins was down to seven days, and their final meeting was with New Line, where Jackson's friend, Mark Ordesky, had been talking up Jackson to CEO Bob Shaye. Ordesky, it must be said, is one of us: as a kid, playing *Dungeons & Dragons*, reading *The Lord of the Rings*, and adorning his boyhood room with Alan Lee posters. He'd been following Jackson's efforts ever since seeing *Bad Taste* and was able to at least get Jackson a chance to pitch the project to Shaye.

Before the meeting even began, Shaye pulled Jackson aside and told him: "Listen, I'm happy to spend an hour with you looking at this film that you've got for us, but you've got to realize that it's probably something that we're not going to want to do."[237] Jackson went through the motions, and Ordesky started the tape: a film that Jackson's manager, Kamins, called "the making of the making of."[238] Shaye watched dutifully, but revealed nothing: no questions, comments, or even expressions. When it was over, silence filled the room. Shaye turned to Jackson and asked, "Why would anyone want movie-goers to pay eighteen dollars when they might pay twenty-seven dollars?" No response, only confusion. "Tolkien has done your job for you. Tolkien wrote *three* books. If you're going to do it justice, it should be *three* movies."[239]

And if *we're* going to do those three movies justice, we'll need a unique approach. An analysis of nearly every scene in the films would be a book

---

236  The bad blood between Fox and Zaentz dated back to the film *The English Patient*. After Fox walked away from production when Zaentz wouldn't give up control over casting, he gave a speech (a rant, really) about the evils of Fox. When told that he would get a fee, Fox reportedly replied, "If he gets one nickel, we're out." Notably, *The English Patient* won nine Oscars, including Best Picture for Zaentz for 1996.

237.  Nathan, *Anything You Can Imagine*, 2018, 83.

238  Nathan, *Anything You Can Imagine*, 2018, 72.

239  Nathan, *Anything You Can Imagine*, 2018, 85.

Why We Love Middle-earth

unto itself...or *three* books, frankly. But we can provide a brief overview of each film, followed by a look at the bigger deviations from the text, discussing which changes—in character, event, and narrative techniques—worked well in conveying "the core of the original" and which might have missed the target a little. We say "a little" because, on the whole, the Jackson adaptation of *The Lord of the Rings* was about as successful as a screen adaptation could possibly be, and in every sense of the word: financially, with more than three billion dollars at the box office; critically, with near-universal praise from the press and seventeen Academy Awards from thirty total nominations; and culturally, as it dominated popular culture, with the trilogy still the "reference" for fantasy films.

Oh, and one last thing: we will be discussing the extended editions of each film, rather than the theatrical release. Despite Jackson calling the theatrical releases "the definitive versions," the majority of fans have come to develop a greater appreciation for the extended editions, thanks to a number of additional scenes that come straight from the book. Then there's the fact that we haven't watched the theatrical versions since the extended editions came out, and it's hard to un-remember things! So now that we've explained our approach to this nearly twelve-hour set of films, let's start at the very beginning—it's a very good place to start—with the 2001 release of *The Fellowship of the Ring*.

# THE FELLOWSHIP OF THE RING

What do Michael Bay and Joss Whedon have in common? Believe it or not, *The Fellowship of the Ring* is the answer.[240] In May of 2001, we lined up to buy tickets for an opening night showing of the latest Bay film, *Pearl Harbor*. Not because either of us were interested in watching Ben Affleck

---

240    We will also accept "allegedly creating toxic work environments" as an answer, but that's a *very* different book.

star in a pretty awful film about how the Japanese attacked a love triangle, but because we knew that the teaser trailer for *The Fellowship of the Ring* would be shown before the movie. The hype: it was real. And in September, we turned our televisions to the now-defunct WB to watch the full trailer attached to the premiere of *Angel*.[241] Anticipation was building; the online Tolkien forums were buzzing with excitement (and consternation). Then, after waiting in line for a midnight showing on December 18, we sat in full theaters, being transported to Middle-earth with hundreds of other Tolkien fans. Three breathtaking hours later, we left the theater...and bought tickets to see it again.

That's the kind of film it was, and we weren't the only ones to see it over and over again, as *Fellowship* grossed over forty-seven million dollars in the first weekend in the US alone.[242] But was it a film that understood "the core of the original"? Let's take a look at some of the significant changes from the text in the light of the Shippey test, starting with the change you notice immediately: the existence of the prologue, where Galadriel narrates more than seven full minutes of exposition and backstory that we would otherwise read in the chapters "The Shadow of the Past" and "The Council of Elrond."

In the prologue—possibly inspired by Bakshi's own use of the technique in his 1978 adaptation—we learn about many important story elements, starting with the forging of the Great Rings for the Elves, Dwarf-lords, and Men, and the power within those Rings. We are informed about the deception of Sauron and his creation of the One Ring in Mount Doom, along with its ability to control the other Rings. Galadriel tells us about the Last Alliance of Elves and Men at the end of the Second Age; we witness the death of Elendil and Isildur's taking of the Ring as she tells us of the defeat of Sauron. We also learn about what happened with Isildur and the Ring afterward, and get a

---

241   Neither of us actually watched the premiere, though one of us did go back and watch that series later on to fill in the gaps in the *Buffy* timeline.

242   Box Office Mojo. "*The Lord of the Rings: The Fellowship of the Ring*" n.d. https://www.boxofficemojo.com/title/tt0120737/.

glimpse of what we know as the Disaster of the Gladden Fields.[243] There's still more, though: we discover that there was a 2,500-year gap between those events and the Ring being found by Gollum when he took it to the Misty Mountains for another 500 years. We even get a clue that the Ring has a will of its own; a sentience, in a way.[244] Finally, we get to see the moment when the Ring was discovered by Bilbo in *The Hobbit*, as the prologue transitions into the film itself.

In the book, of course, we start with Bilbo in Bag End, preparing for his birthday party (and unannounced farewell). So why begin the movie with such a drastic change from the book? This is a great example of those pesky canons of narrative art being different in different media: grabbing the attention and interest of the viewers right away is critical for good cinema, and this was an effective way to get the audience to invest in the story *right now*, rather than wait for an hours-long committee meeting in Rivendell. It's not just effective in this regard; it also fits another cinematic canon: show, don't tell. By reducing the amount of critical story information delivered by "talking heads" (e.g., Gandalf, Elrond, or Galadriel), the audience *sees* the very things Galadriel is talking about. Film is a visual medium, so when crucial story elements can be delivered visually, it's a win.

But does it create a different *result* from that of the book? Does it change, or miss, "the core of the original"? For the most part, not at all—though it does make the core more obvious from the very beginning. Shippey says—and we heartily agree—that "the unquestioned 'core of the original'…is the Ring and what we are told about it: its effect is always corrupting, no-one can be trusted with it, it cannot be hidden, it must be destroyed and it must be destroyed in the place of its forging."[245] The prologue shows us right away

---

243   Discovering that Isildur wasn't as bad as we were led to believe is yet another great reason to read *Unfinished Tales*.

244   At least, the way Jackson portrays it.

245   Shippey, T. A., "Another Road to Middle-earth: Peter Jackson's Movie Trilogy," in *Roots and Branches: Selected Papers on Tolkien*, Walking Tree Publishers, 2007, 370.

that the Ring is altogether evil, corrupting, and that it cannot be used without great risk of harm. To that extent, then, the prologue succeeds.

We do take issue with one particular line, however: that Isildur "had this one chance to destroy evil forever." In Middle-earth, Tolkien has made it very clear that evil will exist until Arda is remade; evil cannot be destroyed "forever" by anyone. Elrond makes that clear in the Council: that when he witnessed the destruction of Morgoth's stronghold of Thangorodrim, "the Elves deemed that evil was ended forever, and it was not so."[246] Of this moment in the prologue, Shippey says, "There is the kernel here of a serious challenge to Tolkien's view of the world, with its insistence on the fallen nature even of the best, and its conviction that while victories are always worthwhile, they are also always temporary."[247] Shippey, too, chalks this up to the difference in the canons of narrative art of the two different media. We agree.

Now let's go to the end of the film for another big change in narrative: the screenwriters' decision to show us the death of Boromir at the end of *Fellowship*. This is actually *two* changes for the price of one—the first of which is a significant change in the structure of the narrative. At the end of *Fellowship* in the books, Boromir has made his play for the Ring: cajoling, reasoning, arguing, and finally threatening Frodo in an effort to obtain the Enemy's powerful weapon. After he returns to the rest of the Company and the hobbits scatter to look for Frodo, Aragorn commands Boromir to go after Merry and Pippin and to guard them. That is the last we see of the Man of Gondor in the books until *The Two Towers*, when we come upon the arrow-pierced warrior who confesses and repents of his deeds before dying of his wounds.

The second change in this scene is the actual inclusion of his fight to protect Merry and Pippin. In the books, we don't get any facts on the fight itself until we get a flashback as Pippin pieces together his memories two chapters after

---

246    Tolkien, *Fellowship*, 2020, 237.
247    Shippey, "Another Road," 2007, 379.

Boromir's death; even that is somewhat lacking in detail, and we are left to assemble a vision of the events through moments as characters look back to the events of Parth Galen.

Today, it's commonplace to watch Jackson's *The Lord of the Rings* films back-to-back; perhaps not on the same day, but perhaps over a long weekend.[248] But when *Fellowship* was released, *The Two Towers* was a year away: that's a *long* time to ask an audience to wait for the emotional payoff of Boromir's character arc. It's also a tough sell to get *The Two Towers* audience to become emotionally invested in a character who is already dying as the film opens—a character they haven't seen in a year. No, moving Boromir's death to the end of the first film was the only reasonable choice for the filmmakers.

At the same time, the decision to show Boromir fighting to protect Merry and Pippin is a perfect example of "show, don't tell": a visual medium cannot afford to relegate an important moment like this to a nonvisual retelling of the incident. Even if the filmmakers left this part out and brought it in via flashback, it would certainly *have* to be a filmed sequence that we see, and not words alone.

What about the core of the original, though? Does the film-watching audience get a different story result from book readers as a result of these changes? We would strongly argue "no": Boromir demonstrates the same all-too-brief arc—confession, repentance, and penance—that he does in the book, and his redemption is brought home to the viewer with perhaps even more poignancy and emotional impact. Similarly, this is a shining moment for film-Aragorn as well, as he becomes a lot closer to book-Aragorn through this scene. We've had our complaints about how insecure film-Aragorn is, notable especially in his scenes in Rivendell, but he speaks of "our people" to the dying Boromir, accepting his role and responsibility as the king. And in a subtle nod to Boromir's brother Faramir, Jackson even has Aragorn "stooping,

---

248    We promise not to judge you if you can't watch them consecutively. Much.

placing his hands upon [Boromir's] shoulder, and kissing [his] forehead" which Tolkien describes as "the manner of his people" when Faramir himself bids farewell to Frodo and Sam in the chapter "Journey to the Cross-roads." Bringing this scene forward serves a cinematic purpose, while remaining true to the core of the original and bringing the films closer to the books for both characters.

Finally, we can't *not* mention the big omission from the adaptation: Sir Not-Appearing-in-Any-Film himself, Tom Bombadil.[249] In the book, Tom is an important—arguably *very* important, while simultaneously not at all central—character in the adventures of the four hobbits between the Shire and Bree. They encounter him after Old Man Willow—an evil-hearted tree, most likely a Huorn—captures Merry and Pippin in the Old Forest. Tom rescues the hobbits, inviting them to his home for food, stories, and song; they spend two nights with him and Goldberry, the River-daughter, with Tom relating his tales almost exclusively in trochaic tetrameter.[250] Tom is unaffected by the Ring altogether: he puts it on and does not become invisible, and he sees Frodo when he is wearing the Ring. He warns them of the neighboring Barrow-downs, through which they must pass to get to Bree, and teaches them a song to sing should they run into trouble. Hobbits being hobbits—and Barrow-wights being evil undead spirits sent by the Witch-king to animate dead bodies—they *do* run into trouble, and Tom once again comes to their rescue. Before he sends them on their way, he gives them daggers "wrought of some strange metal" that "were forged many long years ago by Men of Westernesse," the enemies of Sauron. We'll come back to those daggers in a moment.

---

249 Yes, someone purporting to be Tom Bombadil appears in a ghastly Soviet adaptation of *Fellowship*, shot over a total of nine hours in a single week in 1991, but for Tom's sake, let's not discuss this.

250 Most readers who studied Shakespeare in high school have probably heard the term "iambic pentameter," which is a line of poetry made up of *iambs*: an unstressed syllable followed by a stressed syllable: da-DUM. An iambic pentameter line has five (*penta*, like *pentagon*) iambs: da-DUM da-DUM da-DUM da-DUM da-DUM. A trochaic tetrameter line has four *trochees*, meaning a stressed syllable followed by an unstressed syllable: DUM-da DUM-da DUM-da DUM-da. While not very common in English poetry, trochaic tetrameter is notably found in the Finnish epic poem *Kalevala*, which was a major inspiration to Tolkien.

Why We Love Middle-earth

Tom is also discussed at the Council of Elrond, where we learn that the Elves refer to him as *Iarwain Ben-Adar*, which means "oldest and fatherless." We also learn that, as powerful as he may be, "he would not understand the need" to keep the Ring safe: in fact, "he would soon forget it, or most likely throw it away." Tom Bombadil is rich in thematic material, connecting the story to the most ancient of days before even the coming of Melkor, and touching on themes of pacifism and environmentalism. But the largest *plot* function that Bombadil serves is those daggers we mentioned earlier. In *The Return of the King*, Merry uses his dagger to perform a sneak attack against the Witch-king, "cleaving the undead flesh, breaking the spell that knit his unseen sinews to his will," and clearing the way for Éowyn to strike the killing blow. You might say that dagger is *really* important.

But is it important enough to have a very lengthy digression in the film, meeting two characters that we'll never see again? What would the filmmakers have to cut from the first film in order to make room for Tom and Goldberry, and the incident in the Barrows? From a filmmaker's perspective, cutting Tom also eliminates the need to shoot the entire digression that is covered with the chapters "The Old Forest," "In the House of Tom Bombadil," and "Fog on the Barrow-downs." It also avoids the problem of trying to *explain* who Bombadil is, a question that still vexes Tolkien fans to this day, despite the author himself making it quite clear that he intentionally made Tom an enigma.[251] And from the perspective of the film's audience, the story continues apace, without slowing down for more exposition and a mysterious character whose nature could never satisfactorily be explained. Cinematically, then, not only does it make sense to remove Tom—which necessarily also means removing the Old Forest, Old Man Willow, the Barrow-downs, the Barrow-wight, and the Daggers of Westernesse—it would not make sense any other way.

As for whether it impacts the core of the original, Tolkien himself has some very clear words to say about that: "Tom Bombadil is not an

---

251  Carpenter, *Letters*, No. 144 to Naomi Mitchison.

important person—to the narrative. I suppose he has some importance as a 'comment'... he is just an invention...."[252] Tolkien was never one to mince words, so if he says Tom's not important to the narrative, then I think it's safe to say cutting him has no impact on the core of the original.

# THE TWO TOWERS

With the massive success—critically, with thirteen Oscar nominations and four wins, and financially, with a box office gross of over $850 million—of *Fellowship*, there was precisely zero chance that Jackson's adaptation of *The Two Towers* would fly under the cinematic radar. It wasn't only the nerds waiting for this film's release anymore: Peter Jackson had gotten the world's attention, and cinema-goers around the world were excited for the next film in the series. It's not surprising, then, that it was the highest-grossing film of the year, despite only being out for the last two weeks of 2002. And while it did not garner quite as many accolades (two wins on six Oscar nominations), it was more successful at the box office and was better-reviewed than *Fellowship*, albeit not by much. But did it prove to be its predecessor's equal at conveying "the core of the original," or would the adaptation of Tolkien's second volume of this epic prove to be more challenging to faithfully bring to the big screen?

Structurally, the biggest change was the near-elimination of Tolkien's narrative interlacing—an admittedly rare literary technique (in modern literature; it was common in medieval literature, which Tolkien was understandably emulating), involving separate but interconnecting plotlines told independently with often minimal knowledge of what's happening in the other plotlines—and replacing it with cross-cutting and other techniques. This enabled viewers to follow multiple storylines simultaneously, instead of the way readers have to piece together Tolkien's storylines as his multiple threads and timelines converge, diverge, and leapfrog one another. It's

---

252   Ibid.

certainly simpler for movie audiences who don't have to wait an hour or two into the film to find out what's going on with Frodo and Sam, but it is a very different approach from the text. A proper analysis of Tolkien's interlacing vs. Jackson's intercutting is beyond the scope of this chapter, but we can suggest a couple of helpful reads if you're interested in exploring more.[253,254]

Leaving a thorough discussion of interlacing to the experts, let's start our analysis instead with a sequence of three scenes—two of which were only in the extended edition—that brings us closer to the people of Rohan. First, the filmmakers give us a scene at the Fords of Isen, with Éomer and the Riders of Rohan coming upon the bodies of men and horses; Éomer tells them to search for Théodred, Théoden's son, whom they find alive—but mortally wounded. Much later, in the second of these scenes, after Gandalf has healed Théoden, the king finds out that his son has died, and we witness a funeral procession as Théodred's body is buried in one of the mounds on the road to Edoras. The final scene of this group, which was included in the theatrical release, has Théoden speaking with Gandalf at the tomb of his son after the funeral. In the books, all of this takes place "off screen" as it were, with Théodred dying a week before Gandalf and the others arrived at Edoras.

The first scene sets the stage and actually gives us a bit of a glimpse into the aftermath of the Battle of the Fords of Isen. We find the full story of these battles in *Unfinished Tales*, but as that book was not part of the license, Jackson and his team couldn't adapt that scene precisely. Still, their choice to turn the death of Théodred from something that we would merely be *told* about into something we actually *see* brings an emotional impact that a straight adaptation would miss. It also gave us the moment when Éomer discovered that Saruman was behind these attacks on Rohan.

---

253   Auger, Emily E. "The Lord of the Rings' Interlace: The Adaptation to Film," *Mythlore: A Journal of J.R.R. Tolkien, C.S. Lewis, Charles Williams, and Mythopoeic Literature*: Vol. 30: No. 1, Article 9. https://dc.swosu.edu/mythlore/vol30/iss1/9/

254   Kisor, Yvette. "Making the Connection on Page and Screen in Tolkien's and Jackson's *The Lord of the Rings*," in *Picturing Tolkien: Essays on Peter Jackson's The Lord of the Rings Film Trilogy*, ed. Janice M. Bogstad and Philip E. Kaveny. McFarland & Company, Inc. 2011, 102-115.

The second scene really gives us a close-up look at the culture of Rohan, which—in the books—is deeply rooted in Anglo-Saxon culture, so much so that the Rohirrim speak Old English in the books. So when Miranda Otto, as Éowyn, poignantly sang that funeral dirge, it should come as no surprise that she sang in Old English. In fact, the first line that she sings—*Bealocwealm hafað fréone frecan forth onsended*—is an almost direct quote from a famous piece of Old English literature, *Beowulf*. Translated, the Rohirric funeral dirge is a microcosm of Anglo-Saxon warrior culture: "An evil death has sent forth the noble warrior | A song shall sing the sorrowing minstrels of mead-halls | That he is no more, to his Lord dearest | And kinsman beloved, death took him."

Finally, the powerful scene with Théoden and Gandalf helps us connect more quickly and more deeply to Théoden, comprehending his overwhelming grief. Here, Jackson and his team utilize some of Théoden's dialogue from the book when he says that Gandalf has "come too late, only to see the last days of my house," grieving that "these evil days should be mine...the young perish and the old linger, withering." These are extraordinarily powerful lines, and by utilizing them here, the viewer is given an intensely personal reason behind Théoden's actions later, at the Battle of the Pelennor Fields, as he refuses to "linger, withering." The scene also gives the filmmakers a chance to tell us about the flower that grows on the mounds—*simbelmynë*, or evermind; it's a touch of exposition that is nicely done here. In the book, we learn about it as Gandalf explains on their way up the road to Edoras; here, it's delivered in a more personal and emotional way that serves more than just an expository purpose.

Taken as a set, these scenes give us a close-up look at the culture of Rohan and some of the deep sorrow driving King Théoden. They also set up the importance of Éomer, who is now heir to the throne. And, for those of us who know the books, they also help us understand how close Éomer and Éowyn were to their cousin Théodred. Granted, the whole sequence is an "aside" of sorts, and Tolkien explicitly warned about poor adaptations failing due to "the intrusion of unwarranted matter," but he was speaking of "intrusion" that takes place because the filmmakers fail to perceive "where the core of the original lies." Not only do these scenes avoid that mistake, they demonstrate a rich understanding of the character of Théoden and give us a glimpse of the internal battle between hope and despair that is central to the contrast between Théoden and the Steward of Gondor, Denethor.[255]

Another large set of changes happens in the lead-up to, and the fighting at, the Battle of Helm's Deep. First is Théoden's initial reluctance to fight: he will "not risk open war," and retreats to Helm's Deep *with civilians*. This is a huge change from the books, where he chooses to ride to face off against Saruman, detouring to the Hornburg in order to support Erkenbrand's defense, and leaving his people in Edoras under Éowyn's leadership. Combine this with his rhetorical question to Aragorn, "Where was Gondor when the Westfold fell?" and his momentary hesitation at the news of the beacons,[256] and you end up with a Théoden who is not quite the same as the book version of the character.

Another big change is the absence of Éomer at the Hornburg. In the books, he plays a significant role in the battle, and has some great moments with Aragorn before the battle starts. In the films, he's been banished—in order that he might reappear at the proper dramatic moment and save the day, replacing Erkenbrand.

Finally, the most obvious change is the arrival of the Elves before the battle begins. Of course, there are no Elves at Helm's Deep in the books—but we should remember that Elves *are* fighting elsewhere in Middle-earth! The book says that "Three times Lórien had been assailed from Dol Guldur...

---

255  That's not to say these scenes go by without us griping about *something*. Though it's nearly impossible to *not* weep when Bernard Hill, as Théoden, grieves powerfully as he says, "No parent should have to bury their child," that line takes us both right out of the moment. First, because this is a medieval-type warrior society; they're burying their children *all the time*, one imagines. Second, because Tolkien would have used the Old English word *fæder* (translated as "father") and not the Latin-derived "parent." But neither of these gripes go to the "core of the original."

256  More on this change from the text when we look at *The Return of the King* shortly.

though grievous harm was done to the fair woods on the borders, the assaults were driven back." Even Thranduil's kingdom in the north of Mirkwood was invaded, so the idea of Elves fighting in this war is—in and of itself—*not* a strange concept, even if it seems a bit strange to have them arrive in Rohan of all places.

Did "the canons of narrative art" require these changes from the book? Were these, to some extent, inevitable changes in a good movie? Each of these three changes has its own answer, so we'll start with the easiest one: Éomer's absence from the Hornburg and his replacement of Erkenbrand. Yes, just as the filmmakers chose to replace Glorfindel with Arwen at the Ford of Bruinen in order to avoid introducing yet *another* character we would never see again, while simultaneously introducing us to Aragorn's love interest, Erkenbrand sits on the sidelines (between Glorfindel and Tom Bombadil) so that Éomer gets a heroic entrance, arriving to save the day with Gandalf *and* so that the audience doesn't have to keep track of another character who won't appear again. It fits for so many reasons, and there are really no downsides here to the change; certainly none that impact the "core of the original."

But what about the arrival of the Elves? We think that, in order to show that the Elves are just as invested in the War of the Ring, showing the Elves fighting is crucial. Could they just show some out-of-context, unexplained combat on the edge of Lórien? Sure, that's possible: maybe Haldir could die falling off a *flet* instead of on the Deeping Wall. But, cinematically speaking, it makes good sense to bring the Elves to Helm's Deep—instead of showing fighting going on in multiple places, have them join the main fight that the film has been building up to. And in most ways, adding their presence doesn't impact the "core of the original." After all, the Elves fought and died in the appendices, and their presence at Helm's Deep didn't change the outcome of the battle: they were all going to lose until Gandalf showed up with help and the Huorns arrived to clean up the mess.[257]

---

257  The assistance of the Huorns is only present in the Extended Edition.

While the appearance of the Elves doesn't change the plot line of the original too much, their arrival does demonstrate a particular theme that Jackson and his cowriters appear to have pushed subtly throughout the films: the idea that good is always more powerful than evil, so long as good is united. Tom Shippey argues that Tolkien's original audience (English people in the 1950s) would have readily accepted "the idea that the forces of evil might just be stronger than those of good: it was part of their real-world experience."[258] On the other hand, modern American cinemagoers need a different reason for the failure of good, and Shippey argues that Jackson's decision is to show that reason as "disunity and despair."[259] Early on, Elrond sets the tone in the film version of the Council of Elrond, stating matter-of-factly, "You will unite, or you will fall." Please don't get us wrong: fellowship and unity are *big* themes in Tolkien, but so too is the concept of inevitable defeat and the willingness to recognize that "good" isn't always good enough for victory. Jackson has, to an extent, oversimplified the good vs. evil debate and flattened the peaks and valleys of Tolkien's nuance here. While we see this theme at work even more strongly in the changes to Théoden (stay tuned), we get enough of a glimpse of it here to recognize the change. Still, we can't deny the incredible emotional impact of the arrival of the Elves: the music, Haldir's greeting, and the restoration of the alliance is always a stirring moment—and the way Haldir reacts to his own death speaks more about how the otherwise immortal (or "serially longeval," to use Tolkien's own term) Elves respond to death than all the Elrond and Arwen scenes combined.

A moment ago, we mentioned that this theme of Jackson's—that so long as good unites, it can always defeat evil—was something we saw in the changes to Théoden, so let's expand on that here. Jackson sets up the disunity theme here by starting with a Théoden who is reluctant to fight. After being told of the destruction caused by the wild men stirred up by Saruman, and being

258  Shippey, T. A., "Another Road to Middle-earth: Peter Jackson's Movie Trilogy," in *Roots and Branches: Selected Papers on Tolkien*, Walking Tree Publishers, 2007, 375.
259  Ibid, 375.

told that he must fight, he declines: "I will not bring further death to my people; I will not risk open war." Instead, he evacuates the city and retreats with his people to Helm's Deep. Later, facing what he believes to be the end of his people, he laments that "The old alliances are dead" before we get his famous meme-material line, "Where was Gondor when the Westfold fell?" In other words, Rohan is alone and will lose because they are alone. Disunity. As Shippey points out, "the sense of having been abandoned is set up, of course, only to be reversed, as the elvish army turns up to honour the Old Alliance and man the walls of the Hornburg."[260] This marked change in Théoden threatens to miss the "core of the original"—not just of the character of Théoden, but of Tolkien's theme that evil is sometimes more powerful and that even the victories of good are not permanent—but we confess it is done so skillfully that we nearly forget all about this by the time the Rohirrim charge to the rescue of Gondor in the next film!

The same cannot quite be said for the last change in *The Two Towers* that we'll talk about here: Faramir. Listeners to our podcast know just how much we revere Faramir, and that he is Alan's favorite character in *The Lord of the Rings*, if not the entire legendarium. The Faramir in the books is wise, truthful, honorable, and noble. He knows that Isildur's Bane is "some heirloom of power and peril... A fell weapon, perchance, devised by the Dark Lord." And yet he can say, in all honesty, "I would not take this thing, if it lay by the highway. Not were Minas Tirith falling in ruin and I alone could save her, so, using the weapon of the Dark Lord for her good and my glory." Even after he discovers that it is the One Ring that Frodo is carrying, he says, "I should take those words as a vow, and be held by them." Jackson, on the other hand, removes most of Faramir's honor and wisdom, having him succumb to the temptation of the Ring and declare that it will "go to Gondor" before eventually being persuaded by Sam to let them go.

---

260  Ibid, 376.

Why We Love Middle-earth

Was this change necessary because of the change in medium? We *want* to say that it wasn't necessary at all and that they should have kept Faramir faithful to the book, but...it really *was* an inevitable change. Cinematically, characters are often given a noticeable arc, a journey from one state to another: think Luke Skywalker's transition from naive farm boy to Jedi Master. Characters in books can afford to have more subtle arcs, but a film is a shorter medium, requiring a compressed arc. Book-Faramir's arc is slight and very subtle indeed; Jackson enhanced this arc for the movie audience, making the changes to his character more direct and obvious.[261] That meant he had to *start* in a different place compared to the book version of the character.

Similarly, since Jackson has spent the entirety of the movie telling us that the Ring always and continually corrupts (book-true) and that Men are universally weak (book-false), he would have undermined this theme had he given Faramir the "and I alone could save her" line. Finally, because they chose to move the confrontation between Shelob and Frodo to *The Return of the King*, there needed to be a conflict or peril for Frodo and Sam to face in this film—and Faramir became the sacrificial antagonist. So yes, the difference in the canons of narrative art explain the necessity of the change in Faramir.

But did it demonstrate a failure to understand "where the core of the original lies"? This is a tough question: after all, the changes to Faramir don't affect the eventual fate of the Ring. But we believe the change does demonstrate a lack of understanding about "the core of the original" when it comes to Faramir himself: a noble man in whom the blood of Númenor "runs nearly true." And because Jackson chose to end his arc prematurely—not showing us his romance with Éowyn, his role in the coronation of Aragorn, and his leadership in Ithilien—we don't even get the satisfaction of the completed arc. This doesn't stop us from enjoying the film, of course—but it is one of the changes we would have liked to see handled differently.

---

261  The screenwriters also wanted to give the hobbit characters more influence over those character arcs; note that it is Sam who persuades Faramir to change. Similarly, it's Pippin who convinces Treebeard to fight against Saruman after the Ents initially choose not to—another change from the books. We'll cover this more in the next section.

# THE RETURN OF THE KING

Not surprisingly, given the success of both *The Fellowship of the Ring* and *The Two Towers*, the series had become such a part of the popular zeitgeist of the early 2000s, the release of *The Return of the King* in December 2002 became the climactic moment so many had been waiting for: movie fans, the film industry itself, and—of course—fans of Tolkien's books. The release did not disappoint most of them, setting a record for opening day,[262] and like its predecessors, going on to become the year's highest-grossing film, grossing over a billion dollars worldwide.[263] And, in what many observers believed was an overdue recognition of the accomplishments of the trilogy as a whole, the final installment won all eleven Academy Awards for which it was nominated, including Best Picture.[264] But, in the wake of the larger deviations from the source material in *Two Towers* as compared to *Fellowship*, was *The Return of the King* able to avoid the pitfalls of "exaggeration, and...the intrusion of unwarranted matter owing to not perceiving where the core of the original lies"?

As with *Two Towers*, the largest structural change in *The Return of the King* was the elimination of interlacing, used to tremendous effect by Tolkien in the books, especially as we experience the same moment in time through the eyes of multiple characters: for example, the "deep echoing boom" that happens when the Gate of Minas Tirith is destroyed, which is heard both by Pippin as he races down to find Gandalf at the gate, and by Merry as Théoden prepares to lead the Rohirrim into battle on the Pelennor Fields. Jackson tries to accomplish the same thing through cross-cutting, keeping the viewers focused on multiple storylines at the same time, rather than sticking with one character, then going back to another with the leapfrogging and overlap inherent in interlacing.

---

262  *Return* grossed thirty-five million dollars at the box office on opening day, compared with *Fellowship*'s eighteen million and *Two Towers*' twenty-six million.

263  At the time, only *Titanic* had reached that mark.

264  Its eleven wins ties the mark held by *Ben-Hur* (1959) and *Titanic* (1997), and is still the record for the highest clean sweep.

Why We Love Middle-earth

While the change in technique was significant and noticeable, it's clearly a result of the change in medium, and so we'll spend our time here focusing on the changes in the story itself. We'll do this, as before, by looking at a number of scenes: some of these are changes by addition, others by modification, and others by simple elimination.

The first significant change we want to talk about actually exemplifies all three of these categories: the scene of the lighting of the beacons of Minas Tirith. In the books, Denethor has lit the beacons in time to warn Anórien; Pippin sees them alight, running to the west, as he rides east on Shadowfax with Gandalf toward Minas Tirith. In the meantime, Merry observes as Hirgon presents the Red Arrow to Théoden, officially asking Rohan for aid in Gondor's need on behalf of the Steward. In the films, the Red Arrow is eliminated altogether, with the beacons repurposed to take their place; Denethor, already descending into madness and despair in the films, refuses to light them, and so Pippin is given a role in their lighting.

Let's start analyzing this set of changes by looking at the elimination of the Red Arrow and Hirgon, the errand-rider of Gondor.[265] Significant characters in the story—Tom Bombadil and Goldberry, Glorfindel, Halbarad, Elladan, and Elrohir—have already been left out of the films to this point, so it's no surprise that Jackson and his team removed yet another character whom we won't see again (unless the film chose to show his headless corpse grasping the Red Arrow as the Rohirrim approached the City).

And while the arrival of the Red Arrow is a wonderfully dramatic moment in the books, a visual medium like film demands a visually dramatic moment to accomplish the same plot-related task. It's this difference in "the canons of narrative art" that led to the filmmakers' decision to change the role of the beacons from what it was in the book—a warning system for the land of

_____

265  And the *other* errand-rider of Gondor; but if Tolkien can't be bothered to give him a name, we can't be bothered to analyze his absence in the films.

Anórien in the north of Gondor—to a replacement for the delivery of the Red Arrow: a call to Rohan for aid in a time of need.

So far, then, we are absolutely with Jackson and his team on these two decisions: the elimination of Hirgon and the Red Arrow, and the new use of the beacons: cinematically necessary changes that don't reflect a failure to understand "the core of the original." But what about the timing of the lighting of the beacons? The film shows Pippin lighting the beacon in the City the morning after Faramir and his men are driven in retreat from Osgiliath, which is only thirty to forty miles away from Minas Tirith.[266] Théoden's army has not yet been mustered, will take days to do so, and will have more than three hundred miles to travel when it does—lighting the beacons now accomplishes nothing more than sending Rohan an invite to the afterparty the Witch-king will throw in the Citadel.[267]

Whether it makes sense timing-wise or not, though, let's be honest: the lighting of the beacons is a truly *breathtaking* moment in the films. Sweeping landscapes, gorgeous cinematography, and Howard Shore's soaring musical score result in a truly iconic sequence: in many ways, a genuine improvement on Pippin's mere observation of them from a distance as he travels in the opposite direction.

You've been waiting for the other shoe to drop, so we should get to it: why have *Pippin* light the beacons? Why take this from Denethor and give it to a hobbit? One aspect of this discussion segues nicely into our next set of changes—the demonization of Denethor—so we'll focus on Pippin's involvement for now, and get to what it says about Denethor shortly.[268] By this point in the films, it's become clear that Jackson and his team like to give important moments to other characters, especially the hobbits, something

---

266  In a fit of pedantry (you're used to it by now, right?), we'll also add that in the book, there isn't a beacon *in* Minas Tirith: the nearest one is on Amon Dîn, some forty miles to the northwest of the city.

267  We doubt their name is on the list, and suspect that Mordor bouncers are rather effective.

268  You'd almost think we planned it that way. If we were the types to have a plan.

Shippey calls "democratization" in his essay "Another Road to Middle-earth." He argues that it is seen "in the liking for enlarging the roles of relatively minor characters: just as Sam's stout heart converts Faramir, so Pippin's cunning diversion of Treebeard through the wasted groves near Orthanc converts Treebeard, in Jackson's version only, from neutrality to decision."[269] Even in Rivendell, it is Merry and Pippin who appear to change Elrond's mind about including them in the Fellowship, in contrast to the choice being encouraged by Gandalf in the books. Whenever possible, it appears, Jackson and his screenwriting team give agency and influence to the hobbits in order to enlarge their roles and their centrality to the story. So, while taking it *away* from Denethor is another story altogether—one we'll get to momentarily—giving the task to Pippin is at least consistent with Jackson's democratization of the story and fits the theme in the adaptation of the importance of "small hands." Of course, this is a theme taken from Tolkien's own words that he gives to Elrond in the Council: "Yet such is oft the course of deeds that move the wheels of the world: small hands do them because they must, while the eyes of the great are elsewhere."

While giving the task of lighting the beacons to Pippin is internally consistent with Jackson's apparent objective of giving hobbits control over major story elements, taking that *away* from Denethor is just another step in the demonization of this character. Don't get us wrong: even book-Denethor isn't about to win any Father of the Year awards in Gondor.[270] But the proud and ambitious Denethor, in whom Númenórean blood "runs nearly true," is turned into a callous, greedy narcissist who is, as Shippey says, "the epitome of the 'château general' who sends men to their deaths while living himself in style and comfort."[271] It seems that, at least some of the time, Jackson has a tendency to oversimplify characters: Boromir has been seeking the Ring since Rivendell, Aragorn is unsure about his heritage as king, Gimli is comic relief, etc. Film-Denethor has been rendered essentially one-dimensional, so

---

269  Shippey, "Another Road," 2007, 378.
270  At least not now that Boromir is dead.
271  Shippey, "Another Road," 2007, 377.

much so that viewers no longer feel conflicted about him, as they do when reading the book.

Book-Denethor is far more complex: he actually makes *wise* decisions regarding the defense of the city, bringing in as many troops from the southern fiefdoms as they'll send, delivering the Red Arrow to Théoden to ask for their aid, and lighting the beacons to warn Anórien. Beyond that, he executes a solid defense-in-depth, bleeding the enemy at the crossing of the Anduin before Faramir retreats to the Causeway Forts, then bleeding them again before retreating across the Pelennor, and sending a sortie to rescue the retreating force *and* bleed the enemy even more. He is filled with pride, yes, but he exercises sound operational and tactical judgment. Film-Denethor does *none* of these things, instead refusing to take any steps to defend the City beyond sending his son and a far-too-small cavalry force to charge *buildings*. As Dr. Bret Devereaux, a regular guest on our podcast, has said, "cavalry charges are all about morale impact. Large bodies of infantry in good order cannot simply be run over in the field, so instead a charge aims to break the morale of the defenders, causing them to scatter and then be easily run down. But a ruined city cannot panic and run away."[272] Jackson's choices force the viewer into seeing Denethor as nothing more than a madman, a villain wearing the clothes of a good guy.

This demonization of Denethor works to set up a father-son theme that Shippey points out is "particularly popular in recent (American) film, that of the son trying desperately to gain the love of his father, and of the father rejecting (till too late) the love of his son."[273] In the books, Denethor may love his son—but he places the well-being of Gondor above Faramir, right up until his son is nearly killed. It is the wounding of Faramir that weakens Denethor and his subsequent use of the *palantír* that breaks him, sending him into utter despair. Oddly, for a director who likes his characters to have

272  Devereaux, Bret. "Collections: The Siege of Gondor, Part II: These Beacons Are Liiiiiiit." *A Collection of Unmitigated Pedantry*, March 8, 2021. https://acoup.blog/2019/05/17/collections-the-siege-of-gondor-part-ii-these-beacons-are-liiiiiiit/.

273  Shippey, "Another Road," 2007, 377-78.

recognizable arcs, Jackson's Denethor *begins* in his fully broken state, already succumbing to utter despair, and the father-son relationship suffers for it.

Was this change an inevitable result of the change in medium, a result of the different "canons of narrative art"? Perhaps, in order to put more emphasis on the main characters of Gandalf and Pippin, and even Faramir, it was necessary to oversimplify the admittedly complex character of Denethor, but we think it might have been taken too far, to the point where part of "the core of the original" was lost. Specifically, the way in which Tolkien used Théoden and Denethor as two similarly-situated men—leaders of their respective nations, each having lost a son, each faced with likely destruction of their peoples and rule—who faced their circumstances differently. Théoden, with Gandalf's encouragement, chose to leave despair, and embrace hope, leading to a noble death in battle; Denethor, despite Gandalf's help, chose to embrace despair, leading to his ignoble death. The comparison suffers in the films, in part because of Théoden's transformation taking place without his direct choice, but primarily due to the one-dimensional nature of Denethor.

We've talked about changes through elimination and addition—removing Denethor's decision to send the Red Arrow, and adding Pippin's lighting of the beacons—both of which serve to assist in the demonization of Denethor. The last change we want to discuss is one of modification: when the Witch-king faces off against Gandalf. In the books, the Lord of the Nazgûl enters the City on horseback, riding through the broken Gate that no enemy had ever passed. Gandalf, we're told, sat "waiting, silent and still." Jackson lifts the text of the confrontation almost word-for-word, varying it only slightly: Gandalf commands him to "Go back to the abyss prepared for you... Fall into the nothingness that awaits you and your Master!"[274] The Witch-king's response varies only in the order of the phrases, but he says the same things, calling Gandalf an "Old fool," asking, "Do you not know Death

---

274    Tolkien, *Return*, 2020, 829.

when you see it?"[275] and even lifting his sword with flames running down the blade. So far, so good: if the dialogue is all lifted straight from the book, what's the change, and why is it a problem?

Book-Gandalf simply stands still in response to the Witch-king's threats as the horns of the Riders of Rohan blow in the distance, while atop Shadowfax "who alone among the free horses of the earth endured the terror, unmoving, steadfast." Film-Gandalf gets his staff shattered and is knocked off Shadowfax, who then bolts the scene out of fear. While the text is silent regarding which of these two would win a mano-a-wizard showdown, the idea that the Witch-king could shatter Gandalf's staff with a word and drive off Shadowfax is questionable at best: he is the shade of a mortal Man, albeit an extraordinarily powerful one,[276] while Gandalf is a Maia: an angelic being on the same order as Sauron. Furthermore, this is Gandalf the *White*—or as we call him, Gandalf 2.0—resurrected and enhanced by Ilúvatar, the creator God (big G) of Tolkien's world.

In Letter 156, Tolkien explains that "Gandalf sacrificed himself, was accepted, and enhanced, and returned." *Enhanced*. This is the same Gandalf who fought off all nine Nazgûl at night: "I galloped to Weathertop like a gale, and I reached it before sundown on my second day from Bree—and they were there before me... I was hard put to it indeed: such light and flame cannot have been seen on Weathertop since the beacons of old."[277] Of this moment at the gates of Minas Tirith, Tolkien writes "[Gandalf] alone is left to forbid the entrance of the Lord of Nazgûl to Minas Tirith, when the City has been overthrown and its Gates destroyed—and yet so powerful is the whole train of human resistance, that he himself has kindled and organized, that in fact no battle between the two occurs: it passes to other mortal hands."[278] No. Battle.

---

275   Tolkien, *Return*, 2020, 829.

276   In Letter No. 210, Tolkien says that, by this time in the story, the Witch-king has been "given an added demonic force."

277   Tolkien, *Fellowship*, 2020, 264.

278   Carpenter, *Letters*, No. 156.

Was this change necessary for cinematic reasons? Did it show a lack of understanding of the core of the original? Honestly, we're not convinced that the "canons of narrative art" required this: after all, the confrontation as written would have been just as dramatic and effective. But the scene cannot be addressed in a vacuum, as—and now we tangentially address another change—Jackson and his team had already added an entire invasion of Minas Tirith by trolls and orcs, and would have had to eliminate *that* in order to adapt the confrontation more faithfully. In the book, the Witch-king is the only one to make it through the Gate: even his own forces quail in fear. When he turns tail, they do as well, and the Men hold the Gate through the rest of the battle. By moving the confrontation and adding the invasion, Jackson gets to do what he does well: chaotic battle scenes with massive creatures like trolls. We also get a touching scene between Gandalf and Pippin as the latter expresses his fear of death, in which Gandalf gets lines directly from Frodo's dream at Tom Bombadil's house, about the "pale light behind a grey rain-curtain... turn the veil all to glass and silver, until at last it was rolled back, and a far green country opened before him under a swift sunrise."[279] The drama provided by the invasion, and this tender moment between Gandalf and Pippin, fit the canons of narrative art nicely; it's hard to imagine the film without them. Still, if the confrontation had simply ended with the threat from the Witch-king, followed by the horns, we wouldn't be addressing it here.

There are, not surprisingly, many more significant moments entirely eliminated in Jackson's conclusion to the film trilogy: there is no Ghân-buri-Ghân or any Drúedain at all, for that matter (and the Rohirrim's stealthy approach to the City is removed). There are no Rangers that accompany Aragorn, Legolas, and Gimli through the Paths of the Dead: neither of Elrond's sons appear with them. There is no Prince Imrahil, no Ioreth, no Beregond, and no Bergil. The love story between Faramir and Éowyn—one of our favorite stories of the Third Age—is entirely missing. And, most

---

279    Tolkien, *Fellowship*, 2020, 136.

significantly, the entire Scouring of the Shire is lost, with Saruman's death moved to a moment in Isengard. In a way, it's better to have eliminated these elements than to have compressed them. Tolkien suggests as much in Letter 201, which he wrote to his publisher about a possible film adaptation: "An *abridgment* by selection... would be pleasant... but the present script is rather a *compression* with resultant over-crowding and confusion, blurring of climaxes, and general degradation..." Since the film was already nearly four-and-a-half hours in length, we suppose the elimination of these scenes was in accordance with "the canons of narrative art": specifically, "don't make a six-hour movie."

Over the course of more than eleven hours, Jackson's film trilogy of *The Lord of the Rings* managed to convey the core of Tolkien's original effectively, while enthralling and entertaining viewers around the world: from those who've read everything (e.g., us) to those who've never read a word of Tolkien. We have our quibbles with some choices (Faramir comes to mind), but when considered in its entirety, we only have good things to say about it. This is, unfortunately, not the case for the next films...but that's another chapter.

# SO WHY DO WE LOVE IT?

Jackson's vision of Tolkien's work is visually stunning, includes much of Tolkien's glorious dialogue, and is scored with some of the very best film music of all time. The story is captivating, emotionally moving, and manages to convey many (but not all) of the same themes as the original. The casting and acting are superb; sets, costumes, and visual effects have all set new standards in the industry. Nearly every element of the films has stood the test of time, as nearly twenty-three years have passed since the release of *Fellowship*. For all these reasons, we absolutely love it—despite our slight misgivings over favored characters or events being changed or removed. We each make time to watch the films at least once a year and heartily recommend our listeners do the same: just promise us you'll still read the books, too.

# WHY ALAN LOVES IT

While you might be excused for thinking I don't *actually* love these films as much as I say I do—after all, we just spent a few thousand words pointing out areas where we believe Jackson failed to understand "the core of the original"—I genuinely do. I love them first as great films, aside from any issue with the adaptation aspect. I'm not the experienced film buff that Shawn is, and so I may not be able to explain with any degree of expertise all the reasons *why* they are great cinema—but I feel like I'm on solid ground when I say they are.[280] When I watch Jackson's *Rings*, I see films that succeed on every front: nearly perfect casting and acting, breathtaking cinematography, jaw-dropping effects, spot-on pacing, costumes and weapons that set the standard for the industry, some of the very best scoring of all time, and direction that got the best out of the actors and crew. Even now, more than twenty years later, the movies stand the test of time as films, and I can hardly look away.

As adaptations, they are less perfect—but still quite good. Yes, we can spend time pointing out the weak spots: the places where either the canons of narrative art, or the writer's choices, demanded that Tolkien's story take a back seat. At the same time, there were moments that were nearly perfect in adaptation—not because they replicated a book scene verbatim, but because they conveyed the book so well *despite* changing them: Galadriel's prologue comes to mind, as does the death of Boromir.

But one of the biggest reasons I love these films is because of what they have done for the Tolkien fandom. When *Fellowship* came out in 2001, I was

---

280  After all, that Academy thingy threw a bunch of gold statues their way, and they claim to know what they're doing, so the films can't be terrible, right?

a Tolkien fan in isolation: neither my family nor my friends shared my love for Middle-earth. And while there were message boards (TheOneRing.net was one of my old stomping grounds, I didn't know about fan organizations like the Tolkien Society, or events like Oxonmoot, so meeting people who shared my love of Tolkien was nearly unheard of. Not after these films. In fact, even the day that *Fellowship* was released was a chance to connect with other Tolkien fans: I was attending a "line party" complete with costumes and trivia, and finally knew…I'd found my people.

And while there is a *huge* upside to what Jackson's *Rings* has brought to the Tolkien fandom, I'm not naive or blind. I'm all too keenly aware of the fact that there is, and will always be, a corner of the fandom that detests the films, that detests nearly *all* adaptations for their lack of fidelity to Tolkien.[281] I'm a member of a Facebook group that consists of people who regularly profess their disdain for adaptations.[282] But too easily does that way lead to gatekeeping: it is an infinitesimal step from disliking the films due to inaccuracies, to determining that people who actually *like* the films must not be "true Tolkien fans." Folks, let me be clear: no one—not us, not any Tolkien scholar, not Peter Jackson, *no one*—can tell you whether you are a "true Tolkien fan." And I'm grateful to Jackson's *Rings* films for knocking down the gates and welcoming a flood of new fans to Middle-earth.

# WHY SHAWN LOVES IT

If you're reading this book in order, you may already have figured out why the release of Peter Jackson's *Lord of the Rings* trilogy was such a breath of fresh air to so many longtime Tolkien fans. While there had been adaptations, and while each adaptation had its charms and its share of fans, each of them also had major shortcomings that prevented any of them from feeling

---

281  Many of these people, however, like the BBC Radio dramatization. For good reason: that is, in our opinion, the gold standard of Tolkien adaptations, but sadly, we will have to hold our discussion of it for another day.

282  At least until they read this book and decide I no longer measure up.

remotely like a "definitive" adaptation, if such a thing is even possible. To see Peter Jackson create a trilogy of films that were such phenomenal technical and creative achievements—as evidenced by the critical praise and the many Academy Awards they received—was a treat in and of itself, and not just for Tolkien fans. But to see that Jackson and his collaborators (primarily screenwriters Fran Walsh and Philippa Boyens, of course, but also the many people responsible for the costumes and sets, and of course the conceptual artists Alan Lee and John Howe, who were already established as Tolkien illustrators) had actually read and *understood* Tolkien's books was incredibly gratifying for those of us who struggled with the attempts at adaptation that had come before. Jackson and his screenwriting team hadn't just picked up *The Lord of the Rings* and read it in a vacuum; they were *fans* who had a deeper understanding of the mythology of the Middle-earth legendarium and what makes it tick. And while there are still some places where the text was not quite done justice, somehow these flaws are easier to swallow when it's so evident that the filmmakers came to the production with love and appreciation for the source material.[283]

Jackson's *Lord of the Rings* has its share of moments when it misses "the core of the original," no doubt. But in general, Jackson and his team just *got* Tolkien thematically in a way that previous adapters did not seem to. And Jackson captured the look and feel of Middle-earth better than anyone before or since—from the Anglo-Saxon production design of Rohan, to Gondor's placement on the Roman-Byzantine spectrum, to the breathtaking ethereality of the High Elves like Galadriel and Celeborn (and, let's give credit for distinguishing them from the Silvan Elves like Legolas and Haldir).

But, as much as I loved Jackson's films at the first viewing, it's the experience I've had in the years since its release that has been truly wonderful to me. Because Jackson's films were successful and widely praised, they opened the doors to Middle-earth to more people around me than the more niche

---

283  It must be said that this is certainly not true for all Tolkien fans. We have met many who don't like Jackson's films, and that's okay too.

adaptations that came before. Now, suddenly, there was a new medium and mechanism allowing me to share my love of *The Lord of the Rings* with others: friends, coworkers, and family. Not that these people couldn't read the book, and I would love it if everyone I care about in the world would read it. But that's just not going to happen: it's a big book, full of language that some people aren't going to enjoy, and while it's *my* thing, I can't expect it to be *everyone's* thing. But a few movies? Movies that most people seem to think are pretty solid? That's a much easier sell.

My wife—a cinephile and film history buff who had always appreciated *my* love for Tolkien's writing, but didn't quite share it—fell in love with Jackson's *Lord of the Rings*. We went to midnight shows of every new release. We traveled an embarrassing distance to get a chance to see *The Return of the King* a couple of weeks before it officially released, and saw each of the movies multiple times in the theater. We went to TheOneRing.net's Oscar party in Los Angeles in 2004, and were there (like, way in the back of the room) when Peter Jackson showed up with cast and crew and eleven gold statues.[284] For years, we watched the trilogy at home every few months, and every time it was back in theaters, we were there. It was our thing. And now, we've shared it with our kids, who are only now just starting to get interested in the books...but have been fans of Tolkien's world for a few years now. Even if there were nothing else to love about them, I would love Peter Jackson's films for what they've given me.

So yes, I *do* love Peter Jackson's *Lord of the Rings*, and I would (and do, frequently) recommend them to anyone, even to people who will never read Tolkien's books. A little bit of Middle-earth is better than none, and the world could do a lot worse.

---

284  *Alan*: You were in the back of the room? "Sorry to hear that," he said from the second row. And yes, folks, we were *both* at that Oscar party—we just didn't know each other at the time.

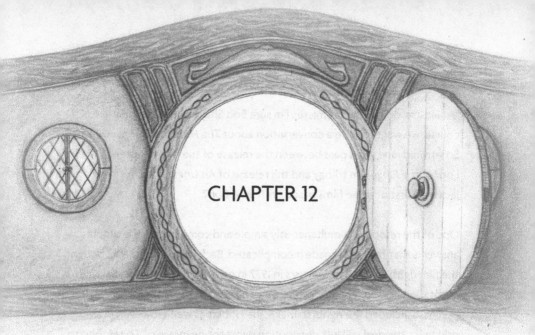

# CHAPTER 12

# BIGGER BUDGET BUST:
# PETER JACKSON'S
# *THE HOBBIT*

*"Why does it hurt so much?"*

—Tauriel, in Peter Jackson's The Battle of the Five Armies

*"Do you really want to know?"*

—Shawn and Alan, watching Peter Jackson's The Battle of the Five Armies

After the massive critical and financial success of Jackson's *The Lord of the Rings*, the natural question presented itself: would Jackson also attempt to adapt Tolkien's first novel, *The Hobbit*? Hollywood is a town built on franchises, and all the Middle-earth signs pointed in that direction. New Line was certainly interested, at least according to Ken Kamins, Jackson's manager:

"At least at one of the premieres I'm sure Bob Shaye said something like, 'Of course, we want to have a conversation about *The Hobbit* at some point.' "[285] So why did nine years pass between the release of the final chapter of *The Lord of the Rings* film trilogy and the release of *An Unexpected Journey*, Jackson's first of three films based on *The Hobbit*?

One of the reasons is simultaneously simple and complicated: the simple answer is that the rights made it complicated. Back when Saul Zaentz bought the film rights from United Artists in 1977 in order to finance Ralph Bakshi's adaptation (see our chapter on Bakshi's *The Lord of the Rings* for more), the purchase included the rights to make *The Hobbit* as well. However, in an odd twist, the deal still left *distribution* rights to any movie of *The Hobbit* to UA. As the rights made their way to different parties, it became even more complicated: the rights to *make* the film were sold to Miramax first, who gave them over to New Line (owned by Warner Brothers), while the rights to *distribute* the film belonged to MGM, who had previously bought out United Artists. If you're following all that, congratulations. And if you're not, the TL;DR version is this: New Line could *make* a film version of *The Hobbit*, but they'd have to deal with MGM, as they still owned the rights to *distribute* any films.

That proved a unique challenge. As Ian Nathan explains in *Anything You Can Imagine*, "[MGM]'s fortunes had fluctuated wildly since the late sixties, changing hands and repeatedly stripped of assets, leaving them permanently orbiting bankruptcy like a black hole. *The Hobbit* represented a financial Catch-22: MGM were in no position to co-finance such a blockbuster production, but they were also unwilling to let go of one of the few assets currently keeping them from being sucked into that black hole."[286] The rights stagnated, and no movement was made toward an adaptation of *The Hobbit* for years.

---

285  Nathan, Ian. *Anything You Can Imagine: Peter Jackson and the Making of Middle-earth.* HarperCollins, 2018, 492.

286  Nathan, *Anything*, 2018, 493.

Why We Love Middle-earth

But there was another reason why it didn't move forward as quickly as one might expect in the wake of the success of *The Lord of the Rings*: Jackson himself was hesitant. Fortunately, the complicated rights situation meant he didn't have to decide one way or the other. Unfortunately, in those intervening years, a split between Jackson and New Line threatened to snuff out any remaining opportunity for Jackson to be involved.[287] But, in 2007, Jackson and the New Line team reconciled and the legal work to resolve the rights situation began. Warner Brothers, who owned New Line, would fully finance the films in exchange for the distribution rights from MGM, but the latter studio would still hold on to international television rights. With that agreement reached, the announcement finally came that Peter Jackson and Fran Walsh would be producers on a two-film adaptation of *The Hobbit*.

Horror and fantasy director Guillermo del Toro—just starting to find mainstream success at the time with *Hellboy* and the Academy Award-winning *Pan's Labyrinth*—was chosen to direct the films, and worked for two years in writing and pre-production with Jackson, Walsh, and Philippa Boyens. But with financial troubles surrounding MGM and other ongoing delays, production had still not been given the green light as of May 2010—and del Toro left the project as a result, but "fully support[ed] a smooth transition to a new director."[288] While other directors surfaced in a few reports, ultimately—to no one's surprise—Jackson was announced as the director of *The Hobbit* in October 2010, and principal photography was to begin a few months later, in February 2011. As one might imagine, this presented significant challenges for Jackson: "Because Guillermo del Toro had to leave and I jumped in and took over, we didn't wind the clock back a year and a half and give me a year and a half prep to design the movie, which was different to what he was doing. It was impossible, and as a result of it being impossible I just started shooting the movie with most of it not prepped at all. You're going on to a set and you're winging it, you've got

---

287  Jackson had requested an audit of New Line's books, since his compensation was based on profit; New Line refused, and Jackson was forced to file suit. See Nathan, *Anything*, 2018, 495-500 for the full story.

288  "Guillermo Del Toro departs 'The Hobbit'", TheOneRing.net, May 30, 2010. https://www.theonering.net/torwp/2010/05/30/36920-guillermo-del-toro-departs-the-hobbit.

these massively complicated scenes, no storyboards and you're making it up there and then on the spot."[289]

Throw in some problems with a labor union—New Zealand Actors' Equity advised its members to boycott the production—and a month in the hospital for Jackson, suffering from a stomach ulcer, and it's a wonder the films (expanded to three by the summer of 2012) got made at all.

In taking a close look at those three movies, we will follow a similar, but not quite identical, structure here as we did in the previous chapter on Jackson's *The Lord of the Rings* trilogy: we'll still focus our discussion on the changes that took place from book to film, and we'll talk about whether those changes were necessary due to the "canons of narrative art"; we'll also discuss to what extent those changes managed to still convey "the core of the original," or how much they missed that core. However, for brevity's sake, we will not break down each film individually, but look at the differences across all three films. After all, we were raised to believe that if you cannot say anything nice about something, don't say anything at all—but that would make for a very short chapter indeed. Our compromise will be merely to say a little less.

# AN UNEXPECTED DESOLATION OF FIVE ARMIES

Well, we had to come up with *some* title for this section, didn't we? We'll be working our way through a number of changes in Jackson's adaptation, but before we start, we thought it might help soften the blow if we take a moment to explain *why* we think *The Hobbit* films struggled so much more

---

289   Hall, Jacob. "Peter Jackson Explains Why The 'Hobbit' Movies Are Such A Huge Mess," Slash Film, November 19, 2015. www.slashfilm.com/541186/peter-jackson-hobbit-movie-problems.

than *The Lord of the Rings* films did in capturing "the core of the original" successfully. Tolkien wrote *The Hobbit* first, in 1937; then he wrote *The Lord of the Rings*—it was a sequel to *The Hobbit*. Jackson, on the other hand, made *The Lord of the Rings* films first, and then tried to turn *The Hobbit* films into a prequel to that trilogy. Prequels, by their very nature, have a tendency to fall into the trap of referencing the later story, and the *Hobbit* films are no exception. From the huge emphasis on Dol Guldur and the Necromancer (which barely warrant a mention in Tolkien's text) to the recycled dialogue ("You have no power here"), from obvious prequel points (Thranduil's mention of Strider) to borrowed plot lines (an Elf-Man romance one-upped by an Elf-Dwarf romance), the films' nature as a set of prequels comes across as heavy-handed and reduces Jackson's ability to simply tell the story of *The Hobbit*.

And it's this fact that leads us right back to Letter 210, which we've referenced over and over: "...the failure of poor films is often precisely in exaggeration, and in the intrusion of unwarranted matter owing to not perceiving where the core of the original lies." Nearly all of the problems that we see with Jackson's adaptation of *The Hobbit* can be identified as exaggerations or the intrusion of unwarranted matter. The sheer number of these moments suggests that, indeed, "the core of the original" has been lost. The noted Tolkien scholar, Corey Olsen, writes: "If, when we look at Bilbo and his magic ring in *The Hobbit*, we are constantly thinking about Frodo and Mount Doom, we will not really be paying attention to the ideas that *this* story is interested in."[290] And we think that's precisely what happened with Jackson and his team here: they wanted the audience to be constantly thinking forward—to Frodo and Mount Doom, to Sauron and the threat of the Ring, to Strider, even to Gimli—and, as a result, lost most of what *this* story was supposed to be about.

---

290    Olsen, *Exploring J.R.R. Tolkien's The Hobbit*, 2012, 14.

That's even the case with one of the scene changes that we both actually *liked* from a cinematic standpoint: the introduction of the dwarves. In the book, the dwarves—aside from their leader, Thorin—are a nearly indistinguishable group of characters. We get their names, and the colors of their hoods and such, but as the story goes, we see virtually no individual characters that stand out. In Jackson's version, we get to spend more than twenty minutes in Bilbo's home, being introduced to each of them and getting to know their characters as individuals, at least to some extent. And throughout the films, some of them—notably Balin, his brother Dwalin, and the comedic Bofur—became nearly as important to the tale as Thorin himself. In addition, Jackson had Thorin arrive much later—on his own—very effectively setting him apart as— in Tolkien's own words—"a very important dwarf."

This change was fun, and entertaining, and helped the audience care about each member of Thorin's Company. Certainly, "the canons of narrative art" that we keep harping on about would almost *require* this sort of effort in a film: why have Thorin and twelve other dwarves if we know nothing about them and they're all as indistinguishable from one another as they are in the book? Cinematically, Jackson needed to either shrink the number of dwarves, or get the audience invested—at least a little bit—in each of them. The former would be a brute-force solution and leave fans even more disappointed, so the obvious answer presented itself—and Jackson did a fantastic job creating very unique individual dwarves with distinct roles in the Company.

And while we like this change a great deal, we still have to acknowledge that it was the first step in a process that changed this tale from being centered around Bilbo to being spread across a wide range of story threads, most of which don't appear (or are given very little page time) in the book: Thorin's quest for vengeance against Azog and the latter's quest to destroy the line of Durin, the focus on Dol Guldur, the White Council, a love triangle including an Elf and a Dwarf, the internal political machinations of Lake-town, and more. The story stopped being *The Hobbit* fairly early on; we just didn't notice it right away.

One place where the story felt most like Tolkien's, though, was the iconic moment from "Riddles in the Dark": after Bilbo has been separated from the dwarves in the goblin caves and finds himself at the shores of the underground lake that Gollum has been calling home for a few centuries. Martin Freeman and Andy Serkis, reprising his role as Gollum from *The Lord of the Rings*, are both at the very top of their game in this scene—so why are we mentioning this here? Because one of the changes that Jackson made in rewriting this scene, while subtle, begins a significant shift away from Tolkien's themes and toward the curse of prequels: setting up the events of *The Lord of the Rings* instead of simply telling the story of *The Hobbit*.

This may sound pedantic, and it wouldn't be the first time we were accused of pedantry in its various forms.[291] In Tolkien's text, Gollum gives one of his riddles and Bilbo is stumped: "He began to get frightened, and that is bad for thinking. Gollum began to get out of his boat. He flapped into the water and paddled to the bank; Bilbo could see his eyes coming toward him. His tongue seemed to stick in his mouth; he wanted to shout out: 'Give me more time! Give me time!' But all that came out with a sudden squeal was: 'Time! Time!' Bilbo was saved by pure luck. For that of course was the answer."[292] In Jackson's version, Bilbo is equally flustered, when Gollum says, "Time's up." This prompts Bilbo to provide Gollum with the previously unknown answer: he now knows this is the answer to the riddle. It is not the cosmic driving force of luck/fate/providence, but his own quick thinking and Gollum's foolish mistake in saying the word *time*, that saves Bilbo. As we said, this is a subtle difference, but it is significant: the theme of "luck"—which is really providence or fate in Tolkien—is present throughout Tolkien's *Hobbit* and plays a big part in understanding the story as Tolkien told it. Instead, Jackson downplays the role of luck[293]—replacing it with conscious character

---

291  We note that accusations are merely accusations and not conclusive evidence of pedantry. This very footnote, however...

292  Tolkien, *The Hobbit*, 2020, 83.

293  In case you think this was an oversight, Jackson goes so far as to put words in Thorin's mouth directly on the subject. After he shoots at, but misses, a white stag in Mirkwood, Bilbo chastises him, saying that it's "bad luck." Thorin responds dismissively: "I don't believe in luck. We make our own luck." .

motives or outside forces, like "the will of the Ring"—seemingly in order to make this the story that sets in motion the events of *The Lord of the Rings*. Of course, this wasn't Tolkien's vision for the story of *The Hobbit* at all, and so it completely misses "the core of the original," even though the canons of narrative art wouldn't seem to require such a drastic change to the thematic material.

The same movement away from "chance" takes place in the recreation of a scene that, while Tolkien's, never actually takes place in his *Hobbit*. In the appendices to *The Lord of the Rings*, we read about Thorin and Gandalf: "But at last there came about by chance a meeting between Gandalf and Thorin that changed all the fortunes of the House of Durin..." Gandalf was staying in Bree and was pondering how "Sauron might use [Smaug] with terrible effect," when Thorin stood in front of him. The dwarf-king-in-exile tells Gandalf, You have often come into my thoughts of late, as if I were bidden to seek you." Later, when retelling the story, Gandalf says that disaster "has been averted—because I met Thorin Oakenshield one evening on the edge of spring in Bree. A chance-meeting, as we say in Middle-earth." Chance— which, in Tolkien's *Hobbit*, nearly always refers to providence.

In Jackson's retelling, however, after a few minutes of conversation, Thorin asks, "This is no chance meeting, is it, Gandalf?" and Gandalf admits that he has arranged this meeting. In fact, Gandalf manipulated events to make this meeting happen precisely so that he could then manipulate Thorin into attempting to retake his former kingdom of Erebor. It's another attempt to ensure the audience is thinking about these films *in the context of* the later story as told in Jackson's *The Lord of the Rings* films. He falls into the prequel trap again, as he has Gandalf placing pieces on the chessboard for the later story instead of telling *this* story. There is no need to do this in order to adapt the story to the screen: the "canons of narrative art" do not demand the removal of luck/providence, nor do they demand that a prequel constantly reference the later story—yet that is what Jackson does here and, in so doing, continues to miss "the core of the original."

While not all of Jackson's changes relate to this theme of luck/providence, there's one more that we want to discuss here because it really sums up the way Jackson has treated the theme throughout the films: Gandalf's farewell to Bilbo. In the book, Gandalf and Balin come and visit Bilbo several years later, and Bilbo observes that "the prophecies of the old songs have turned out to be true, after a fashion!" In essence, Gandalf asks, why wouldn't they? He adds, "You don't really suppose, do you, that all your adventures and escapes were managed by mere luck, just for your sole benefit? You are a very fine person, Mr. Baggins, and I am very fond of you; but you are only quite a little fellow in a wide world after all!" When read in context, it is clear that Gandalf is telling Bilbo that there was a greater power, a providence, involved in ensuring Bilbo's "adventures and escapes" in order to bring about the greater plan. This is reiterated when Gandalf reminds him that he is just one little guy in a big world and that only providence and fate would create the sort of series of events that he encountered and survived.

In the films, we still get that line about not supposing that the adventures and escapes were managed by mere luck: the line is verbatim from the book.[294] But then, instead of making it clear that providence has been at work through "luck" all along, Gandalf follows this up with prequel-focused dialogue: "Magic rings should not be used lightly, Bilbo." Good advice, yes—but placed, as it has been, directly after the line about "mere luck," Jackson is conveying the message that it was *the Ring* that managed Bilbo's adventures and escapes! Not only does Jackson work very hard at eliminating the notion of luck/providence, he replaces it with the will of the One Ring, completely gutting one of Tolkien's most consistent themes in *The Hobbit*. Bilbo's finding of the Ring wasn't the start of all the problems: it was the start of the *solution*. Jackson and his team knew that being found by Bilbo was not the Ring's doing when they wrote the prologue to *The Lord of the Rings*: "Something happened then that the Ring did not intend." Somewhere along the line, they forgot about it.

---

294    Right up to the moment where it eliminates the crucial, "just for your sole benefit."

Moving on past the issue of luck and providence, we want to touch on yet another prequel-trap problem: Jackson treating Thorin coming under the influence of dragon-sickness in a manner nearly identical to the way he treated Frodo being under the influence of the One Ring. Bilbo says of Thorin, "He doesn't sleep. He barely eats," echoing Sam's lines about Frodo near Cirith Ungol in the first trilogy of films. Thorin acts the way Denethor does when talking about the Ring: advocating isolationism, and demonstrating a willingness to fruitlessly throw lives away. The concept of dragon-sickness is elevated to the level of the power of the One Ring in *The Lord of the Rings* in what appears to be a conscious attempt to echo the later movies, as prequels are so often wont to do.

This is a perfect example of the "exaggeration" Tolkien talked about in Letter No. 210, as "dragon-sickness" is mentioned only *once* in the entirety of Tolkien's story. Even then, it's about the old Master of Lake-town: no dwarf is ever said to have suffered from "dragon-sickness." They have, however, been known to suffer from greed. In other words, Jackson has replaced an *internal* character flaw (a selfish desire for wealth) with an *external* influence ("dragon-sickness"). This drastically diminishes the experiences of Frodo in *The Lord of the Rings*, because his suffering really *did* come from the external influence of the Ring—book-Thorin was simply greedy, and Gandalf says as much in the book: "Pride and greed overcame him in spite of my warning."[295] This exaggeration—perhaps useful cinematically, in order to give Thorin a more dramatic character arc—shows a significant failure to understand "the core of the original," and the film suffers for it.

It seems that this same dragon-sickness that has infected Thorin has also had an influence on Jackson's character of Thranduil.[296] In the book, our favorite line of dialogue from the Elvenking is when he speaks to Bard before the battle. Bard has just called the dwarves fools and suggests that he and the

---

295  Tolkien, *Unfinished Tales*, 2020, 345.

296  Even though the Elvenking, or the King of the Woodland Realm, in *The Hobbit* is clearly Thranduil, we are not given his name until *The Lord of the Rings*: he remains nameless in Tolkien's story.

Elvenking should attack now. The Elvenking responds quite rationally: "Long will I tarry, ere I begin the war for gold... Let us hope still for something that will bring reconciliation." He then acknowledges that the Men and Elves have the advantage of numbers "if in the end it must come to unhappy blows." This is important because Tolkien's elves are not evil or bloodthirsty—he says, of the Elvenking and his people, "Still elves they were and remain, and that is Good People." That's why he will wait to attack, it's why he still hopes to reconcile with Thorin, and it's why he describes the possible battle as "unhappy blows."

It's hard to see Jackson's Thranduil as "Good People" in any sense of the word through most of the films, as he has been turned into another of the multiple antagonists in the story. Whether this is a demand of the "canons of narrative art" may be debatable, but it seems to us that it was more of a choice by Jackson to make the films—the final film in particular—darker and heavier in tone. Again, trying to match *The Lord of the Rings* instead of telling the story of *The Hobbit*. And another example of exaggeration that reveals a lack of understanding of "the core of the original."

There were so many changes to the films that showed either "exaggeration" or "the intrusion of unwarranted matter" that we could spend another several pages going through them, but a simple list of bullet points will suffice:

- Were-worms (mentioned in the book, yes—as a mythical, not real, creature)

- Azog in nearly every other scene (and Bolg the Orc appearing at all)

- Alfrid, the sly servant of the Master of Lake-town

- The repeated attempts to portray pipe-weed as some sort of narcotic

- Radagast's "Rabbits of Unusual Size"[297]

---

297    Blatantly stolen from *The Princess Bride's* Rodents of Unusual Size.

- Bilbo's already-apparent "addiction" to the One Ring

- Six Flags Over Mirkwood's new flume ride: The Barrels of Certain Doom

- Attempting to drown a dragon in molten gold

- Kili and Tauriel's adolescent crush[298]

- Nuclear Galadriel

- Thranduil's Elk of Condescension

Before you get too upset at us for saying some unkind things about Jackson's *Hobbit* films, let's be clear: we really liked *The Lord of the Rings* films. The *Hobbit* films, even taken strictly as cinema—forgetting that they were an adaptation of Tolkien's book—simply weren't all that good. And the experts agreed: *Rings* earned a total of thirty Academy Award nominations, winning seventeen of them. *The Return of the King* alone holds the record for eleven wins (tied with *Titanic* and *Ben-Hur*). On the other hand, the *Hobbit* films were nominated for a grand total of seven (none for the final movie), and won only a single award: a scientific and engineering award. Critics agreed as well: the average score on Rotten Tomatoes for the three LotR films is 93 percent, while the average for the *Hobbit* films is 65 percent, a score actually lower than that of the Rankin/Bass version of *The Hobbit* from 1977.

That last comparison is an interesting one, because it highlights both the risk of making a movie too short and the risk of making a movie too long. We lamented the failure of the Rankin/Bass version due, in part, to its compressing the book into seventy-five minutes. Jackson's version has the opposite problem, stretching a 95,000-word book into nearly *nine hours* of film. Jackson runs the *Hobbit* films, then, at a pace of 179 words per

---

298  Arguably, this entry should have received its own paragraph, but we know there is absolutely nothing we can say that will comfort those who appreciate this fanfic "ship." Perhaps we can salvage some of your respect by saying we have no quarrel with Tauriel herself, only the absurd idea of an Elf-Dwarf romance and the poor and childish way it was written in the movie. Never mind the fact that it manages to cheapen both the friendship between Legolas and Gimli *and* the love between Aragorn and Arwen.

minute of film—while *The Lord of the Rings*, with a length of over eleven hours, was filmed at a pace of 705 words per minute. It's no wonder, then, that stretching out *The Hobbit* to a length of nearly *four times* that of *The Lord of the Rings* led to quite a bit of that "exaggeration" and "intrusion of unwarranted matter" and the loss of "the core of the original."

# So Why Do We Love It?

It should come as no surprise, given the discussion above, that we don't love these films nearly as much as we love Jackson's first film trilogy. But we confess that, after rewatching them in light of the Rankin/Bass and Bakshi adaptations, Jackson's *Hobbit* films seem...less terrible than before.[299] Jackson's vision of Middle-earth, demonstrated so well in his *Rings* films, still comes through, and there are many entertaining and moving moments. Yes, it almost completely misses all the important themes from Tolkien's story... yes, there are far more eye-rolling and cringey moments...but there are many positive elements as well. Most importantly, these films served as an entry into Middle-earth for many younger fans: those who were too young to watch *The Lord of the Rings* in theaters nearly a decade before. Fans who might never have read the books otherwise have watched these movies, bought *The Hobbit*, read it, and become immersed in Middle-earth.

Does that mean we recommend watching it? Weeeellllll, "recommend" is a strong word. We think it's worth watching at least once, even if it's only for the fantastic acting of Martin Freeman and a few of the dwarves, the rich visuals, and Howard Shore's music: but it will depend on your ability to forget Tolkien's version of the story long enough to enjoy the adventure these films provide. At the end of the day, it's a different story—one that we don't enjoy nearly as much as Tolkien's story, but that can be enjoyable enough on its own for a bit of fun.

---

299   Unlike Rotten Tomatoes, we'd give it a higher score than the Rankin/Bass edition.

# Why Alan Loves It

While I may not *love* Jackson's retelling of *The Hobbit*, I dislike it a lot less than I used to. I'm still really disappointed with Jackson's obvious dismissal of the role of luck and providence, and I roll my eyes more often than not. But it's still Middle-earth...or, to be more precise, Middle-earth-*adjacent*. I adore Freeman's acting, am still moved by Shore's music (though it is not the gold standard that his *Rings* score was), and genuinely love those moments where the dialogue is lifted straight from Tolkien's text. The scene of Thorin's death and his reconciliation with Bilbo—along with the funeral scene in the extended edition, nearly ninety seconds of wordless shots filled with poignancy—still bring me to tears. But, unlike *Rings*, I don't find myself going out of my way to watch it.

# Why Shawn Loves It

Honestly, there's been so much criticism leveled at Peter Jackson's *Hobbit* movies, and we've covered most of it here already, so I feel a little bit guilty piling on...but not that guilty. In case we haven't made the point by now, *The Hobbit* had no business whatsoever being made into three movies, let alone three movies as dark as *The Lord of the Rings;* but two—the original plan— might actually have worked. I can remember waiting with anticipation in the years between the trilogies, reading about how Jackson was going to bring in this or that bit from beyond *The Hobbit* (usually from the appendices of *The Lord of the Rings;* for example, the material about the White Council and Dol Guldur) and being excited that he was going to add all that stuff. So I don't think that any amount of additions to the source material would have doomed the films, even if all that stuff did just turn *The Hobbit* into a prequel to *The Lord of the Rings* instead of allowing it to tell its own story. Not to mention all the other stuff that was added that wasn't from the appendices, much of it not from Tolkien at all (looking at you, Alfrid).

But, for all of its flaws, Jackson's *Hobbit* trilogy does some things well. The casting of Martin Freeman as Bilbo was spot-on—not only does he do a great job portraying the everyman-in-over-his-head written by Tolkien, but he also manages to capture many of the quirks Ian Holm gave the character in the *Rings* movies. Andy Serkis is, of course, brilliant as Gollum, even if the "Riddles in the Dark" scene misses some of the core of the original. And, say whatever else you will about him, Peter Jackson has absolutely nailed the look and feel of Middle-earth, once again.

In the last chapter on Jackson's *Lord of the Rings*, I mentioned that the flaws of those films are easier to swallow because the filmmakers had love for their source material and their project. And that, to me, is the missing piece of the puzzle that is *The Hobbit*. While Jackson no doubt loves Tolkien's book (if not perhaps as much as he loves *The Lord of the Rings*), it is absolutely clear that the love for the project that made *The Lord of the Rings* work was simply not there for the production of *The Hobbit*. Whether because Jackson was hesitant to make it in the first place, or because he felt like he was winging it after stepping in for del Toro, or because he just got sick at a critical time; the absence of that love is felt, and I think that's why *The Hobbit* trilogy failed to be everything it could have been.

With that said, it's still the second-best adaptation of Tolkien's works to hit the screen so far—and that has not changed with anything I've seen recently. So, while it's not something I've any interest in rewatching year after year (or even once every five years), I would definitely say I love that it's there, and that it has brought yet another new generation of fans to Tolkien's world.

PART III

# CONCERNING FANDOM:
# EXPRESS YOURSELF
# AS A TOLKIEN FAN

## CHAPTER 13

# EXPLORING THE TOLKIEN FANDOM

Up to now, we've spent a lot of time in this book talking about the work of others: writers, artists, scholars, actors, set designers, filmmakers...and of course, Professor Tolkien himself. In this last section of the book, we want to talk about *you:* the Tolkien fan.

As we discussed in Part I, Tolkien's aim in his fantasy—or, for what it's worth, what he believed was the mark of successful fantasy—was to enable readers to engage in a kind of "Secondary Belief." This means creating a "Secondary World" which the reader's mind can enter, and which is believable even though they know it is fictional, because that world has an "inner consistency of reality": consistent rules that make sense within the confines of that world (such as, for example, Elves are immortal, but they're not always happy about it; wizards are magical in their way, but they don't go around casting Delayed Blast Fireball on unsuspecting trolls; and eagles will never, ever fly over holes in the earth to drop jewelry into them), and a world that feels real and lived in. The second part of the equation (the real-and-lived-in part) is largely achieved by Tolkien's magnificent world-building: the fully developed mythology, the centuries' worth of epic history, the languages that show signs of having developed over time, just like real-world languages do. And these exist over a variety of cultures across the Middle-earth landscape: Elves, Dwarves, Hobbits, and many nations of Men, each with their own history, mythology, language, and (certainly to judge by the incredible scenes we've been treated to in visual adaptations) aesthetics of visual art. Tolkien's invented world did not just introduce us to one fantasy culture, like J.K. Rowling's Ministry of Magic or Frank Herbert's Fremen of Arrakis; it introduced us to an entire world of them.

So perhaps it is no surprise that different fans latch onto different aspects of Middle-earth. Some fans connect deeply with a particular culture: some love the Rohirrim, while others delve deeply into Dwarf-culture. Some love Elves; and maybe they're really fond of the Noldorin Elves, while others can't look past the whole Fëanor thing (we know, it takes a lot to look past it) and latch onto the Sindar, or the Silvan Elves. Some cosplay as beautiful Elvish princesses or rugged Rangers, while others prefer to live out their Middle-earth fantasies baking *lembas* or devising menus and recipes for mushroom-filled Hobbit meals that would make Mrs. Maggot proud. Still others latch onto a specific aspect of Tolkien's world-building, like languages or maps. Some show their fandom by writing essays, giving lectures—or, dare we say, recording podcasts and writing books—while others make it a mission to track down rare (or otherwise valuable, objectively or subjectively) editions of Tolkien's published books.

Simply put, there are as many ways to be a Tolkien fan as there are...well, Tolkien fans. That's right, you are unique. Whether you're only just now being introduced to the exciting world of Middle-earth, or you've been steeped in it for years, there is no one else in the world who is going to be a fan of *exactly what* makes you a fan of Tolkien's work, and in *exactly the same way* that you are. But in this next section, we explore some of the many ways Tolkien fans do express themselves; some of the niches of fandom we've come across during our time in the fan community. We hope that these last few chapters will help you find your precise niche in the Tolkien fandom.

# CHAPTER 14

# EMBRACE YOUR INNER DRAGON: COLLECTING TOLKIEN

*"You may be interested to hear that a reprint of
The Fellowship seems already to be needed. But I do not suppose
the first printing was very large."*

—J.R.R. Tolkien, from a September 1954 letter to Naomi Mitchison less
than two months after the publication of The Fellowship of the Ring[300]

As we mentioned in the first chapter of this book, the initial print run of
*The Hobbit* was 1,500 copies. It was published in September of 1937, and
by December of that year, that entire print run had sold out. The second
printing of 2,300 copies lasted until early 1942.[301] In recent years, a first-

---

300   Carpenter, *Letters*, No. 154.

301   Over four hundred copies from the second printing were lost in a warehouse fire caused by a bombing in
      November 1940, during World War II, making this already-small printing even smaller in the end. For more
      on this and the history of printings of *The Hobbit* and *The Lord of the Rings*, we recommend visiting
      TolkienBooks.net.

edition copy of *The Hobbit* sold at auction for £137,000 (about $171,000 today), believed to be the most expensive Tolkien book ever sold. The copy in question had been signed by J.R.R. Tolkien and gifted to one of his former students, and was in near-perfect condition with the dust jacket intact—a rare find indeed. Still, it's not uncommon for first-edition UK *Hobbit*s in less prime condition, without a dust jacket, to go for upwards of £6,000 (about $7,500).

In 2015, the London-based collectibles dealer Stanley Gibbons ranked *The Hobbit* at number two on the list of the most expensive first editions published in the twentieth century, behind F. Scott Fitzgerald's *The Great Gatsby* (the list was compiled prior to the record-breaking sale mentioned in the previous paragraph, though *Gatsby* still has that impressive sale beat, so *The Hobbit* is still at number two). *The Lord of the Rings* weighed in at number six. While it's not entirely clear whether it's the enduring appeal of Tolkien's works, the fact that they've been printed so many times and in so many languages, or just the delightfully obsessive nature of Tolkien fans, Tolkien collecting has always been a big part of the fandom.

# SOUNDS FUN! BUT...

Yes? What concerns do you still have? What do we have to do to get you into a brand-new Tolkien collection today?

## It Just Seems Like It'll Take Up a Lot of Space. And Time. And Money.

Weeeellll...yeah. It can. But it doesn't have to. There are many different ways to collect Tolkien, and many different kinds of collectors. Chasing down rare and expensive first editions is just *one* way to be a Tolkien collector.

Speaking to us on *The Prancing Pony Podcast* a few years ago,[302] our friend Jeremy Edmonds, founder of the Tolkien Collector's Guide website and community (tolkienguide.com), suggested that *anyone* can consider themselves a collector, if they have lots of Tolkien books (no specific number; just the right size for what you're interested in right now) and they had a purpose for getting them.

What qualifies as a "purpose"? Well, how about "I love reading Tolkien and I just want to have a copy of all his published works"? That absolutely qualifies you as a collector.

How about, "I really love *The Hobbit*, and I want to own a copy of every edition that's been published in English"? Yep, you're a collector too.

"I really love *The Hobbit*, but I don't need all the English editions. However, I'm a trained classicist and I'd like to have a copy of *The Hobbit* translated into Latin, and a copy of every translation in every Romance language so I can compare the syntax." Yes, you too are a collector.

There are so many ways to be a collector that there's no right or wrong way to do it. Whether your interest is in collecting various editions of a particular book, or books on a certain theme (like collecting Tolkien's various linguistic journals and papers), books illustrated by a particular artist (or just different artists in general), there is no wrong way to be a collector. And of course, there's lots of collectible material that's not even *by* Tolkien: scholarly writings *about* Tolkien, fan fiction, fanzines and media, "ephemera" (material meant to exist only for a short time, like materials related to plays, musicals, and movies), and stuff related to the movies—even those old Burger King glasses with Frodo and Gandalf on them—can be collectible. And in the twenty-first century, digital collecting is becoming a thing, too: collecting (legal) scans of fanzines and papers, ebooks, and so on...so you can be a

---

302    Episode 224.

collector without even dedicating a shelf to it in your living room, just a few gigabytes on your hard drive.

And even if you intend to collect physical books, keep in mind that rarity alone is not going to make something valuable. Chad High, an admin and moderator at the Tolkien Collector's Guide website, spoke to us and observed that value is subjective, and depends on both an individual collector's desire to have a certain item, and the level of competition for that item: rarity typically contributes to the second factor (competition, and desirability for a wider group of collectors), but value can also be derived purely from an item's worth to a single individual. At heart, High says, an interest in collecting stems not from a desire to invest and make money on appreciating value, but from "a passion for the world that J.R.R. Tolkien created, and wanting to connect with the man and his works in some way."

## I Don't Know. Collecting Still Seems a Little... Obsessive? Hoardy?

We know there's a stereotype out there about collectors, that they obsessively hoard books like bars of gold in Fort Knox, never taking their precious trophies out to read or enjoy them or let others see them. And while we suppose it takes all kinds of people to move the world, our experience of Tolkien collectors (including ourselves, though we have friends who have forgotten more about this hobby than we will ever know) is that they are Tolkien fans first and foremost, and are motivated by love and appreciation just like any other fan; not to mention generosity, as much as desire. It's no surprise that the collectors we've spoken to tell us there's a real joy and satisfaction in finding that perfect new item to add to one's collection (and we've felt it ourselves), but they've also told us that there are unexpected joys to be had from helping others make their way through the world of collecting, too. High told us that, next to finding just the right item, another thing that makes his day as a collector is helping others "with information or advice on how to do the same thing for their collection and their item that they want." And Jeremy Edmonds says that a great day for him as a collector is when he discovers something he didn't even know he wanted: "It happens more than you think, even after decades of collecting. Other collectors sharing their discoveries and recent acquisitions with each other is a fantastic part of the community...and sharing that discovery with others is truly what drives me and a lot of other passionate collectors that I know."

But of course, there are bad days, too: finding that perfect item when you don't have the money or the means to make the purchase, and having to see someone else snap it up; getting taken advantage of by shady sellers; items getting lost in the mail: all of these are very real risks and experiences. But they're all part of the game, as it were. Andrew Ferguson, also known as Trotter on Tolkien Collector's Guide, advises new collectors to "get used to this, as you are not going to get every item that is missing from your collection. It is an important part of being a collector." *C'est la vie*. But clearly, the image some people have of collectors as weird little goblins hiding in caves full of moldy old books, obsessively adding up the values of their decaying first editions while guarding the door against intruders, is completely false. The collectors we know, even the most well-hoarded, do it for the love...and for the community.

## How Will I Know When My Collection Is Complete?

That's easy. It will never be complete! Or it will be complete when you feel like you've got everything you need; when you look at your glorious collection, sigh contentedly, and go to sleep that night without a single desire in the world.[303]

---

303  But seriously, take it from us: it will never be complete.

# Okay, You've Convinced Me. But What About All That Collector Jargon? Edition? Impression? Limited Edition? Help!

You've come to the right place, young Padawan. (Wrong fandom? We don't care.)[304]

First of all, an "edition" is all the copies of a book that are printed from the same setting of type. In the earlier days of printing (and we're not just talking about, like, Gutenberg-early, but even several decades ago), type was set manually. The printer would set the type (i.e., put little dies in the shape of each letter on a big machine to spell out all the words) and print off as many copies as had been ordered.

If all those copies sold, and the publisher had to order more (like *The Hobbit* in December 1937), the printer would print more. But unless serious changes were needed, the new batch of copies would be printed from the same typeset as the previous batch; setting type manually was a painstaking process, and typically the printers would keep the type set in storage waiting for the next printing to be ordered.[305] When the order for new copies came in, the type would be taken out and new copies printed, but because the

---

304 For this section and the next, we are again indebted to Jeremy Edmonds of Tolkien Collector's Guide (tolkienguide.com) and his appearance on Episode 224 of *The Prancing Pony Podcast*. For more information, we also recommend *ABC for Book Collectors* by John Carter and Nicolas Barker.

305 Sometimes the printer *didn't* keep the type ready for another printing. Because Rayner Unwin had feared *The Lord of the Rings* would not be successful, in 1954–55 the printer ended up putting the type for *Fellowship* away after the first printing (in their defense, putting all that type away would have freed up a *lot* of those little metal letter blocks in their inventory). When the book sold like hotcakes and Allen & Unwin ordered a second printing, the printer reset the type in a hurry and reprinted the new copies with numerous errors introduced through the rush reset. While technically this could qualify as a new edition, it is always referred to as the second impression of the first edition. According to Hammond and Scull's *Reader's Companion*, the facts behind this resetting were not discovered until 1992.

typeset had not changed, this was not a new edition, but a new "printing" (or "impression"), thus, the first edition, second printing.

These days, it's all done with computers, and it's a whole lot easier to set type on a computer than it was in the days of manual typesetting. But the fundamentals are still the same: if a new print run is ordered from what is essentially the same text, that's a new *impression*. If significant changes are introduced to the text, this is considered a new *edition* and the first print run is the first impression of that edition. As an example, *The Lord of the Rings* underwent many impressions for the first ten years after it was published; the second edition didn't come out until 1965, in response to the Ace Books fiasco.

## The What?

Oh man. We *totally* forgot to mention this earlier. Our bad. Quick digression here. It won't be long, we promise.

The original US edition of *The Lord of the Rings* was published in hardcover by Houghton Mifflin (which still publishes US hardcover and paperback editions of Tolkien's works, though it has since been acquired by HarperCollins, which publishes the UK editions) between 1954 and 1956. However, it seems that the pages which were bound and published by Houghton Mifflin had actually been printed in the UK for Allen & Unwin, and exported from the UK to the US publisher. Because of this, *The Lord of the Rings* for those first few years existed in a sort of limbo/loophole/insert-other-ambiguous-l-word-here in American copyright law. This placed it, arguably, in the public domain in the United States.

At least, *someone* argued that.

In 1965, Ace Books (still well known today as a publisher of science fiction and fantasy books) decided to capitalize on this perceived loophole and publish the first paperback editions of Tolkien's works in the United States. They sold their paperback editions for the low-low price of seventy-five cents per volume, making it possible for budding fantasy fans and bud-smoking hippies to acquire a complete copy of Tolkien's magnum opus for just a little over two bucks.

There wasn't much that Tolkien, Allen & Unwin, or Houghton Mifflin could do about this at the time, except to revise the text of *The Lord of the Rings* for the purpose of obtaining a fresh American copyright. So that's just what Tolkien did, and sent it to Houghton Mifflin in August 1965. This new version of the text was published in the US in (legal) paperback by Ballantine Books in 1965, after which point the changes were made to the UK edition by Allen & Unwin for their *second edition* in 1966. Houghton Mifflin published their second hardcover edition in the US in 1967.

As for Ace Books, they did the right thing by agreeing to pay royalties owed to Professor Tolkien and to let their pirate edition go out of print—but not before selling some 100,000 or more copies. Ace paperback copies can still be found from time to time on the collectors' market, and are quite sought after by some collectors. Of particular note are the artworks for the covers, done by frequent Ace cover illustrator Jack Gaughan. Though they are somewhat idiosyncratic—with a very Moses-on-the-mountain-looking Gandalf on the cover of *Fellowship*, and a Nazgûl on the cover of *Two Towers* riding a creature which can only be called a "pega-bat" (or "bat-asus")—as Hammond and Scull note in their *Reader's Guide*, they "are comparatively true to the story (or perhaps one should say, they deviate from it less)"[306] than the art for the authorized Ballantine paperbacks released shortly thereafter, notoriously painted by Barbara Remington with their mysterious psychedelic fruits and emus. We're not kidding.

---

306    Scull & Hammond, *Reader's Guide*, 2017, 563.

# Wow.

Yeah. But we digress. Back to book collecting.

The good news for collectors is that all of the information you need to determine when a book was published, which impression it is, and even (usually) which edition it is, is all contained in the book itself. Typically, the publisher will include all the relevant information on the copyright page; for example, a 2020 US hardcover edition of *Unfinished Tales* with illustrations by Alan Lee, John Howe, and Ted Nasmith indicates on the cover page:

> First published in hardback by HarperCollinsPublishers 1992... First published in Great Britain by Unwin Hyman 1980

Followed by copyrights for the text in 1980, then the illustrations in 2007 and 2020. The presence of the 2020 copyright tells us we are looking at the 2020 edition of *Unfinished Tales*.

Most books will clearly indicate which impression of the edition you're holding, too, as long as you know what to look for. Sometimes (particularly with older books) one gets lucky enough to see very clearly printed on the copyright page: "Third impression," or whatever. But even if it's not that obvious, the impression number is usually hidden in plain sight. Near the bottom of the copyright page is usually a row of numbers, either counting down:

10 9 8 7 6 5 4 3 2 1

Or counting up:

1 2 3 4 5 6 7 8 9 10

Or alternating in a way that looks almost random until you look at it closely:

1 3 5 7 9 10 8 6 4 2

The lowest number in that row tells you which impression the copy is from. Why did they do it this way? Simple, really. When setting the type for the first impression of the edition, the printers would just include all the numbers from 1 to 10 (or sometimes more) to be ready for the next few impressions. When the time came to print the second impression, all they had to do to mark the printing as such was remove the little 1. Then remove the 2 for the third impression, and so on. Of course, like Nigel Tufnel's amplifier, sometimes impressions go to eleven...for these, the printers would just start the process again with a row of numbers from 11 to 20.

As for what makes a "special edition" or "collector's edition," that's really all up to the publisher. HarperCollins does tend to release collector's editions of Tolkien's books from time to time in hardcover, usually printed on higher-quality paper with better bindings, often with slipcases and other goodies like maps, art, or even supplemental media like audio CDs. These certainly make for a lovely presentation and add color and oohs and ahhs to any Tolkien collector's "shelfie,"[307] and are absolutely worth collecting. But these should not be confused with *limited* editions, which are typically—well, as the name suggests—limited to a number of copies (250 or 500 is a common number), usually hand-numbered and often signed by an artist or editor, even Christopher Tolkien himself.

# WHAT ABOUT OTHER
# TERMS LIKE "FINE"

---

307  What's a "shelfie?" It's a picture of your bookshelf taken by you yourself, of course, usually for posting on social media and earning the admiration and envy of your fellow Tolkien nerds.

# AND "VERY FINE"?
# WHAT'S THAT ABOUT?

In addition to the edition and the impression, you're also going to want to know the condition of a book that you're considering buying to add to your collection. That's where terms like "Fine," "Good," "Fair," and so on come in. Here's a quick guide to book conditions for the newbie collector. If collector value is what you're after, be aware that books acquired in the first three categories below can be expected to appreciate in value, as long as they are properly cared for:

- "As New," sometimes called "Very Fine"—the absolute best, perfect, pristine condition a book can be in. It's relatively rare to find books in "As New" condition, particularly books that were published a long time ago, because "As New" or "Very Fine" means that the book is virtually untouched since publication: it's never been placed on a shelf, thumbed through, or perhaps even opened—most likely it's been sitting in a box in a warehouse somewhere since the day it came off the press.

- "Fine"—almost as good, and a bit more within reach for any book that's had a previous owner: it may have been opened or read, but there is no damage or wear to the binding or paper. Aside from the normal aging that time subjects all of us to (books *and* people; we're certainly beginning to feel it), a book in Fine condition is more or less as good as new.

- "Near Fine" or "Very Good"—will show some signs of wear, but has no tears on either the binding or the paper. Depending on the seller, "Near Fine" may be slightly a cut above "Very Good" and may include only the hardest-to-spot flaws and blemishes.

Anything below this point is not going to retain collector value, but that doesn't mean books in these conditions are worthless. For certain collectors, particularly those who "just want the words" and are looking for particularly rare items, it may be worth considering books in the following conditions. Just keep in mind that these will be for your own use as reading copies, and you won't be able to sell them to put your kids through college:

Why We Love Middle-earth

- "Good"—this is more or less your average, run-of-the-mill "used book" that you'd find easily in a secondhand bookstore or thrift shop. It should not be missing any pages, but may have other defects that should be noted by the seller.

- "Fair"—books in this condition will show significant wear, and even tears and damage. Title pages, endpapers, and other stuff may be missing, but all the text pages and illustrations will be present. Other defects may be present that should be noted by the seller.

- "Poor"—caveat emptor. A book in Poor condition should have all the text, but illustrations, maps, and other stuff may be missing. There may be coffee stains, blood stains, or worse. But the text should more or less be there, or else the book won't even qualify as Poor.

Keep in mind that hardcover editions that still have a dust jacket will list two conditions: the first refers to the book, and the second refers to the dust jacket. So, if you find an old copy of *The Two Towers* in "Very Good/Good" condition, that means the book is in Very Good condition (with wear but no damage, as noted above), but the dust jacket is just Good (i.e., average, and may have some damage). It's worth noting that the dust jacket can make up to 90 percent of the value of the collectible book; while dust jackets are now highly prized for their beautiful cover art, blurbs, author information, and so on, once upon a time they were considered disposable and were discarded when the buyer brought the book home. For this reason—not to mention their fragility and the general ease with which a dust jacket can sprout legs and walk away—old dust jackets are extremely valuable, and very rare to find with the oldest books on the market.

# What About Collecting Stuff Besides Books? Toys, Figurines, Etc.?

That's another rabbit hole (hobbit-hole?) we could spend a *long* time going down. While collecting books is certainly attractive to many Tolkien fans—

after all, our Professor was a writer—and holds a place of prominence in many online collector communities like Tolkien Collector's Guide, the truth is that there is a *lot* more Tolkien-related stuff that can be collected. Brandon Wainerdi, a Director of Social Insights at Funko—a toy company that makes collectibles such as the wildly popular Pop! figures—told us "there is a misconception that collecting is all about books. And, indeed, it is a large part of it, just for the sake of the breadth of work and the number of editions and resources published." Wainerdi says "you could only collect Tolkien books for the rest of your days, and still never be close" to completing your collection, but there are "so many [other] avenues" available to collectors.

Toys and action figures based on *The Hobbit* and *The Lord of the Rings* have been around since the 1970s, when the first animated adaptations came out from Rankin/Bass and Ralph Bakshi, and of course the popularity of Peter Jackson's movies saw a huge surge in movie-related toys and memorabilia: not just action figures and playsets, but life-size swords (plastic ones, and also prop-quality replicas) and so much more. Although cool and no longer being manufactured, and certainly worth collecting if you like them—after all, it's *your* collection—be aware that items like this don't tend to appreciate in value as much as you think, even if kept in the box. Wainerdi reminds us that toys related to the Peter Jackson movies were mass-produced, which means there are a lot of them out there. They can still be very fun as toys, and even well-made, but they are unlikely to take on the rarity that tends to contribute to appreciating value. Even toys marked at the time as "special" or "collector's items" may not appreciate in value as much as one might assume.

Speaking of Pop! figures—those delightfully big-headed coal-eyed figurines available in the likeness of everyone from Mike Ehrmantraut from *Breaking Bad* to Eleven from *Stranger Things* to LeBron James and Billie Eilish— oh, yeah, there are a lot of them based on Tolkien. Fellowship heroes, Ringwraiths, even an extra-large-sized Balrog from *Fellowship of the Ring* (which we love, really we do, but we need to talk about those wings). And there's more to Funko than just Pops: the now-discontinued Rock Candy line focused primarily on great female characters of pop culture, including Tolkien's own Arwen and Éowyn.

For years, even before the movies, there have been board games and video games (as discussed earlier in this book) based on Middle-earth. Not to mention chess sets, which are ubiquitous enough that they have their own section on the Tolkien Collector's Guide website, aside from board games. And there is so, so much art that we will need to give it its own chapter in a future book: prints and originals from high-profile artists like Alan Lee and Ted Nasmith as well as up-and-coming artists like Jenny Dolfen and Emily Austin—both of whom were featured in the 2023 edition of the Tolkien Calendar, and the latter of whom we were fortunate to get to work with on this book. All of the aforementioned artists are primarily inspired by the books, though there are also many artists inspired by the film adaptations, and a sizeable community has sprung up around the collecting and reselling of "alternative movie posters" (AMPs), unofficial posters for movies (usually older movies) which are true works of art, in contrast to the typically cobbled-together-from-still-images official posters released by the studios; the AMP phenomenon has touched on seemingly every pop culture universe with any cultural impact, from *Star Wars* and Disney to Universal monster movies and Godzilla, and there are more than a few *Lord of the Rings* and *The Hobbit* AMPs to be found.

If you're interested in collecting Tolkien, our advice is simply: go for it! As Edmonds said on our podcast, there is no minimum size or minimum value you have to achieve to call yourself a "collector." Collect what you want; the advice we hear from collectors is to pick an area/topic/type of book you're interested in (at least to start with) that will satisfy the "thrill of the hunt" for you right now, and focus on that. Don't worry about the future. And don't worry if your interests change over time, either. Walking down one road of Tolkien collecting may very well open up new pathways where you least expect them. Your interests may change over time, and that's cool too. There is simply no right or wrong way to collect.

And, since you're here because you presumably love these books—and movies—anyway, don't you already have *some* kind of a collection? You're not starting something new, just adding to what you already have.

# WHY ALAN LOVES IT

If there is one aspect of the Tolkien fandom that has grabbed me more than most, it is collecting. Maybe it's the kid in me who had to have all the Matchbox cars;[308] or maybe it's the adolescent in me who needed to complete sets of baseball or football cards.[309] Whatever the cause, the collecting bug has most definitely bit me—and I have to scratch that itch from time to time!

Of course, like most collectors, I suffer from a shortage of both time and money: I can't afford to buy whatever my heart desires, and I don't have the time to hunt down special finds at bargain prices. And so I've had to set a reasonable—and, I hope—achievable collector's goal: I want to collect a UK first edition, first impression copy of each of Tolkien's works *after The Hobbit* and *The Lord of the Rings*, as those (and earlier academic works) are well beyond the means of a humble podcaster. And though I have many, I still have yet to track down certain volumes—so I have temporarily settled for US first edition, first impression copies of some works (such as *Farmer Giles of Ham*). I'd also be happy to ignore my first impression standard to obtain later printings of first editions of *Hobbit* and *Rings*, as those *might* just be obtainable without selling off a kidney.

I'm also a complete sucker for limited editions—not just *collector's* editions, mind, but the actual numbered editions—which are usually signed by the

---

308  Don't even *talk* to me about the substandard Hot Wheels.
309  Adolescence goes into one's thirties, right? Right??

artist and, sometimes, by Christopher Tolkien.[310] I have a few of these, and they are the pride of my collection.

That's how I ended up with a dozen copies or so *each* of *The Hobbit*, *The Lord of the Rings*, and *The Silmarillion*. But you don't have to collect like I do—or even collect *what* I collect—in order to enjoy collecting Tolkien. Maybe you want foreign-language paperbacks...maybe you want all the deluxe editions sorted by color...maybe you have significant resources and want a copy of each impression of *The Hobbit*. Whatever you choose, find something that drives you—but that won't drive you to bankruptcy!

# WHY SHAWN LOVES IT

I never really considered myself a "collector" until...oh, a couple of years ago, when we had Jeremy Edmonds on our show. I mean, sure, I suppose I have more Tolkien books than the average person; and I certainly want more. But I've never really chased after the limited editions, signed copies, first impressions, or any of that stuff. I've always "just wanted the words." And yes, "just wanting the words" could explain much of my collection, like the shelf of mass-market paperbacks that first opened the door to Middle-earth for me many years ago, now held together by a little hope and a lot of packing tape; or the reprints of linguistic journals *Vinyar Tengwar* and *Parma Eldalamberon* which I display as proudly as if they were original printings.

But of course, "just wanting the words" doesn't explain the multiple copies of *The Hobbit*—including two facsimile first editions[311]—and *The Lord of the Rings*, or the hardcover illustrated copy of *The Silmarillion* I bought at a moot one year just so I could get it signed by Ted Nasmith. And it doesn't

---

310  There are collectors who seek volumes signed by the Professor himself, but again—as with 1/1 copies of *The Hobbit* and *The Lord of the Rings*, and the Undying Lands, some things will be forever beyond my mortal reach.

311  First printed in 2016, the "facsimile first edition" is a replica of the first edition of *The Hobbit*, complete with the first-edition text; most notably Bilbo's sanitized version of the encounter with Gollum in the caves in Chapter Five. This facsimile edition made the first-edition text more accessible to readers for the first time in decades. Shawn bought two of them.

explain the figurines on the shelf, nor the works of art—many prints and a few originals, purchased directly from the artists—that hang on my walls. It doesn't explain my ongoing hunt for a complete set of the Ace Books paperbacks. And it certainly doesn't explain the three boxes of action figures from the Peter Jackson films that I hoard in my attic. So yes, I've made peace with it: in my own small way, I am a collector.

But only in a small way. There are a handful of rarities that I am on the lookout for, and there are one or two Holy Grails that I would snap up regardless of price (within reason, I guess) if I ever saw them out in the wild. But they are few and far between.

So it was quite an epiphany for me to realize that collecting doesn't necessarily mean just going after the rarest, or most valuable, "collectible" items. And it's representative of the Tolkien fandom as a whole, I think: just like being a Tolkien fan in general, you can express your love for collecting however you want to. And when I stare at my bookshelf, I sometimes have the beautiful thought that, at the end of the day, all of us Tolkien fans are collectors, in one way or another.

# CHAPTER 15

# TALK LIKE AN ELF-GYPTIAN: TOLKIEN'S INVENTED LANGUAGES

*"This idea of using the linguistic faculty for amusement is however deeply interesting to me... The instinct for 'linguistic invention'—the fitting of notion to oral symbol, and pleasure in contemplating the new relation established, is rational... In these invented languages the pleasure is more keen than it can be even in learning a new language—keen though it is to some people in that case—because more personal and fresh, more open to experiment of trial and error."*

—*J.R.R. Tolkien, "A Secret Vice"*[312]

*"The invention of languages is the foundation. The 'stories' were made rather to provide a world for the languages than the reverse."*

—*J.R.R. Tolkien, from a 1955 letter*[313]

---

312  Tolkien, J.R.R., edited by Dimitra Fimi and Andrew Higgins. *A Secret Vice: Tolkien on Invented Languages.* HarperCollins, 2016, 15-16.

313  Carpenter, *Letters*, No. 165.

Tolkien's invented languages—by which we mean primarily the Elvish languages, Quenya or "High-elven" and Sindarin or "Grey-elven," though he did some work on other languages of Middle-earth as well, including Khuzdul (Dwarvish) and Adûnaic (the language of the Men of Númenor)—are among the most unique features of his Secondary World. While Tolkien was not the first fantasy author to ever dabble in "conlanging," that is, constructing fictitious languages for his fictional world,[314] he certainly went farther along with it than any fantasy writer before him, and farther than most fantasy writers to come after him.[315] Of course, it helped that Tolkien was a linguist by training, and he actually knew what he was doing. He had actually been playing around with language invention since he was a child, first when he was taught a language invented by two cousins, and then later when he created his own language called *Nevbosh* ("New Nonsense") with one of the same cousins. He had always shown a tremendous aptitude for real-world languages; he started learning Latin from his mother when he was only four years old, and had added Greek, French, and German to his polyglot repertoire before he was in his teens. By the time he graduated from high school, he was teaching himself Gothic—an extinct East Germanic language now known only from just a few surviving texts—and was scribbling in it in his textbooks, as one fan discovered when she found one of those textbooks in a used bookstore decades later.[316] And of course, his knowledge of Finnish,

---

314  The idea of developing a fictitious language for an imaginary place in a work of fiction is at least as old as the sixteenth century, when a friend of Sir Thomas More named Peter Giles created an alphabet for, and four lines of poetry in, a language he invented for the Utopians of More's *Utopia*. More recently, but still predating Tolkien, Edgar Rice Burroughs created snippets of languages for the apes in his *Tarzan* novels, as well as for the inhabitants of Mars ("Barsoom") and Venus ("Amtor") in two series of pulp science fiction books. The Martian or "Barsoomian" language first explored in Burroughs's 1917 novel *A Princess of Mars* was expanded by linguist and professional conlanger Paul Frommer for the 2012 film adaptation *John Carter*.

315  Much like Edgar Rice Burroughs before him, George R.R. Martin wrote bits of Dothraki and High Valyrian speech for his *A Song of Ice and Fire* book series, but the languages weren't properly developed until linguist David J. Peterson was hired to do the job for the HBO series *Game of Thrones*. For more on how these languages were developed, as well as Peterson's tips on creating your own conlang, check out his excellent book *The Art of Language Invention*. Even Klingon, that gold standard of conlang, started out with just a few made-up words; actor James Doohan—yes, Scotty—created the first words of Klingon spoken at the beginning of 1979's *Star Trek: The Motion Picture*. The Klingon language was developed more fully for *Star Trek III: The Search for Spock* in 1984, by (once again, a professional linguist) Marc Okrand, whom we interviewed on *The Prancing Pony Podcast* in Episode 88.

316  Carpenter, *Letters*, No. 272.

Welsh, and Old English is well-known; plus, as we noted in Part I, he did actually work for a dictionary.

So it can easily be deduced from all of this that, while Tolkien was neither the first, nor the last, author to introduce invented languages into his fantasy work, he certainly took a unique approach to his conlanging—an approach informed by a lifetime spent studying and inventing languages, becoming intimately acquainted with the close relationship between languages and the histories and values of the cultures that speak them, and contemplating the relationships between sounds and meanings, which often seem random in the real world, but according to Tolkien, need not be so.[317] He took very much the approach we might expect from a scholar and linguist who, as his friend C.S. Lewis put it, "had been inside language."[318] This unique approach—and indeed, the unique position that language held in Tolkien's fantasy world; for if nothing else, the Professor was certainly unique in making language part and parcel of his fiction—has led to a huge amount of interest in Tolkien's invented languages on the part of fans, which has led not only to clubs and books dedicated to learning and conversation in Elvish and Dwarvish languages, as well as a great deal of philological study in the way Tolkien's languages developed in his own lifetime, it has even sparked an interest in language creation for many Tolkien fans who wish to follow in the Professor's footsteps.

But it is worth noting that Tolkien's approach to language invention was always the approach of a philologist; meaning that it was always the approach of a person who studied language and its evolution over time, rather than the approach of someone who studied language for purposes of conversation. Tolkien was a scholar of ancient tongues, not a United Nations interpreter. While this may seem like a hair-splitting distinction, in reality it has a significant

---

317  Readers interested in Tolkien's ideas about the relationship between the sound of a word and its meaning should look into the critical edition of *A Secret Vice*, edited by Dimitra Fimi and Andrew Higgins (interviewed on *The Prancing Pony Podcast*, Episode 20). This edition includes a short "Essay on Phonetic Symbolism" by Tolkien that explores this concept.

318  Curiously, this phrase appeared in the obituary of Tolkien published in *The Times* on September 3, 1973. Lewis actually died in 1963, ten years before Tolkien, but Carpenter states unequivocally that this phrase was "undoubtedly written by C.S. Lewis long before Tolkien's death."

impact on how fans approach the study of Tolkien's languages. As Carl F. Hostetter, a noted scholar of linguistics in Tolkien, celebrated member of the Elvish Linguistic Fellowship, editor of two journals on Tolkien's languages, and most recently editor of Tolkien's own manuscripts in the volume *The Nature of Middle-earth*, put it in a 2006 essay "Elvish as She Is Spoke," the information Tolkien left behind about the languages he created essentially amounts to

> ...a sequence of more-or-less complete and more-or-less variant and even conflicting versions of historical grammars...describing *versions of his invented languages as they were conceived at various points in his lifetime;* together with a smaller number of more-or-less variant and even conflicting versions of lexicons containing what are by the standards of living languages and even of many dead languages quite small and selective vocabularies... Even assuming that the sometimes profound differences among the versions of the languages could somehow be smoothed out into a cohesive and consistent system, we are thus left at best with what amounts to traditional historical grammars of two poorly attested, dead languages.[319]

In other words, Tolkien didn't write phrasebooks, grammars, or vocabulary lists for his fans (or even for himself) on "how to speak Elvish." Hostetter even asserts in his essay that one of the reasons Tolkien didn't include more Quenya or Sindarin in his books is because he—Tolkien himself, the creator of the languages—*was not fluent in them.*[320] Creating standardized Elvish languages for everyday use was not what Tolkien was interested in; he was interested in creating these languages for his own philological and conlanging pleasure, using them to come up with personal names and place-names for his mythology that weren't just gibberish, and exploring the ways languages

---

319  (Emphasis added.) Hostetter, Carl F. "'Elvish as She Is Spoke,'" in *The Lord of the Rings 1954-2004: Scholarship in Honor of Richard E. Blackwelder*, edited by Wayne G. Hammond & Christine Scull. Marquette University Press, 2006, 238-39.

320  It's important to note here that Hostetter is not being inflammatory with this statement, nor does his view seem to be a controversial one. Hostetter was, in fact, one of a few people trusted by Christopher Tolkien himself to be an editor of Professor Tolkien's linguistic papers, which he has done as editor of the journal *Vinyar Tengwar*, a publication of the Elvish Linguistic Fellowship.

might diverge over time among disparate tribes of the same Elvish race, separated by geography, experience, wisdom, and grief. Okay, and maybe occasionally writing a snippet of sweet poetry to give to Galadriel, or a sexy greeting to give to Frodo to impress some Elves he meets randomly on the road. But not a standard language, meant to be taught to fans to learn and then exchange greetings in it themselves, certainly not with such prescriptivism as to put forth any idea that *this is the way to say XYZ in Sindarin/Quenya*. Another way of saying this is to say that Tolkien's exercise in conlanging was a *diachronic* one, primarily focused on examining changes over time; not a *synchronic* one, focused on reporting out the proper way of speaking Quenya or Sindarin at any given point in time. So instead of a standardized grammar, what we have from Tolkien are various vocabulary lists, conjugation charts, and syntax notes forming a "historical grammar" (in Hostetter's words) that shows how the languages developed over time— and "time" in this case meaning not simply the "in-universe" time of the language's development as Elves migrated from place to place in the history of the legendarium, but also "real time" as Tolkien the creator changed his mind about things over the course of decades of writing.

So one would be hard pressed—spoiler alert; we're going to say it's impossible—for fans to come up with one single, standardized, "proper" version of Quenya or Sindarin to learn and speak to one another, which we know Tolkien would agree with, bless, and call the correct mode of speaking his language.[321] This makes it different from Klingon, or High Valyrian or Dothraki, or other fantasy and science fiction conlangs one might look to that were developed with conversational usage in mind, and that continue to be developed by their original creators, Marc Okrand and David J. Peterson. Tolkien didn't conlang in quite the same way they did, and he didn't do it for

---

321 Even the forms of Quenya and Sindarin presented in the "finished" publication *The Lord of the Rings* cannot be said to be the "final" or "standard" form of these Elvish languages, because Tolkien made changes after *The Lord of the Rings* was published. Famously, the Quenya greeting recited by Frodo to a group of passing elves in Book I, Chapter 3: *"Elen síla lúmenn' omentielvo"* ("A star shines on the hour of our meeting") was not the original form of the greeting. The form in the 1954 edition was *"Elen síla lúmenn' omentielmo"* (with an M instead of a V in the last syllable). It was changed in the second edition, published in 1965... because this is Tolkien we're talking about.

the same reasons they did; and it's debatable whether Tolkien would even approve of fans' attempts to extract a single, "correct" form of "King's Elvish" to use for everyday conversation from his inherently historical, philological, diachronic linguistic exercise.

But that hasn't stopped fans from doing it, and some of them have done it very well. One of the most important names in this space is that of David Salo, himself a professional linguist by trade, who (much like Okrand with Klingon and Peterson with the languages of Martin's world) was hired to fill in the gaps in Tolkien's languages for their adaptation to the screen: all of the dialogue in Quenya, Sindarin, Khuzdul, and the Black Speech (at least, any such dialogue that didn't appear in the books, which is virtually all of it) in Peter Jackson's *The Lord of the Rings* and *The Hobbit* movies was translated into Elvish by Salo—an effort which required a great deal of invention on Salo's part, working from what Tolkien left behind to the extent possible. Since of course the Peter Jackson movies were many fans' first introduction to Tolkien's works and languages, many fans have understandably been interested in learning the languages as used in the movies, and have taken up the baton from the work of Salo (and others) to continue to develop the languages and use them conversationally.

The newly constructed, conversational, standardized forms of Tolkien's languages thus created are often called "Neo-" languages—as in "Neo-Quenya," "Neo-Khuzdul," etc.—to distinguish them from the (admittedly very mutable) forms of the languages that appear in Tolkien's own writings. And while Neo-Elvish, Neo-Khuzdul, and the rest have their fair share of detractors, with some critics calling them the conlanging equivalent of fanfiction, and deriding the exercise as "artificial" or even "silly," there are nonetheless very active and knowledgeable communities online dedicated to the art of reconstructing Tolkien's invented languages, with many well-respected individuals offering lessons, grammar and vocabulary resources, and even original compositions such as Neo-Sindarin poetry.[322]

# WHERE CAN I FIND OUT MORE?

Well, as is hopefully obvious from the last few paragraphs, it really depends on what you're after. But we'll start by telling you *don't skip the appendices!* At the back of *The Lord of the Rings* (which may be the back of *The Return of the King* if working from a three-volume edition, obvs) are two appendices focused on the languages and writing systems of Middle-earth: Appendix E ("Writing and Spelling") and Appendix F (particularly the first part, "The Languages and Peoples of the Third Age"). Once you get through that, the Appendix to *The Silmarillion* ("Elements in Quenya and Sindarin Names") provides a great basic vocabulary list of words and roots that appear in commonly found names.

After you read those, if you're interested primarily in the diachronic study of how Tolkien developed his languages over time, there are more of Tolkien's own writings to guide your way. *The Lost Road and Other Writings* (that's Volume V of The History of Middle-earth) contains some excellent linguistic material including the *Lhammas* ("assortment of languages") and the *Etymologies*, a lengthy glossary of Elvish roots with examples of some of the character and place-names they appear in. Volumes IX and XII of The History of Middle-earth, *Sauron Defeated* and *The Peoples of Middle-earth*, also contain some excellent linguistic material on the languages of Men of Númenor and the Dwarves.

---

322  The authors of this book would rather not take sides in what can often be a rather heated and angry debate between the "Neo-" adherents and those who insist that only Tolkien's own diachronic study of his languages should be considered. On the one hand, we've always been more interested in Tolkien's own words than fanfiction, and neither of us has ever had much interest in learning conversational Elvish. On the other hand, we don't go in for gatekeeping, and we happen to have noticed that even Tolkien attempted to reconstruct fragmentary languages for the purpose of writing in them: see Letter 272 in Carpenter's collection, and the story of Tolkien's interest in Gothic.

Then it's time to start shopping online for the journals of the Elvish Linguistic Fellowship (ELF—get it?). Since 1988, the ELF has dedicated itself to scholarly study, education, and publication of material related to Tolkien's languages, and in that time they have released a lot of material that's worth looking at, primarily in the form of two linguistic journals. *Vinyar Tengwar* ("Newsletters" in Quenya) started as a simple newsletter for the ELF, but for many years, under the editorial eye of the aforementioned Carl F. Hostetter, has been entrusted with the editing and publication of short essays and commentaries by J.R.R. Tolkien himself, on linguistic matters varying from Catholic prayers translated into Quenya to...Elvish telepathy,[323] along with commentary from the editors, who are some of the most knowledgeable people in the world on the matter of Tolkien's languages. As of the publication of this book, fifty issues of *Vinyar Tengwar* have been published, and they are all conveniently available for purchase online, collected and bound in sets of ten.

The other journal published by the ELF is *Parma Eldalamberon* ("Book of Elven Tongues"), edited by Christopher Gilson, which since the 1990s has been dedicated exclusively to publishing longer-form essays, grammar, and vocabulary lists written by Tolkien himself. Published somewhat sporadically—there have only been twelve issues since 1995, though each of them is a book in its own right—*Parma Eldalamberon* is also only sporadically available, except on the collector market; only around half of the issues are currently available for purchase. Fortunately, one of the issues that *is* available for purchase is an absolute must-have: issue 17, *Words, Phrases and Passages in Various Tongues in The Lord of the Rings*, which collects Tolkien's notes on the etymologies (i.e., word origins) of nearly all of the Elvish, Dwarvish, and Black Speech terminology used in the book. It's a word-nerd's dream, and a great introduction to this series of journals. Fans

---

323 Appearing in *Vinyar Tengwar* issue 39, "*Ósanwe-kenta*" or "Enquiry into the Communication of Thought" by Tolkien is an amazing analysis of telepathy among the Elves (as well as the Valar and Maiar, and yes, it is a thing in the books) that goes off on some fascinating tangents into the nature of the relationship between body and mind, and free will. It is among the most beloved entries in the history of *Vinyar Tengwar*, and often quoted on *The Prancing Pony Podcast*.

interested in finding out more should check out the ELF's website, elvish.org, or go straight to the *Parma Eldalamberon* website at eldalamberon.com.

If learning conversational Elvish is more what you're after, David Salo's book *A Gateway to Sindarin* is a popular introduction to Neo-Sindarin, and was originally published not long after Peter Jackson's *Lord of the Rings* films came out, so has the benefit of coming out after much of the *Vinyar Tengwar* and *Parma Eldalamberon* material, which has been considered in Salo's reconstruction of the language. Even more recently, linguist Fiona Jallings has incorporated further publications and fan discussion online into a more comprehensive and up-to-date version of Neo-Sindarin "using Tolkien's creation as a roadmap"[324] in *A Fan's Guide to Neo-Sindarin*. Both are great resources for learning the language of the Grey Elves of Middle-earth (or something close to it). If, on the other hand, you're wishing to explore the language Tolkien called the "Elven Latin" and learn to speak and write Neo-Quenya (after all, how else are you going to write your own Elvish poetry to recite while wearing your epic Galadriel cosplay?), there are fewer options, but linguist Helge Fauskanger has some Neo-Quenya material available at his website, ardalambion.com.

Or maybe you prefer beards to pointy ears, and would rather learn some Dwarvish? Aye, you could do that. Though there is considerably less material about Khuzdul available from Tolkien himself, David Salo (again, proceeding from his own considerable effort in translating dialogue for Peter Jackson's movies), the creators of *Lord of the Rings Online*, and others have assembled a workable form of Neo-Khuzdul, which one can find helpful lessons for at the website of The Dwarrow Scholar, dwarrowscholar.com.

---

324    According to the publisher's own words.

# What if I Want to Follow in the Professor's Footsteps?

There is always the possibility that, after learning about Tolkien's own language invention, you'll be inspired to invent your own. We'll admit that we've never gone down that road—we already have families, podcasts to record, and a book to write, and couldn't possibly find the time to add conlanging to our lists of hobbies—but our hats are off to you. To be honest, Tolkien's *A Secret Vice*, the essay and lecture that served as his own personal "coming out" as a conlanger and which has recently been published in a critical edition edited by Dimitra Fimi and Andrew Higgins, is a wonderful piece of inspiration that may just push you down the road of creating your own language, if you're already flirting with the idea. There are also many other essays by Tolkien of a linguistic bent that word-nerds and conlangers may be interested in; "English and Welsh" and "On Translating Beowulf" (both available in *The Monsters and the Critics and Other Essays*) explore some of Tolkien's personal predilections toward language; his personal aesthetic tastes, sounds he enjoyed, and so on.

And for the polyglottally inclined, there are so many real-world languages that Tolkien was familiar with and inspired by that one might be inclined to study:

- Dig the sounds of Quenya? Why not study Finnish?

- Sindarin? You'll want to look into Welsh.

- Khuzdul? Adûnaic? Tolkien acknowledged that both bore some intentional similarities to Hebrew.

- How about the rich, alliterative, and poetic language of the Rohirrim? That's just straight-up Old English.

Besides these very clear real-world influences that show up in the pages of the legendarium, Tolkien was also familiar with Latin, Greek, French, Spanish, Italian, German, Icelandic, Gothic, and other languages. And if this suddenly makes you feel like you haven't done nearly enough with your life, we're right there with you.

# But Where Can I Learn About All Those Weird Runes and Letters?

Or maybe you're one of those kids who loved playing with their Little Orphan Annie decoder ring growing up. We understand...I mean, at least the interest. Even we are too young to remember the decoder ring, except for the scene in *A Christmas Story* where Ralphie discovers that the whole thing is just a "crummy commercial" for Ovaltine, which is pretty amazing...and we feel for him. Childhood is full of little disappointments like that, isn't it?

But we digress.

If you love codes, ciphers, secret alphabets, and passing notes to your friends that they don't understand—and who doesn't?—then Tolkien's invented scripts may be of even more interest to you than the languages themselves.

# What's the Difference?

We're talking about the difference between *translation* and *transliteration* here.

A *translation* is changing the words of a message from one language to another. This is what most people think of when they think of learning a new language. If you want to tell your significant other or family member you love them, you can say *I love you* in English, or *te amo* in Spanish, *Ich liebe dich* in German, or *je t'aime* in French (or whatever else in any other language you may happen to know how to say it in). The words are different—sound different, are spelled differently, are in different order—from language to language (though, in many cases, including these, the words from one language may be related to words in another language; that's a word-nerd rabbit hole we don't have time for here). If someone hands you a card on Valentine's Day that says *jag älskar dig*, and you don't speak Swedish, you might ask them (very confusedly) what it says, to which they might reply: "It says 'I love you' in Swedish." This is *translation*. The words of the message have been converted from a language you don't speak (Swedish) to one you do (English) in an effort to convey the meaning...though you still may wonder why this particular person has told you they love you, in which case we wish you the best.

A *transliteration* is changing the text of a message from one writing system to another: to another alphabet, to put it simply, though not all writing systems are properly called alphabets—there are syllabic systems like some Japanese writing, logograms in Chinese, hieroglyphs for those who like to keep it *really* old school, etc. *Transliterating* a message doesn't change the words; rather, it changes the symbols with which they are written. This enables a reader who doesn't read a script to get a sense of (more or less) what a phrase in another language sounds like, even though it doesn't actually reveal the meaning of the message itself. If, instead of being handed a Valentine's Day card in Swedish, someone handed you a card in Greek that says σ'αγαπώ, you may understandably be at a loss for what this phrase is even supposed to sound like, let alone having a clue what it means. If your well-meaning Greek friend *transliterates* that message for you as *s'agapo*, you suddenly understand more or less how the phrase sounds...but are no closer to its meaning than you were when your Swedish friend gave you the card that said *jag älskar dig*. *Transliteration* changes the letters into a script you can read (but not understand). *Translation* is required to understand its meaning...which, as you've probably guessed from all of the examples in the preceding paragraphs, is again "I love you."

We hope this illustrates the difference between translation and transliteration. And if these examples are just too hard for you to relate to, we understand. It's rare for us to receive multitudes of cards expressing true love from speakers of exotic European languages, too.

With those definitions out of the way, we can get back to Tolkien. One can *translate* a word from English (or the real-world language of one's choosing) into one of Tolkien's Elvish languages, or vice versa. The most well-known example, thanks to Gandalf's beard-tearingly frustrating forgotten password episode at the Doors of Durin on the way into Moria, is that *mellon* is the Sindarin word for *friend*. If you're reading *The Lord of the Rings* in Spanish, you may think of *mellon* as the Sindarin word for *amigo*—which, of course, is the Spanish word for *friend*, and *friend* is the English word for *amigo*. Each of these three words—*friend, amigo, mellon*—means the same thing, but each is pronounced and spelled very differently. They are *translations* of each other. And each of them can be *transliterated* from the Latin alphabet (which is the native writing system for English and Spanish) into, for example, the Tengwar—the Elvish script devised by Tolkien for his Elvish languages, and thus the native writing system for Sindarin:

[325]

|  | **Latin Alphabet** | **Tengwar** |
|---|---|---|
| **English** | friend | byị̃p̃ |
| **Spanish** | amigo | ịṁ̃ty̆ |
| **Sindarin** | mellon | ᴅʌᴛᴛᴄᴍ |

---

325  We are indebted to our good friend Chad Bornholdt—"Chad in Texas" to regular listeners of *The Prancing Pony Podcast*—for this example of the difference between translation and transliteration, as well as lots and lots of additional help in preparing this chapter.

Every one of the words in the chart above *means* the same thing: *friend*. But, as is hopefully obvious, the words are pronounced very differently in the three different languages presented, and they look very different, even when transliterated in the Tengwar script invented by Tolkien.

Which brings us back to the Tengwar themselves. According to the in-universe history presented in the legendarium, the Tengwar (plural of Quenya *tengwa*, which means simply "letter") were invented by Fëanor (yes, the very same jerk who led an entire kindred of Elves into exile and war in *The Silmarillion*, but who happened to invent a lot of really cool things, including writing systems) while the Elves were still in Valinor. Fëanor based his script on an earlier script, the Sarati, invented by a famous (to Elves, at least) loremaster named Rúmil—and which Tolkien also invented himself, natch.

As the Tengwar were used for writing down many different languages over the centuries of Middle-earth history—first Quenya, then Sindarin, later Adûnaic and Westron—there are various "modes" for writing in Tengwar. The most well-recognized mode may be the Mode of Beleriand, commonly used for writing Sindarin; this is the mode used on the West-gate of Moria, which appears in *The Fellowship of the Ring*, and is no doubt familiar to fans of both the books and the Peter Jackson movies. This mode is most like the Latin alphabet, in that it uses individual letters for both consonants and vowels. However, perhaps even more popular among fans who write and read Tengwar (and certainly lovelier to look at, by most accounts) are the many modes that use *tehtar* or diacritical marks for vowels: these are the various dots, slashes, and curlicues that surround the letters in many Tengwar inscriptions found in books, websites, and of course, tattoos. Modes that use *tehtar* include the Quenya Mode, the Mode of Gondor (used primarily for writing Sindarin), and the infamous Black Speech Mode used on the inscription on the One Ring. In the years since Tolkien's books have been published, fans have adapted these modes into modes for use in the modern world, for languages such as English (for which, of course, we have Tolkien's own inscriptions to go on), Spanish, and many others.[326] Each of these modes presents slight variations in the values of certain letters, the placement of *tehtar* (whether the *tehta* is placed above the consonant that precedes the vowel, or the consonant that follows it), and in some cases, even the values of the *tehtar* themselves, each adapted slightly to the phonology of the language for which the particular mode is used.[327]

# I'M REALLY MORE OF A DWARF FAN, HONESTLY...

We can certainly understand that. If that's you, you may be more interested in Tolkien's tough-looking, Norse- and Old English-inspired angular runes, called *Certar* (in Quenya, though more commonly known by their Sindarin names, *Cirth* or *Certhas*)[328] than those loopy, flowing Elvish scripts. Though the Dwarves didn't *only* use runes—in one rather well-known example from *The Lord of the Rings* (again, like the Tengwar of the West-gate, from the Moria section of the book), a Dwarven chronicle is found written both in Cirth and in Tengwar—they did tend to favor the Certhas for most of their chirographical purposes. As Tolkien himself states in Appendix E to *The Lord of the Rings*, Tengwar were primarily intended for "writing with brush or pen," while the Certhas were "devised and mostly used only for scratched or incised inscriptions," which is why they are angular in shape rather than rounded like the Tengwar. In Tolkien's in-universe history, the Certhas were

---

326 In the Tengwar column of the "friend chart" above, the English *friend* is written in English Orthographic Mode, while the Spanish *amigo* is written in Spanish Mode. *Mellon* is written in the Mode of Beleriand, exactly as it appears on the West-gate of Moria in the famous phrase, "Speak 'friend' and enter."

327 This "localization" of Tengwar modes is not just fan obsession. Even within Tolkien's own writings, the values and placement of *tengwar* and *tehtar* vary by mode. For example, the consonant sounds B and G never appear on their own in Quenya, so the letters that signify those sounds in Sindarin actually are used for MB and NG in Quenya. And in the Black Speech, O is rare, but U is a very common vowel sound, so the *tehta* that signifies O in most modes is used for U in the Black Speech.

328 Both names are based on the singular Sindarin noun *certh*, which means "rune." *Cirth* is the simple plural we will use to refer to any group of more than one rune, while *Certhas* is the collective plural form preferred by Tolkien when referring to the runic alphabet as a whole. Further complicating matters, Tolkien also used the term *Angerthas* to refer to a couple of the best-known runic writing systems; see below.

also invented by Elves, but "became known to many peoples, to Men and Dwarves, and even to Orcs, all of whom altered them to suit their purposes and according to their skill or lack of it."

Eventually, Tolkien tells us in Appendix E, the Elves largely stopped using the Certhas, but one type, called the *Angerthas Daeron* or "Long Runes of Daeron,"[329] developed in Beleriand in the First Age by a poet and loremaster who once had a major beef with Beren on account of his own lifelong schoolboy crush on Lúthien, did manage to catch on in Moria, where it was adapted into the *Angerthas Moria* (or "Long Runes of Moria") and became the favorite script of the Dwarves. One can perhaps guess why the Dwarves—a race so fond of smithing and chiseling in stone—would end up favoring the Certhas; they liked them so much, it seems, that they even developed runes for writing in pen on paper.

The primary example of Dwarvish writing in runes on paper in the published legendarium is Thrór's Map, which Gandalf gave to Thorin in the first chapter of *The Hobbit*, and which contained two messages in runes: one which described the secret side door into the Lonely Mountain, and one written in moon-runes which was only seen later by Elrond, and which explained the secret to finding the keyhole. Interestingly, these runic inscriptions on the map were not written in Certhas, but in runes based on ones that were once used in the real world: the Anglo-Saxon runes called *futhorc* (derived in turn from the Elder Futhark runes used by the early Germanic peoples, and related to the Norse runes called Younger Futhark). Why Tolkien chose to use the Anglo-Saxon runes this one time in the legendarium is not entirely clear; all we know for sure on the matter comes from a 1947 letter not included in Carpenter's collection, but quoted in John Rateliff's *The History of The Hobbit*, in which Tolkien states that he used the Anglo-Saxon runes

---

329  Before you start pulling your hair out and gnashing your teeth at what appears to be *yet another* Sindarin word for "runes," let us clarify for you that *Angerthas* really is just two Sindarin words put together: *and*, "long" plus *certhas*, and can be translated as "long rune-rows." The mutation of C in *certhas* to G in *angerthas* is called "lenition" or softening and is very common in Sindarin, which just happens to be one of the many reasons the authors of this book have always been scared to attempt learning Sindarin.

"on the translation principle"—meaning apparently that since he rendered the Common Speech as English and the Dwarves' names (which would have been in a more antique and Northern dialect) as Norse, he rendered Dwarvish writing as something akin to ancient Scandinavian writing; and since at the time *The Hobbit* was not intended to be part of the larger legendarium, he probably didn't think it made much sense to use one of the Elvish writing systems. All we know for sure is that he stated in a 1938 letter to the editor of the *Observer* that there was "doubtless an historical connection" between the runes on Thrór's Map and the Anglo-Saxon runes, and later, in a 1963 letter to Rhona Beare, stated only that the Certhas themselves "have no supposed historical connexion [sic] with the Germanic Runic alphabet." Finally, going back to the 1947 letter quoted in Rateliff, we know that Tolkien was "rather sorry" that he had used the Anglo-Saxon runes on the *Hobbit* map, and we can only imagine it nagged at him for the rest of his life...which is kind of sad, but also humorous, when we think of how relatively impressive Tolkien's creativity is, even when he botches something with an accidental inconsistency, compared to us on our best days.

Much like Tengwar, then, there are various ways to write any given word in Certhas. Here's an example showing a well-known phrase that's near and dear to our hearts, written in various modes:

| | THE | PRANCING | PONY | PODCAST [330] |
|---|---|---|---|---|
| Angerthas Daeron | ᚻᚻ | ᛈᛕᚾᛏᛦᛁᛦ | ᛈᛆᛏᛁ | ᛈᛦᛆᛢᚾᛈᛐ |
| Angerthas Moria | ᚵᛏ | ᛈᛏᚾᛢᛚᛁᛦ | ᛈᛆᛢᛍ | ᛈᛦᛆᛣᚾᛈᛐ |
| Thrór's Runes | ᚦᛗ | ᚲᚱᚠᛏᚺᛁᛦ | ᚲᚠᛏᛘ | ᚲᚠᛘᛚᚠᚺᛏ |

---

[330] Thanks again to Chad Bornholdt, "Chad in Texas," for help with this chart showing the various modes of Certhas.

# So Where Can I Get My Decoder Ring?

The best place to start learning Tengwar or Certhas is undoubtedly Appendix E to *The Lord of the Rings*, in which Tolkien explains not only the pronunciation of words in his invented languages (a fantastic resource even if you're *not* interested in studying the language or the scripts, but just, say, planning a session to read some of Tolkien's text aloud...or, uh, starting a podcast), but also the in-universe history of the scripts and some of the most important modes. But Tolkien doesn't exactly make learning the one-to-one correspondences between the letters and their sounds all that intuitive; instead of offering up a table of each letter with a sound value next to it (y'know, like a normal person), Tolkien offers tables of the letters, but then explains their sounds in text in the surrounding pages, with explanations like this:

> The normal letters, Grade 1, were applied to the 'voiceless stops': *t, p, k*, etc. The doubling of the bow indicated the addition of 'voice': thus if 1, 2, 3, 4=*t, p, ch, k* (or *t, p, k, kw*) then 5, 6, 7, 8=<u>*d, b, j, g* (or *d, b, g, gw*)</u>. The raising of the stem indicated the opening of the consonant to a 'spirant': thus assuming the above values for Grade 1, Grade 3 (9–12)=*th, f, sh, ch* (or *th, f, kh, khw/hw*), and Grade 4 (13–16)=*dh, v, zh, gh* (or *dh, v, gh, ghw/w*).[331]

I mean, yeah, it's about as clear as the water in Mordor that Sam reluctantly filled up his water bottle with; but, just like that water, back when that was all we could get, it was enough. Some of us actually (improbably) taught ourselves to write in Tengwar on the basis of nothing but explanations like that. But fortunately, these days, there are lots of resources online to help you on your way. The website *Tecendil* (tecendil.com) offers not only a Tengwar Handbook with tables and explanations for how to use *tengwar*,

---

331   Tolkien, *Return*, 2020, 1120.

*tehtar*, and even special marks like punctuation and capitalization markers in various modes, but also a Tengwar transcriber if you just want to get a reliable transliteration of your boyfriend's or kid's name before you go to the tattoo parlor to get your arm inked. And while the Certhas aren't quite as widespread in usage among Tolkien geeks (or their tattoo artists), there are sites like ring-lord.tripod.com/cirth where one can find articles, tables, and more to help elucidate Tolkien's sometimes challenging commentaries on the script.

But languages—and writing systems—are designed for the purpose of communicating, and the best way to build fluency in either the languages or the writing systems is to find friends to communicate with. Find a Facebook group online, join a club, find a smial (a Hobbitish word meaning "burrow," also used to mean the local chapters of some fan groups) or other local group, or just find a chat group online of people who want to learn together and take turns writing messages to each other, in translation *or* transliteration. It's a fun hobby, a great way to kill time when you're bored at work...and it feels like passing notes in class that your teacher won't be able to read when she catches you.

# Nice! Is There Anything Else the Authors Want to Talk About for a Page or Two, But Aren't Sure Where Else to Fit It in the Book?

We thought you'd never ask.

The thing is, Tolkien was certainly fond of his invented languages, and they are a big part of the appeal of Middle-earth to any word-nerd who encounters his work. But that's to say nothing of the pure, unadulterated joy and love of Tolkien's mother tongue—English—that is to be found in his work. Tolkien was a master of the use of the English language, and understood the history of and the spectrum of meaning conveyed by a single word better than any other writer we can think of. As the authors of *Ring of Words: Tolkien and the Oxford English Dictionary* (three writers who, like Tolkien himself, worked at the above-mentioned dictionary—not just any dictionary, but the "definitive record of the English language," according to its own website) put it: "Many authors before and since have taken an interest in the words they use—to do so is arguably intrinsic to being an author—and many have invented words in the course of their writing; but few writers can have found so much of their creative inspiration in the shapes and the histories of words themselves." They add that:

> In many cases Tolkien's unique perspective on language led him to choose a particular word for very precise reasons, and careful examination of such a word from a similar perspective—including consideration of how it is dealt with in the OED—can take us on a philological adventure which brings to light connections and resonances which may not be immediately apparent.[332]

If this kind of thing sounds exciting to you, then by all means, pick up *Ring of Words: Tolkien and the Oxford English Dictionary*, a journey in three parts that covers not only Tolkien's time working for the titular OED (primarily on the W-words that happen to have particularly complicated Germanic etymologies, as noted above), but also Tolkien's skills as a wordsmith and particularly his penchant for breathing new life into forgotten or nearly forgotten words (like *weapontake* and *dwimmerlaik*, both of which, not coincidentally, come up in proximity to the Rohirrim, whose language was

---

332    Gilliver, Marshall, and Weiner, *Ring of Words*, 2009, vii, ix.

                                              Why We Love Middle-earth

based on Old English and whose diction was based on archaic forms of English), and finally, a glossary of sorts of some of the most interesting words from the remote past of English Tolkien managed to dig up for his writing... and one notable addition to the OED inspired by Tolkien himself: that's *hobbit*, of course.

If studying Tolkien's use of English is on your to-do list, you'll also want to get yourself access to a good etymology resource online, like the Online Etymology Dictionary (etymonline.com) or better yet, online access to the *Oxford English Dictionary* itself, which can be subscribed to for a fee, or accessed through membership in many public and institutional libraries. The OED is truly a dictionary like no other: whereas most online and print dictionaries give a definition and pronunciation with a short etymological note, the OED leans into the etymology, with citations from texts going back to the early Middle Ages to show how words change in form, sound, and meaning over time. It's a philologist's playground.

It's safe to say that language is such an intrinsic part of Tolkien's literary creation that there isn't just one way to appreciate the language and languages of Tolkien's writing. It's no mystery that Tolkien has introduced many readers to the world of philology, and why so many readers of a philological mindset find themselves so drawn to Tolkien.

# WHY ALAN LOVES IT

It's fair to say that collecting Tolkien is to me what Tolkien's languages are to Shawn: the corners of the fandom that have called to us each most deeply. But, thanks to seven years together on the podcast, we've each gifted one another with the appreciation for our particular niches. I'd like to think I've helped Shawn find joy in collecting Tolkien,[333] just as he has definitely helped me expand my interest in, and love for, the languages of Tolkien.

A disclaimer of sorts: I've never been very good with other languages. Maybe it's a cop-out, maybe it's a self-fulfilling prophecy, but it has always been this way for me. Despite my love for, and relative skill with, the English language, I have always found other tongues quite difficult. I tried French and German in high school; the latter at least interested me enough to continue it in college—yet neither has stuck with me. Attempts later in life to learn Italian, Swedish, or even Icelandic have also failed to one degree or another. And you can *forget* about languages that use other alphabets![334] So, even though I loved the way Tolkien's languages *sound*—or even *look*—I've never really studied them as functional languages.

Instead, my emphasis has been on understanding how Tolkien uses English—understanding the history and etymology of words, and learning how Tolkien utilized his own deep knowledge of philology to craft language so precisely, complete with hidden double meanings and more. Diving into my own language more deeply has given me an even greater understanding of Tolkien—as well as a greater appreciation for the gift of languages that he possessed.

# WHY SHAWN LOVES IT

I've loved languages for as long as I can remember. I fell in love with a set of Spanish flashcards longer ago than I can even clearly place in the timeline of my life; but it was probably around kindergarten—I learned how to count to twelve, words for basic colors and family relationships, and that's about it until I learned more as an adult (but I digress). In fifth grade, I taught myself

---

333  Though, like him, I credit Jeremy Edmonds from the Tolkien Collector's Guide for really opening his eyes to how collecting can be satisfying, no matter what aspect of Tolkien one chooses to collect.

334  I'm looking at you, Shawn, Mr. I taught myself the Greek alphabet in the fifth grade and wrote in Phoenician in high school. (Actually, I'm duly impressed.)

the Greek alphabet...and then I taught it to the guy who sat behind me in homeroom, so we could pass secret notes to each other. It was probably a year later that I taught myself the Cyrillic alphabet (sadly, that one didn't stick; but even today I can stumble my way through transliteration of a simple Russian inscription), and by eighth grade my best friend and I were spending Louisiana history class in the back of the classroom, looking up Phoenician letters in the *World Book* encyclopedias on the shelf behind us and writing notes to each other in fake Phoenician cipher.[335] I also used to spend way more time than most kids flipping through the pages of my *American Heritage Dictionary*, reading about word origins and connecting related words to each other through the Indo-European Roots Appendix.

So when I read Tolkien—and specifically, when I got to Appendix E—I was enthralled. I taught myself the Tengwar, and then encouraged a couple of my friends who were also reading *The Lord of the Rings* at the same time, to learn them...although we didn't really get into the habit of writing in it.[336] But I internalized the information, and the love of philology, and even Tolkien's rudimentary lessons in topics like articulatory phonetics (which you can learn enough about to be dangerous based on a reading of Tolkien's appendices and a little supplementary research on your own). As the internet became a thing, I continued geeking out on word origins...and when I found other Tolkien fans online via social media and podcasting, the word-nerds quickly became my tribe.

During my time on *The Prancing Pony Podcast*, I always made an effort to bring my love of language into our discussions. I was fortunate to have Alan as a willing accomplice; while he doesn't consider himself as much of a word-nerd as I do, he definitely has a passion and a love for Tolkien's unique use of language and enjoys delving into the histories of words and the hidden facets of meaning that Tolkien's deep knowledge of philology affords him

---

335  Yeah, so we were nerds. How did *you* slack off in history class?

336  Probably because, despite our budding love of Tolkien, we were still far too invested at the time in learning how to play grunge music riffs on our budget guitars to impress girls.

as a writer. And I like to think I awakened a love of words and language in the hearts of many of our listeners; more than a few people over the years have reached out to me to tell me that insights I raised on the podcast helped them uncover a love for language themselves—like zombies, word-nerds tend to spread the infection—and our Philology Faire segments (in which we talk about the history of certain interesting words that Tolkien uses in the text, usually but not always English words) were always a fan favorite.

I like to think that Tolkien would be proud. After all, Tolkien was a *philologist*—in every sense, both professionally as a scholar of language, and also in the literal sense as "one who loves language"—and the fact that he's awakened a love of language in so many of his readers, I find quite beautiful. Much like his religious views, which he almost never wore on his sleeve, but wove into his writing in subtle and poetic ways that inspire and enlighten, Tolkien's love of language appears on every page of his legendarium, not just the ones that have Elvish words on them. And I truly believe that, in a way, to love Tolkien is *to love language*: not just because of the obvious, that Tolkien's world was created in language (because, y'know, writer), but also because language is at the heart of Tolkien's world, and is highly valued by the creator and the characters within it. It is, like the man who wrote it, a world that exists—again, in the words of Lewis—"inside language."

# CHAPTER 16

# THE BEST KIND OF HOMEWORK: TOLKIEN STUDIES

*"The analytic study of fairy-stories is as bad a preparation for the enjoying or the writing of them as would be the historical study of the drama of all lands and times for the enjoyment or writing of stage-plays. The study may indeed become depressing. It is easy for the student to feel that with all his labour he is collecting only a few leaves, many of them now torn or decayed, from the countless foliage of the Tree of Tales, with which the Forest of Days is carpeted."*

—J.R.R. Tolkien, "On Fairy-stories"[337]

*"There are, I suppose, always defects in any large-scale work of art; and especially in those of literary form that are founded on an earlier matter which is put to new uses—like Homer, or Beowulf, or Virgil, or Greek or Shakespearean tragedy! In which class, as a class not as a competitor, The Lord of the Rings really falls..."*

—J.R.R. Tolkien, from a 1954 letter to Robert Murray, S.J.[338]

---

337    Tolkien, "On Fairy-stories," in *Tales from the Perilous Realm*, 2008, 371.
338    Carpenter, *Letters*, No. 156.

When *The Lord of the Rings* was first published volume by volume in the 1950s, it met with a mix of responses from the literary and critical community. Some literary giants praised Tolkien's work, like the English poet and fellow Oxford alumnus W.H. Auden, who would write later in 1956 in the *New York Times Book Review* (a little over a year after his initial positive review of *Fellowship* in the *New York Times*) that "[n]obody seems to have a moderate opinion; either, like myself, people find it a masterpiece of its genre or they cannot abide it."[339] And it'll surprise no one to hear that Tolkien's good friend C.S. Lewis praised the book in 1954 in *Time and Tide*, saying the book was "like lightning from a clear sky: as sharply different, as unpredictable in our age as [William Blake's] *Songs of Innocence* were in theirs. To say that in it heroic romance, gorgeous, eloquent, and unashamed, has suddenly returned at a period almost pathological in its anti-romanticism, is inadequate... it makes not a return but an advance or revolution: the conquest of new territory."[340] High praise indeed.

There were other critics who praised Tolkien's work (including many who, unlike Lewis and Auden, didn't go by their first two initials...but where's the fun in naming them?). It received positive reviews in *The New Republic*, *Nebula Science Fiction*, and elsewhere. Of course, there were negative reviews as well, such as the notoriously bad review given by American critic Edmund Wilson, who insinuated in his 1956 review in *The Nation* that *The Lord of the Rings* was "juvenile trash," stated flat-out that "except when [Tolkien] is being pedantic and also boring the adult reader, there is little in *The Lord of the Rings* over the head of a seven-year-old child," that it was "a children's book which has somehow got out of hand," and that Tolkien had

---

339   Auden, W.H. "At the End of the Quest, Victory," in *The New York Times*, January 22, 1956.

340   Lewis, C.S. "The gods return to earth," in *Time and Tide*, August 14, 1954.

"little skill at narrative and no instinct for literary form." He also attacked Auden for liking it.[341]

But, despite the mixed critical response to Tolkien's work, it wasn't long before some academics began to look seriously at Tolkien's work as a piece of literature, worthy of academic study and analysis. *Master of Middle-earth*, a short but influential early work of Tolkien studies by scholar Paul H. Kocher, was published in 1972, while the Professor was still alive. This means it was also published before *The Silmarillion*, *Unfinished Tales*, and the twelve volumes of The History of Middle-earth (not to mention many other essays and manuscripts published in the past fifty years), and so Kocher relies a great deal on speculation and inference for his analysis of Tolkien's works. But the book has held up remarkably well—much of what Kocher guessed in his analysis ended up confirmed by Tolkien's posthumously published writings or by Christopher Tolkien's commentary on them. And even where some details may have proven to be wrong in hindsight, Kocher's analysis reveals a thorough understanding of what mattered to Tolkien as a writer, and he spilled a great deal of ink on topics in Tolkien's writing that are still major focuses of study today, like the nature of evil of Middle-earth, the enduring "inner consistency of reality" of Tolkien's sub-creation, the importance of Tolkien's faith to his writing, and his mastery of language to give color and depth to his secondary world. Kocher even devoted a chapter to several non-legendarium works, including perennial fan favorites like *Leaf by Niggle*, *Smith of Wootton Major*, and *The Homecoming of Beorhtnoth*

---

341  Wilson, Edmund. "Oo, Those Awful Orcs! A review of The Fellowship of the Ring," in *The Nation*, August 14, 1956. It's worth pointing out that, while Wilson may not be the household name that Tolkien has become despite being the target of vicious mockery in this review, Wilson was no literary slouch. Often dubbed "America's greatest reader," Wilson was a writer and critic for publications such as *The New Yorker* and *Vanity Fair*, and wrote over a dozen works of literary criticism. He simply doesn't seem to have appreciated the fantastical; in addition to despising Tolkien's work, Wilson famously called the work of H.P. Lovecraft "hackwork." For what it's worth, unlike Tolkien, who we know was fond of responding to fan letters with personalized and detailed answers to even the most challengingly geeky questions (many of which are published in Carpenter's *Letters*), Wilson was famous for *not* responding to fan mail. Wilson famously sent a pre-typed form response letter to almost every fan letter or inquiry he received: a form letter in which he not-so-graciously declined to "read manuscripts... do editorial work... deliver lectures... autograph books... supply personal information [or] photographs of himself..." or really much of anything else out of his way. We'd rather read the work of someone who appreciates his fans, thank you very much.

*Beorhthelm's Son.* So Kocher's *Master of Middle-earth* remains a valuable addition to the bookshelf of any aspiring Tolkien scholar, if you can track down a copy.

Another rather early entry in the field was from Jane Chance, an American professor of medieval literature and gender studies whose 1979 work *Tolkien's Art: A Mythology for England* established her as also a leading Tolkien scholar. Like Kocher, Chance went beyond just *The Hobbit* and *The Lord of the Rings* and into *Homecoming, Farmer Giles,* and other non-legendarium works. Unlike Kocher, Chance had the benefit of publishing her book after the publication of *The Silmarillion* in 1977, but despite this, she treats *The Silmarillion* only briefly. A second edition of the book, released in 2001 during the height of anticipation for Peter Jackson's films, expanded the work but still did not go into as much depth on *The Silmarillion* as it did other works. Chance's focus is largely on looking for, in the words of Tom Shippey in a 1980 review of the book, the "seeds" of Tolkien's mythology in the medieval literature that he spent his hours at his day job studying. While this is an approach we ourselves tend to enjoy at times, Chance's work has been reevaluated by many modern Tolkien scholars in recent years, who have argued that it relies too much on applying allegorical interpretations to Tolkien's work, often from angles that Tolkien most likely did not intend and most certainly would not approve of; and that her limiting *The Silmarillion* to brief treatment only at the back of the book was an error in not recognizing the importance of this book that Tolkien spent virtually his entire life writing. There's still a lot to enjoy in this first book by Chance, with a few of these caveats in mind, and in the last two decades she has continued to publish new work on Tolkien and his mythological sources, as well as Tolkien and gender, and continues to be a valued voice in Tolkien scholarship. But it is typical of these early works, published during what Tom Shippey called "the Age of Innocence of Tolkien studies" in the 1970s,[342] that though they are

---

342  Shippey, Tom. "Foreword," in *A Tolkien Compass,* edited by Jared Lobdell, Open Court Publishing Company, 2003. Lobdell's *Compass* was first published in 1975, so is itself another entry in the bookshelf from the "Age of Innocence."

often foundational, they are also all too often incomplete, and superseded by the many writings that came after them.

In the early 1980s, as *The Silmarillion* and *Unfinished Tales* were out and new History of Middle-earth volumes started coming out on an ongoing basis, a new crop of scholars, like Tom Shippey and Verlyn Flieger (both of whom the PPP is thankful to count among the group of Tolkien scholars who have not only appeared on the podcast, but also given talks at our events), began to publish works that incorporated all the new material, unlike the works from the "Age of Innocence." Shippey's *The Road to Middle-earth* and Flieger's *Splintered Light* (both of which were mentioned in Part I of this book) were published in 1982 and 1983 respectively. Both have been updated, and both remain absolutely current and invaluable works of Tolkien studies; and their authors have continued publishing new monographs and essays in the years since. It wouldn't be a stretch to say that the work of these two scholars was fundamental in bringing new legitimacy to the field of Tolkien studies.

Of course, though there weren't too many books out on the subject yet, there were lots of essays flying around, largely within the relatively closed circles of Tolkien- and Inklings-focused fan groups. *Mythlore*, the journal of the Mythopoeic Society (a United States-based organization dedicated to the study of the Inklings and other "mythopoeic" literature), first appeared in early 1969 as a more casual fanzine with some scholarly articles in it; as time went on, the focus gradually became more scholarly and less fanzine-y. On the other side of the pond, the Britain-based Tolkien Society's[343] journal *Mallorn* was first published in late 1970, and gradually underwent a similar shift from a magazine full of art, poetry, and scholarly essays to be more singly focused on scholarship.[344]

---

343  We want to make it absolutely clear that, although the Mythopoeic Society started out as an American organization and the Tolkien Society a British one, both organizations today welcome (and boast a large number of) members from all over the world. See our chapter in this book for more information about both organizations and the benefits of membership.

344  Both *Mythlore* and *Mallorn* would eventually become fully peer-reviewed scholarly journals; see below.

And ever since the dawn of the twenty-first century and the renewed interest in Tolkien's works across the broader spectrum of pop culture (not least of all thanks to a huge new crop of fans introduced to the books by Peter Jackson's films), the field of Tolkien studies has exploded. *Mythlore* became a fully peer-reviewed[345] academic journal in 1999 (*Mallorn* followed in 2016). Two new journals dedicated to academic study of Tolkien appeared in the new century: *Tolkien Studies*, first published in 2004, and the *Journal of Tolkien Research* in 2014. In addition to these journals, there are more moots and conferences[346] taking place among Tolkien fans around the world than ever before, all of them putting out calls for presentations and lectures on new academic topics. There are more blogs than there are Orcs in Moria, and podcasts—some with a more academic bent than others[347]—putting out great scholarship online for no cost. And there are books, so many books; collections of essays and also monographs[348] coming out constantly from academic presses such as that at Kent State University and the recently launched Signum University Press, the publishing arm of a digital-first university offering graduate programs in Tolkien studies and adjacent disciplines such as Germanic philology and medieval literature.[349]

And Tolkien studies is gaining more mainstream acceptance than ever before. Despite the fact that there have been scholars for decades—like Kocher, Chance, Shippey, and Flieger—willing to tackle serious study of Tolkien's works, Tolkien studies have not always been respected by mainstream scholarship, with the possible exception of linguistic study. It was hard for

---

345 "Peer-reviewed" means that the academic articles in the journal are reviewed by a panel of "peers," i.e., scholars with expertise in Tolkien studies. This peer review ensures that submitted articles meet acceptable standards of accuracy, originality, and significance in the field. It's a bit like a stamp of quality for academic research.

346 Discussed in the next chapter!

347 As always, we tip our hats to the Tolkien Professor, Dr. Corey Olsen.

348 A book focusing at length on a single, specialized academic topic.

349 Signum University and its associated press are both well worth looking into for anyone interested in jumping into Tolkien studies. Signum University's graduate programs are focused on affordability and accessibility, and they offer numerous non-degree programs for those who just want to casually learn about a new interest. Signum University Press takes that same democratizing philosophy to academic publishing, with a goal of nurturing emerging scholars alongside more familiar already-published scholars. Signum also hosts moots throughout the year, which is a great way to break into the community and learn more.

graduate students to get the green light to do dissertations on Tolkien, or for working professors to count publications on Tolkien toward their tenure requirements. But even in the last decade, serious academic study on Tolkien (as well as other fantasy, science fiction, horror, etc., authors and titles) has gained acceptance and become a field one can pursue as a professional academic. Score one for the fans!

# SO THERE'S PLENTY OF ACADEMIC STUFF ON TOLKIEN TO READ. BUT I CAN'T WRITE MY OWN, CAN I?

I mean, look, we know that not everyone who loves Tolkien as a fan—even a rabid, dyed-in-the-wool, Fingolfin-quoting, pointy-ear-wearing *fan*—is going to ever have any interest in dipping their toes into Tolkien studies. Much like every other topic covered in every other chapter of this section of the book, it's going to appeal to a certain niche. And even if you find yourself in that niche as a new or intermediate fan of Tolkien, we'd be surprised if you're not at least a *little* intimidated by the thought of pivoting your geeky fan-love of Tolkien into serious (or not-so-serious) academic study. We know it seems like a daunting task, outside the comfort zone of the average fantasy geek, to submit a paper on your favorite author to the discerning and probably cruel eyes of your peers and have them tear it apart, stomp on it, grind it into the mire like Orcs on some particularly chaotic battlefield,[350] and ultimately deem it unfit for publication. Or if it is accepted, the thought of getting up on a stage and speaking into a microphone about that topic for twenty to forty minutes might be a little scary for all but the most unjustifiably

---

350   We're totally thinking of Nirnaeth Arnoediad, the Battle of Unnumbered Tears, here. But your mileage may vary.

confident and attention-seeking members of the Tolkien fan community; and Eru forbid someone suggest the insurmountable task of coming up with 100,000 or more words on Tolkien for a book and submitting that for publication, review, and sale on the open market (okay, so at some point, this sentence stopped being about you and started being about us...recalibrating).

Have we scared you away yet? No? Good! Because we're here to tell you that the field of Tolkien studies is not nearly as scary as all that. We have found the field of Tolkien studies, and the scholars who participate in it, to be incredibly welcoming to newcomers, even those who don't have a PhD (or who have a PhD in an unrelated field, like math or science). In our years as podcast hosts and as active members of the international Tolkien fan community, we've met many, many people who have written essays on Tolkien that have been published in academic journals. We've also met more than a few people who have gone on to write entire books on Tolkien, and they're not just the well-known names you might think. We've also met several people who edit for journals or presses. And do you know what? They're all fans, just like you and us.

We're not going to claim this is unique to Tolkien scholarship (because, frankly, this is all we know), but we have observed that Tolkien scholarship is very democratic. Perhaps because Tolkien is such a popular author, the scholarship surrounding Tolkien's works has been quite thoroughly popularized as well, due in no small part to the efforts of organizations like Signum University, the Mythopoeic Society, and the Tolkien Society. Organizations like these have made scholarship more accessible to fans through their journals (for example, the Tolkien Society posts all back issues of *Mallorn* more than two years old online for the general public; more recent issues are only available to members) as well as events (such as moots or conferences, or online seminars open to the general public). And there are numerous blogs, and yes, podcasts (not just ours) that bring Tolkien scholarship to a broader audience. All of this makes the bar of entry to one's own academic pursuits that much easier, because it's easier to see what others are writing about and talking about; and these are often the sparks that ignite new ideas in scholarship.

And, as mentioned above, in recent years it has become even more within reach for those who are interested in pursuing Tolkien studies in a more official and professional capacity to complete coursework and academic tracks in Tolkien studies or Inklings studies, at the right institutions of higher learning. Signum University offers online degree programs, as we mentioned above; and there are certainly many academics who studied in traditional brick-and-mortar universities who did MA and PhD work focused on Tolkien in related fields, like medieval studies and English literature.

But even if you don't have, or aren't interested in pursuing, traditional academic credentials, that isn't remotely a barrier to getting a paper or talk accepted in the world of Tolkien studies. All you need is an exciting idea about something in Tolkien's works that you want to write about, and the ability to organize your thoughts in a way that is compelling and persuasive. If you can do that, you can find an audience for your Tolkien scholarship.

# SOUNDS AWESOME! HOW DO I GET STARTED?

We strongly recommend starting by simply seeing what's already out there. Read articles, and books—not just Tolkien, and not just the super-well-known household names in scholarship like Shippey and Flieger and Garth, but lesser-known scholars as well. Look for books that focus on whatever it is that fits your niche interest in Tolkien; in our experience there are a lot of interesting books focusing on the intersection of Tolkien's work with other academic disciplines: from the obvious ones like linguistics, religion, and philosophy, to less obvious topical crossovers with botany, astronomy, gender studies, and queer studies. Explore essay anthologies on a specific topic or group of related topics;[351] these often feature chapter contributions from different authors, and are a great way to introduce lesser-known names in scholarship. You don't necessarily have to buy expensive books from academic presses, either. Many essays are available for free online through services like Project MUSE. Read as much as you can, and learn about the kinds of questions asked by scholars and researchers; this will get your creative juices flowing. And if nothing else, if you're interested in writing an article on, say, how Tolkien was inspired by seventeenth-century mercantile theory in the development of the myth of Númenor, it's important to first know what *other* authors have said about how Tolkien was inspired by seventeenth-century mercantile theory in the development of the myth of Númenor.[352] One pro tip, suggested by Sørina Higgins, former editor-in-chief of Signum University Press, is to read the latest scholarship first when researching previous scholarship on a topic. That way it's easy to see what current questions people are interested in right now, which earlier scholars made the most impact on the field (i.e., the ones who are cited the most in more recent essays and articles!). It can even help you identify people with ideas similar to yours worth networking with; after all, as Higgins says, scholars tend to be "very friendly and generous" with their time, particularly where their work is concerned.

In addition to reading scholarship, attend as many moots as you can. Ever since the COVID pandemic, many moots now offer online attendance for a significantly lower registration price than attending in person. While it's unavoidably true that attending a moot online isn't quite as socially engaging as being physically present in a conference center with a few dozen fellow Tolkien fans, attending online offers a perfectly good entry to the aspect of moots that's most relevant to this chapter: presentations. Most moots put out a public call for papers ("CFP") requesting submissions for presentation topics from the general public, and (assuming it's a big enough moot and

---

351  For example, *Tolkien and the Classical World*, edited by Hamish Williams and published by Walking Tree Publishers (2021). It features chapters contributed by various authors, all exploring different ways in which Tolkien was influenced by ancient Greek and Roman sources.

352  We're not gonna lie. We would totally read this.

long enough to have enough room on its agenda) will often schedule talks by a variety of presenters of varying experience levels: presentations from seasoned writer-speakers who present at several conferences a year, all the way down to newcomers giving their first moot presentation (and invariably getting a ton of love and support from the audience in doing so). The highest-profile moots will even have one or two (or more) keynote addresses delivered by true Tolkien luminaries, the household names of Tolkien scholarship. What this all means is that attending a moot is absolutely the best way to immerse oneself in Tolkien studies for an entire day or weekend, and also to hear speakers at various levels of experience. And did we mention the Q&A sessions? Most moot schedules allow for at least a few minutes of questions from the audience at the end of each talk, which gives audience members a chance to talk directly to the people doing the scholarship. It's always fun to hear an audience member ask a really brilliant question of a speaker, pulling at some thread or turning over some stone that was only hinted at in the presentation...and sometimes, that great question turns into next year's great presentation topic.

So now, you've familiarized yourself with what others are doing, and you're ready to make your own great contribution to the field of Tolkien studies. Great! Here are some things to keep in mind as you begin.

The first one is so simple it's easy to forget: start with a question. Don't think of a paper or academic essay as on a particular "topic," because that can lead to output that is broad and unfocused. Instead, think of a particular question to be answered through the research. Higgins suggests that the questions that lead to the best research papers are those that are "honest, interesting, generative, personal, and new." Think of a question that you are interested in, that you *really* want to know the answer to, and that you honestly do *not* know the answer already (because if you know, or think you know, the answer already, it may bias you toward research that supports the answer already in your head). And make sure it's a question that someone hasn't already asked and answered in exactly the same way before in the many decades of academic study on Tolkien's works—this is where reading a lot of essays, and then a lot more, and then topping that off with a few more, can be very helpful. If it turns out someone else has already addressed the question you want to ask, then don't Denethor out in despair! Just think of a new angle on the question, or a way to respond to and/or build on what's come before. Combine ideas, even seemingly unrelated ones: recent studies in botany, medicine, or astrophysics may yield exciting new questions to ask about characters and events in Tolkien's works. And we've heard surprisingly great presentations at moots that juxtaposed Tolkien's work against other genres of storytelling as wildly different as monster movies and anime, or against hard-hitting social issues facing us in the twenty-first century. As long as there are new things happening in the world, there will be new things to bring to bear as context for our understanding and appreciation of Tolkien.

Higgins cautions, though, against taking on too much or too little. If the scope of your question is too big, it'll be impossible to prepare properly for it: there will be too much existing scholarship on it, and you won't be able to take all of that in to write something that's sure to bring something new to the field. On the other hand, a question that's too small is not going to yield enough material for a decent paper. Open-ended questions are your bread and butter; avoid questions like "Did Tolkien do X?" or "Are there similarities between Y and Z?" Ask questions that can't be answered with a simple yes or no, and consider "why," "how," and "when." Once you have a question in mind, go back to reading. If you haven't read all the available scholarship on a particular topic (don't forget: chronologically backward!), do so now. That will help refine the question into something truly unique.

There are loads of resources out there in the world for how to write a great paper or give a great presentation, so we won't attempt to reinvent that wheel here. But if you're struggling, again, reading other scholars' work or listening to their talks at moots can help. Pay attention to how they structure their arguments, how they present their evidence, what details they spend time on. It'll inspire you, give you pointers, and frankly, it's just a lot of darned fun...if you're a nerd like us (which we assume you are, if you're still reading this chapter).

But we do want to talk about something that is bound to happen from time to time, when you're writing and submitting papers (or writing and submitting anything, really): *rejection*. We're sorry; we know you don't want to think about it, but it's going to happen someday. The most important thing to keep in mind, which we hear over and over again,[353] is not to take it personally. There are so many reasons why a paper or presentation may be rejected. Maybe the venue you chose already has everything they need, and they are quietly rejecting everything else that comes through the door. Maybe they're looking for a particular theme that you didn't touch on, or maybe they recently published something that was similar to your topic in theme. Or maybe the editor just isn't that interested in the particular topic you chose. Are you starting to see a pattern? Any one of these scenarios could get you rejected, and every one of them has *absolutely zero* to do with you and your writing. If you get specific comments, do a quick revision to address them (Sørina Higgins suggests no more than an hour or so) and then resubmit it somewhere else. The point is not to get overwhelmed or think it's all on you.

But with that said, it is a good idea to have others read your paper or presentation before you submit it. Find a group of friends or fellow Tolkien fans who're willing to read what you've written. Make sure they're going to be honest with you. If all your friends are too protective of your feelings to tell you that your arguments are weak and unconvincing, your prose reads like it was written by a slightly drunk sixth grader, and your jokes are corny, then (a) please introduce us, because we would love to have friends who don't tell us that *every day*, and (b) go find someone who will be honest with you. Local writers' groups are usually willing to be brutally honest

_____

353  Because we have lots of friends in this arena and we talk to them, not because we're constantly getting rejected. That's our story and we're sticking to it.

when workshopping; or writing consultancy services can be found to give professional feedback for a modest fee.

# What if I'm Not Ready for All That Just Yet?

Nothing says you have to, or should, jump straight into the deep end here. Unless you're lucky or absolutely brilliant, your first-time-out-the-gate research paper speculating on barter economy reforms instituted among the Drúedain during the chieftainship of Ghân-buri-Ghân is going to need a little work before it's ready to submit to a peer-reviewed anthology published by a prestige academic press. Submitting an idea to a moot—especially a smaller, regional one—is a great way to develop an idea before blowing it out into a full article. And, in case we haven't made this clear already, going to moots is a heck of a lot of fun.

Online communities are also great places to workshop and develop ideas, and get comfortable with the idea of strangers reading (and judging) your work. Fan communities you may already belong to on Facebook, Reddit, Discord, and elsewhere are full of people who want to read your academic work and would love to give you feedback on it. Or, if you think this is something you'll be doing a lot of, why not start a blog and publish your insights regularly? Most of the Tolkien fans we know love reading blogs about Tolkien, and there are some excellent ones out there. Start one, write something interesting, and you may very well get shared or even—as the kids say (we think?)—go viral. Pro tip: allow readers to comment on your blog. It'll help you gain valuable feedback that will improve your writing (as will all the practice), and you'll get some very interesting questions which may lead to new research and writing. Just be gracious in responding to your commenters; scholarship is about sharing ideas, but also about challenging ideas in a way that is constructive and contributes to our collective body of knowledge about Tolkien's work.

So conquer your fears, take a deep breath, and jump into the conversation in whatever way seems best to you. We look forward to reading, or hearing, your contribution to the exciting world of Tolkien studies.

# WHY ALAN LOVES IT

Shawn and I have each had the privilege of speaking at Tolkien conferences and moots around the world—both together, and individually. So while we can identify with the nerves that make themselves known when presenting a paper in front of a live (or even virtual) audience, I confess that presenting an *academic* paper is not in my experience. All my writing in the last decade has been for a more casual audience: podcast listeners.

Don't get me wrong: writing the episodes takes a lot of *studying Tolkien*. But it isn't proper "Tolkien Studies," and the show has rather prevented me from diving deeper into this niche—for now. I already have several questions I'd like to try to answer, and plan on being a pest at Oxonmoots, Mythmoots, and more for years to come. And if I weren't still paying off my JD, I'd go after a PhD in Tolkien Studies!

In the meantime, I love Tolkien Studies because it gives me an endless supply of insights about Tolkien and his works. I may not always agree with the conclusions that the author of a paper reaches, but that's part of what makes this such an interesting field. Do yourself a favor: subscribe to one or more of these journals—or access some for free, like the Tolkien Society's older *Mallorn* journals—and enjoy the dedicated hard work that Tolkien scholars have done to bring you their insights.

# Why Shawn Loves It

When I was a freshman in college, majoring in literature, I took a class on modern epics. For my final, I wrote a paper comparing the tale of Túrin Turambar—primarily using *The Silmarillion* as my source, but also some of the *Narn i Hîn Húrin* version from *Unfinished Tales*—with the Siegfried myth as told by the German opera composer Richard Wagner in his four-opera cycle *The Ring of the Nibelung* (Wagner was on the syllabus; Tolkien most certainly was not). One has to admit that, in the grand scheme of possible freshman final paper topics that could have compared Tolkien to Wagner, Túrin/Siegfried[354] wasn't the most boneheadedly obvious connection I could have come up with. The most boneheadedly obvious, of course, is the Ring itself; despite Tolkien's cheeky complaint in a 1961 letter to Allen & Unwin that "both rings were round, and there the resemblance ceases."[355] But I didn't pick the low-hanging fruit; I saw Wagner's lone-wolf dragon-slaying hero with a magical sword and I thought myself very clever for recognizing a similarity to what I thought of—at the time—as a pretty deep cut from Tolkien's writings.

I was eighteen, y'all. Cut me some slack.

The paper didn't do very well. I didn't fail or anything; it just didn't do very well by the admittedly high bar of my usual academic performance. I think I got a B+ on it, and just barely managed to hang onto my A for the semester. I was angry. I thought my professor just didn't "get it." The professor didn't accept the clear evidence that I presented in support of my thesis. Or he didn't think I should be writing on Tolkien; heck, he obviously didn't *know* anything about Tolkien (judging from the fact that he questioned my assertion that the utterly English Professor Tolkien was Catholic, not Anglican).

---

354 For you non-opera fans, Siegfried is the German equivalent of the Norse hero Sigurd, mentioned earlier in this book.

355 Carpenter, *Letters*, No. 229.

Of course, I realize now—and you can probably see already—that the fault was all with me. If my professor didn't "get it," it's because I didn't do a good enough job of giving it to him. If he didn't accept my evidence, then it wasn't presented correctly (or it wasn't the right evidence). If there was a chance I shouldn't be writing on Tolkien, I should have wowed the teacher so much he had no choice but to accept my choice of topic; and if he didn't know anything about Tolkien, then it was my job to educate him: right down to the (understandably surprising, if you're not a Tolkien fan) information that Tolkien was in fact a Catholic. In other words, my paper just wasn't written all that well.

The other reason the paper didn't do as well as I wanted it to was because the question it set out to answer wasn't a good question, as we've discussed in this chapter. There was nothing to it except, essentially, "Did Tolkien read Wagner?" and/or "Was Tolkien inspired by Wagner?" which is absolutely *not* the kind of open-ended question that makes for good academic essays. The question, and my approach to answering it, were also fundamentally flawed in the sense that whether or not Tolkien read Wagner doesn't matter one scale on Glaurung's slimy belly, because we know that both Tolkien and Wagner read the Norse *Völsunga Saga*, which is well attested in secondary sources as an inspiration to both of them. Which, if course, is something that I would have found out quickly if I had done even the tiniest fraction of the proper research and managed to get a hold of Tolkien's Letter 131 to Milton Waldman (ironic, considering that I now seem to reference this once at least once a week) in which he states *quite clearly* that yes, Túrin Turambar was "derived from elements in Sigurd the Volsung" as well as other myths. In other words, I didn't even scratch the surface of the research I should have done to write that paper properly, and if I had done the research, I could have reduced my entire paper to the paragraph I just now wrote as an adult, sitting at my desk in my sleep shorts.

In hindsight, not only did I have absolutely no right to be angry at the result, but I should be thankful that I got a B+...which I chalk up to the fact that I got along very well with that professor, and he was a fan of my prose style.[356]

So, yeah, my first foray into the world of Tolkien studies wasn't great. It kind of broke all the rules that have been established in this chapter.[357] But as I got older and I continued reading deeper and deeper into Tolkien's *Biography*, *Letters*, and the scholarly works we've been talking about in this book, I got much better about my own analysis—not to mention better at recognizing what's truly a significant question to ask, and what's not. I'm no academic, and there are people out there who can research, analyze, and write circles around me. But, like anyone who keeps at something for a long enough time, and with apologies to Monty Python, "I got better." And while I still haven't really done any serious academic research and haven't given many academic presentations on Tolkien, I suppose one could say that it was the hunger for that kind of analysis that led me to approach the text the way I always have done on *The Prancing Pony Podcast*.

The world of Tolkien studies is endlessly fascinating to me, and frankly is the reason why I personally will never run out of things to read about Tolkien. Even if someday there are no more unpublished manuscripts left behind to publish, if eventually the seemingly endless (but sadly, certainly not endless) hoard of papers left behind by Professor Tolkien eventually runs out...there will always be new scholarship. New analysis, new insights, and new generations of scholars approaching the work for the first time. Tolkien studies is truly a fountain that will never run dry, and like the fountain that feeds the stream that fills Galadriel's mirror, it will continue to reveal many things: things we wish to behold, and also things unbidden that are often stranger and more profitable.

---

356  Really, can you blame him?

357  Which, as Geoffrey Rush's Captain Hector Barbossa said in *Pirates of the Caribbean*, was "more what you'd call 'guidelines' than actual rules." Longtime listeners to *The Prancing Pony Podcast* surely saw this one coming.

Why We Love Middle-earth

# CHAPTER 17

# FELLOWSHIPS OF THE RING: FAN ORGANIZATIONS AND CONFERENCES

*"I have heard about the Tolkien Society.[358] Real lunatics don't join them, I think. But still such things fill me, too, with alarm and despondency."*

—J.R.R. Tolkien, from an August 1965 letter to W.H. Auden[359]

Fan organizations have been part of the Tolkien fandom since not long after the publication of *The Lord of the Rings*. According to Charles E. Noad, who wrote on the history of the Tolkien Society in the 2010 issue of *Mallorn*, the

---

358 The "Tolkien Society" in question was not the current Tolkien Society headquartered in the United Kingdom, but what would become the Tolkien Society of America, later a part of the Mythopoeic Society. We still don't think *real* lunatics join either of these fine organizations; just moderate lunatics like ourselves.

359 Carpenter, *Letters*, No. 275.

journal of the Tolkien Society, the first "organized Tolkien fan grouping"[360] was likely organized in 1960 by around 30 fans based in California, called (fittingly enough) The Fellowship of the Ring.[361] By the time *The Lord of the Rings* was published in paperback in the United States in 1965—first by Ace Books and then later in the authorized Ballantine Books edition—there was a new American fan club in existence: the Tolkien Society of America, founded by a student named Richard Plotz in New York. Plotz wrote to Tolkien in 1965 to invite him to join the Society; and though Tolkien's thoughts on the group are painfully apparent in the letter to W.H. Auden quoted above, the Professor was (as always, when corresponding with fans) kind to Mr. Plotz, writing back (Letter No. 276) to say that he would be "pleased to be associated with [the Society] in some informal capacity," though he did not feel right about joining a society of fans of the works he himself had written.

# THAT'D BE WEIRD.

Indeed.

Not long afterwards, on the West Coast, another Tolkien society formed at California State University Los Angeles in 1967 by a fan named Glen GoodKnight expanded its focus to include members of the Inklings, such as C.S. Lewis and Charles Williams, and rebranded itself the Mythopoeic Society. The Mythopoeic Society held a Narnia Conference in 1969, and the following year had its first-ever annual conference, called "Mythcon." The Mythopoeic Society became such a force to be reckoned with in fantasy fandom that in 1972, the Tolkien Society of America merged with the Mythopoeic Society, and it became *the* preeminent fan organization in the United States dedicated to Tolkien and the other Inklings. Today, the Mythopoeic Society is a thriving entity, holding Mythcon annually, publishing

---

360   Noad, Charles E. "The Tolkien Society – the early days." *Mallorn* No. 50 (2010), p. 15.

361   According to Noad, this early Tolkien fan club was exclusive – one needed the personal approval of its founder Bruce Pelz to join it. Still, there was an "offshoot" of the group in the United Kingdom, and a fanzine exclusive to the English membership in addition to the one for members in the United States.

Why We Love Middle-earth

books and the renowned academic journal *Mythlore,* and giving the prestigious Mythopoeic Award every year for outstanding achievements in mythopoeic fiction and scholarly writing. They are not an exclusively-Tolkien organization, but nevertheless stand tall in the fandom community.

On the other side of the pond, there were British members of the Tolkien Society of America; but despite it being the land Tolkien called home for nearly all his life, there was as yet no fan organization based in the United Kingdom. That started to change in 1969 when a retired civil servant named Vera Chapman – revered in Tolkien circles as "Belladonna Took"—undertook the formation of a British-based Tolkien fan organization in an attempt to disassociate her beloved Tolkien's works from "the drug-ridden writings of hippiedom"[362] which were apparently all too often sharing space with Tolkien's works on the bookshelves of fans motivated by the counterculture of the day. The first meeting of the UK-based Tolkien Society[363] was in January 1970, and it wasn't long before they got the Professor's attention just like Plotz's American organization had some years before. For Tolkien's 80th birthday on January 3, 1972, the Tolkien Society sent him a happy birthday message via telegram, and Chapman was promptly thanked by the Professor's secretary that night, and by a personal letter from the Professor himself a month later. Apparently emboldened by this personal connection, Chapman approached Tolkien in 1972 and asked him if he would be interested in serving as the Tolkien Society's honorary president, to which Tolkien replied, "Certainly."[364] Professor Tolkien remains the Tolkien Society's President *in perpetuo* today,[365] and the Tolkien Society continues to grow and thrive in its mission to promote the life and works of J.R.R. Tolkien,

---

362  Noad, "The Tolkien Society," 2010, 17. Noad, for his part, acknowledged that this *might* have been "not an altogether unproblematic stand to take, in that it may betray a tendency towards too prescriptive a view of Tolkien appreciation."

363  Henceforth, we will just call it the "Tolkien Society," as it is the only organization by that name in existence today.

364  Noad, "The Tolkien Society," 2010, 22.

365  In practice, the Tolkien Society's head is its Chair. Serving in the role of Chair since 2013 is Shaun Gunner, whose leadership has led the Tolkien Society to increase its membership more than fivefold, and firmly established the Tolkien Society as a global fan organization.

through local "smial" chapters all over the world, highly active social media communities, an annual in-person (and online) Oxford conference called "Oxonmoot," frequent webinars and online events, and the publication of its news bulletin *Amon Hen* and literary journal *Mallorn*.

# SO AS AN (AMERICAN/ BRITISH) FAN, SHOULD I STICK TO THE (MYTHOPOEIC/TOLKIEN) SOCIETY?

Though one might be mistaken into believing that the Mythopoeic Society today is for American fans, and the Tolkien Society for British fans, in actuality both of these organizations have impressive membership figures worldwide, and membership in either (or both) can be rewarding for fans no matter where they are located. Fans anywhere can benefit from these organizations' websites, snail mail or electronic delivery of their newszines and academic journals, and the relative ease of joining online conferences in the twenty-first century.

And there are organizations in non-English-speaking countries (or not primarily English-speaking countries) as well. One of the best known is the Deutsche Tolkien Gesellschaft in Germany, founded relatively recently in 1997, but already boasting nearly a thousand fans. DTG members can meet up at the annual *Tolkien Thing* ("Tolkien Moot") as well as the weekend-long party *Tolkien Tage* ("Tolkien Days") featuring talks as well as entertainment; the DTG also publishes the bilingual, interdisciplinary academic journal *Hither Shore*. Another well-known European organization is Forodrim, founded in Sweden in 1972. Forodrim is notable for its "guilds," subgroups devoted to special interests within Tolkien fandom, such as singing, history, and languages. But these are just a sampling of the organizations that have gained some recognition worldwide; as Scull and Hammond note in their entry on Fandom and Popularity in *The J.R.R. Tolkien Companion and Guide*, fan organizations "today are active in most countries of Europe, as well as in Russia and Japan."[366]

Even more recently, another organized fan group has collected around Signum University and its open-access arm, Mythgard Institute. First launched in 2011 by podcaster and academic Corey Olsen, "the Tolkien Professor," Signum and Mythgard bring fans together from all over the world through online seminars, for-credit academic courses, and podcast recordings. It also has hosted an annual multi-day conference called "Mythmoot" since 2012, as well as single-day regional moots in the US, UK, and now Australia. Signum also offers Signum Academy Clubs, online groups for children and teens focused on writing, foreign language learning, translation of ancient texts, and more.

All of the organizations above have active websites and online presences, so the best place to find out more—or join—is your device. Tell them Alan and Shawn of *The Prancing Pony Podcast* sent you!

# YOU KEEP USING THIS WORD... WHAT'S A "MOOT"?

As is probably apparent, most of these fan organizations have at least one major annual conference. Some of them, like Signum, have various regional ones as well. And many of these conferences are called "moots." It's reasonable to wonder why.

---

366   Scull & Hammond, *Reader's Guide Part 1*, 2017, 392-3.

The answer, of course, goes back to Tolkien himself, who used the word *moot* in *The Lord of the Rings* to describe a meeting of the Ents, called "Entmoot" or in some cases simply "the Moot." According to the *Oxford English Dictionary*, the primary meaning of this word is "a meeting, an assembly of people, especially one for judicial or legislative purposes," and—like many obscure words favored by Tolkien—it goes back to Old English and even older Germanic roots. It's really just another, more archaic-sounding noun derived from the verb *meet*, not used in everyday conversation anymore because we already have the far more ubiquitous (and far less interesting) noun *meeting*.

The use of the word *moot* to mean a meeting of Tolkien fans—not Ents—goes back at least as far as 1973, when a fan named John Abbot suggested an "Oxford Moot" in a fanzine called *Nazgul, or The Wakefield Charivari*.[367] The first Oxonmoot[368] hosted by the Tolkien Society was held the following year, and because apparently Tolkien fans love a good archaism, the term seems to have stuck. For our part, we love this peculiar little term, for a couple of reasons. First of all, it feels like *ours*. Though many moots now invite discussion on a host of authors besides Tolkien, and even other forms of storytelling like film, most of them are still largely by and for Tolkien fans, and the use of the term *moot* is a sure marker that you'll find some Tolkien fans present. Secondly, though, we find the word *moot*—with its monosyllabic Germanic simplicity—so much warmer and alive than its Latin/French-derived synonyms like *conference* or *convention*. You may have to go to a *convention* for a corporate desk job. You'll be invited to a *conference* with your child's teacher. But a *moot* is Tolkienish, and that means geeky comfort.

But moots are not just a bunch of fans sitting around a table talking about hobbits and elves. At a moot, you can expect informative and eye-opening presentations and roundtable discussions, often including at least one or

---

367  The Tolkien Society website, "The Origins of Oxonmoot." https://www.tolkiensociety.org/society/events/oxonmoot/origins-of-oxonmoot/

368  Note that the spelling is *Oxonmoot* – not *oxen*. The *Oxon-* in the prefix is not the plural of *ox* but is actually derived from the Latin name of Oxford, *Oxonium*. *Ibid*.

Why We Love Middle-earth

two keynote presentations by notable Tolkien scholars, artists, authors, and more. The biggest moots are multi-day affairs with presentations during the day; and dinners, happy hours, gaming, cosplay contests, entertainment, pub quizzes, and more fun with fellow fans and friends by night.

# SOUNDS FUN! ANY OTHER ORGANIZED FAN GROUPS I SHOULD KNOW ABOUT?

Well, since you asked...we're not sure if this qualifies as "organized" (unless perhaps you mean "organized chaos"), but the fan community that has grown up around *The Prancing Pony Podcast* through our social media spaces, our Patreon community, and Discord server, has become very much like an online "smial" or fan organization. Members of our community have formed lasting friendships, discovered Tolkien together, and we've enjoyed getting to know them better. Since 2021, we've even hosted our own almost-annual PPP Moot! Our first official gathering of fans of *The Prancing Pony Podcast* was online only, but we quickly followed that with an in-person moot (with an option for online attendance) in fall 2022, in Milwaukee to coincide with the "J.R.R. Tolkien: The Art of the Manuscript" exhibition at the Haggerty Museum of Art at Marquette University – which kindly hosted us and welcomed moot attendees to the exhibition.

We plan on hosting many more PPP Moots over the coming years, and even hope to keep them going long after the podcast itself has finished. We hope to see you at one!

# WHY ALAN LOVES IT

Having hatched my love for all things Tolkien and Middle-earth on my own, for the longest time I'd considered my fandom a singular affair. As I mentioned elsewhere in this book, I did not know about fan groups until the Jackson adaptations came out, and it was a couple of more years after that before I discovered organizations like the Tolkien Society.

I look back at my years as a young fan and I can't help but wonder how much my experience would have been enriched had I known about, joined, and taken part in these groups and events. While I can't change the past for me, I hope I can encourage those of you who are newer to the Tolkien fandom to consider joining one or more of these organizations. There is no easier way to find your people, to connect with like-minded individuals from all around the world—folks who love Tolkien as much as you do, if not more!

Joining organizations is one thing, and we certainly encourage that. But as Shawn has suggested below, it is the fan *gatherings* that are the highlight. Hardly a year has gone by since the start of *The Prancing Pony Podcast*— aside from 2020 when such in-person gatherings were simply not possible— where I've not found a way to attend either the Tolkien Society's Oxonmoot or Signum's Mythmoot. I don't go to present papers—though Shawn and I have delivered the keynote at one of Signum's regional moots and recorded live podcast episodes at both moots—but to see my people. To connect with others who love these works as much as we do, to stay up until all hours of the night at a pub, or by a fireside, to explore deep questions about Middle-earth...or to tell our own stories, sometimes entirely unconnected to Tolkien (but never unaffected). If you are able to do one fan-related activity, make it this one: attend a moot, in-person if you are able.

# WHY SHAWN LOVES IT

Pinning down what I love about Tolkien fan organizations and moots is tough, because ultimately these entities are about people, and there are as many reasons to love them as there are incredible people who make them what they are. But I'll start with the obvious: I *love* going to moots. There's simply no other feeling in the world like spending time with other fans talking about Tolkien, sharing ideas, exploring likes and dislikes, learning, and everything else that geeks do when they're together; when everyone around you gets your jokes, understands the love you have for this fantasy world, and everyone lifts each other up in a sea of geeky passion and mutual inspiration. The fact that I have so many friends in the Tolkien community, and this is where we see each other in person, is the icing on that magical cake.

Most of the moots that happen are hosted by fan organizations like the Tolkien Society and Signum, so it's great to be plugged into them for that reason alone. And in recent years, the bar to entry on moots is lower than ever before, because many moots now offer the option to attend parts of the conferences online. It's not the same as being together in a room, sharing food and drink with members of your community; but it is still a whole lot of fun to attend a moot online, and nothing says you can't break bread with friends over videoconferencing.

But there's a whole lot more to fan organizations besides just moots: there are print publications like the Tolkien Society's *Amon Hen* and *Mallorn* to give us something tangible to hold onto, and these days most fan organizations have online communities on Facebook, Discord, and other platforms, where one can join webinars, discussions, and just hang out with other members of the community. And while it's true that one can find friends and like-minded geek communities without the formal structure of a fan organization, the costs to join these organizations are usually not steep at all, and more than worth what you have the potential to get out of it. The real question is, why *not* join one?

# CHAPTER 18

# NOT ALL TECHNOLOGIES ARE AN EVIL: ONLINE CONTENT

*"I love the internet. It's never been easier to connect with my fans, or deliver news and information to people all around the world who want to read my works."*

—Not a real quote by J.R.R. Tolkien at all, at all

It feels like kind of a shame that Professor Tolkien didn't live to see all the amazing content that's sprung up on the internet for Tolkien fans. We can only wonder what he might have thought of the internet at all. Granted, considering his reactions to other types of technology that were new when he was still around—like the automobile, which he famously called the "infernal combustion engine" and blamed for the "destroying" of his beloved

Oxford,[369] or the tape recorder, which he first encountered in 1952 in the home of some friends, and spoke into it only after first reciting the Lord's Prayer in Gothic into it to "cast out any devil that might be in it"[370]—he probably would have hated it. But for fans of Tolkien, there is much to love online. It would be impossible to do more than scratch the surface of what's available online in this chapter, and the nature of online content is that it's constantly changing; by the time this book goes to print, and certainly in a couple of years, there will be so much new stuff out there that we'll look back and laugh at how incomplete this chapter is. But we present this chapter to you simply to show examples of the depth and breadth of stuff there is available for Tolkien fans online. We trust you to turn to your search engine for more.

Of course there are more websites than it's possible to name here, and there are websites for every subset of fandom mentioned already in this book (and more): for collectors, there are sites like Tolkien Collector's Guide (tolkienguide.com), TolkienBooks.net, Tolkien Library (tolkienlibrary.com), and many more to help you find information about collecting and connect with other collectors online. For fans of Tolkien's languages, there's the Elvish Linguistic Fellowship (elvish.org), the online Elvish dictionary Parf Edhellen (elfdict.com), Helge Fauskanger's Ardalambion (ardalambion.net), and the Tengwar website Tecendil (tecendil.com) for Elvish fans. Fans interested in Dwarvish can find a wealth of information at the Dwarrow Scholar website (dwarrowscholar.com). Those interested in Tolkien studies should definitely check out Signum University's website (signumuniversity.org), or learn more about the incredible work being done on Tolkien and digital humanities by our friend and cohost of *The Rings of Power Wrap-up*, James Tauber, at the Digital Tolkien Project (digitaltolkien.com). And every major fan organization

---

369 From a 1944 letter to Christopher Tolkien (No. 64) and a 1956 draft of a letter to Michael Straight (No. 181), respectively.

370 The friends were George and Moira Sayer, and Tolkien's "whimsically" fearful reaction to the device was documented in the liner notes to the LP issue of the recordings, *J.R.R. Tolkien Reads and Sings His The Hobbit and The Fellowship of the Ring*. The recordings are now available as part of the four-CD *J.R.R Tolkien Audio Collection* set.

we've mentioned in this book has a website, too, from the aforementioned Signum University to the Tolkien Society (tolkiensociety.org) and the Mythopoeic Society (mythsoc.org).

There are more blogs out there devoted to Tolkien than we could possibly mention here. Some are more academic, while others are devoted to more casual fan musings. Some of them are actually written by some of the biggest names in Tolkien scholarship. Wayne G. Hammond and Christina Scull have maintained a blog called *Too Many Books and Never Enough* (wayneandchristina.wordpress.com) that remains one of the greatest resources online for bite-size Tolkien scholarship. Dimitra Fimi, Michael D.C. Drout, John Garth, and other Tolkien scholars have websites with blogs they keep current with news and observations. But our favorite site for a mix of general fandom news, Tolkien-related travelogue, and accessible research is TheTolkienist.com, run by one of the most likable individuals in Tolkien fandom around the world, Marcel Aubron-Bülles—who also offers a newsletter called the Roving Ranger.

And of course, for news about Tolkien's books and their many adaptations, there's TheOneRing.net, which for almost twenty-five years (founded in 1999) has been a mainstay of the Tolkien fan community. While still generally containing more information about adaptations than some of the other sites we've talked about, there's a lot there for book fans as well, including "The Library," which offers a place for more scholarly articles on Tolkien's work.

Great Tolkien content can also be found at other outlets not dedicated to Tolkien, too: without a doubt, one of the best places we know of is Tor. com, online presence of the legendary science fiction and fantasy publishing house Tor Books. For years, Tor.com has featured Tolkien content regularly, from news and reviews, to research and character studies, to truly one-of-a-kind content like *The Silmarillion Primer*, a thirty-plus-part summary, breakdown, analysis, and guide to Tolkien's most notoriously hard to digest work by fantasy writer Jeff LaSala.

Speaking of one-of-a-kind content, there are some fan projects out there that truly defy categorization. Emil Johansson's LotrProject (lotrproject.com) is one such project: featuring interactive maps of Middle-earth, timelines of the major events of the First through the Fourth Ages, and fascinating statistics on all sorts of topics from the life expectancy of characters by race to searchable databases of keywords frequently used in Tolkien's texts, it's a powerful research tool if you know how to use it,[371] and a classic example of a labor of love in the Tolkien community, as the effort to build it all must have been staggering.

Take all that we just said about a "labor of love" and multiply it by a thousand for ArdaCraft (ardacraft.me), a nine-plus-year project to recreate Middle-earth in "one of the largest and most detailed Minecraft maps ever created." That's right, just install their mod and you too can explore Middle-earth in all its magnificent glory *in Minecraft*. And for those of us who are too old or too uncool to know our creepers from our illagers,[372] there's a YouTube channel by the ArdaCraft team, allowing you to passively enjoy videos that sweep across the painstakingly recreated landscape in all its 3D majesty.

# GREAT! WEBSITES...LOTS OF WEBSITES. ANYTHING ELSE?

Oh, sure. At the risk of sounding like we're talking to our parents, there's a whole lot of online content out there besides just websites. The Tolkien Society, which gives awards every year to outstanding entries in Tolkien scholarship and fandom, expanded its "Best Website" category in 2020 to a "Best Online Content" category, to allow for nominations of the many non-HTML-based creations out there, like YouTube channels and podcasts.[373]

---

371  In other words, great for quick lookups of information you need to win online arguments.

372  Shawn's son told us these are actual things in *Minecraft*. We'll just have to take his word for it.

373  At the risk of tooting our own horns like Boromir in an orc-fight, *The Prancing Pony Podcast* was proud to win the Best Online Content award in 2020 (the year the category was expanded) and again in 2022. Thanks, Tolkien Society!

Obviously, we will suggest you listen to *The Prancing Pony Podcast* (if you haven't already), which focuses primarily on Tolkien's books. We also launched *The Rings of Power Wrap-up* in 2022 to discuss, analyze, dissect, gossip, and speculate all about Amazon's *Rings of Power* series. And, because we are—above all—*huge* fans of alliteration, in 2023 *The Prancing Pony Podcast* launched *Today's Tolkien Times,* a daily short-format video podcast focusing on a different topic each day, such as Tolkien Tuesdays (delving into the biography of the Professor himself), Word-nerd Wednesdays, Third Age Thursdays, and Fandom Fridays.

But of course there are a lot of great podcasts out there produced by others. *The Tolkien Experience Podcast,* hosted by Tolkien scholars Sara Brown and Luke Shelton, interviews a notable Tolkien fan or scholar in each episode to learn more about their personal experience of Tolkien's work, from initial discovery to current impressions. And of course, we must tip our hats again to the person who really put Tolkien podcasting on the map, Corey "The Tolkien Professor" Olsen, whose current podcast *Exploring The Lord of the Rings* takes listeners on a sentence-by-sentence journey through Tolkien's magnum opus (yes, even slower than we go), followed by a "virtual field trip" through the places of Standing Stone Games's *Lord of the Rings Online* game. Or, if YouTube is your platform of choice, you can't go wrong by subscribing to the reigning high king, Nerd of the Rings (youtube.com/c/NerdoftheRings) who walks viewers through character profiles, journeys, Middle-earth history, and more. Finally, don't forget the Logan's Run of social media:[374] TikTok. Use the hashtag #TolkienTok to find some incredible content creators, but especially The Obscure Lord of the Rings Facts Guy (@donmarshall72) and the always entertaining @knewbettadobetta. Just don't stop with those two!

All this is only a taste of what's out there online, provided to help whet your appetite to go in search of more. You can always find more content

---

374  If you're too young to understand the reference, that's the point. *Logan's Run* was a 1976 film (based on a book of the same name) in which anyone who reached the age of thirty was killed.

by searching and through social media—there are more Tolkien-related Facebook groups (including many by and for fans of the content creators we've been talking about), subreddits, and chat forums than you can brandish a Barrow-blade at. Tolkien fans being generally decent people, most of them tend to be among the friendliest fan communities we've encountered online. Good content creators are always out there promoting themselves, so social media groups are a great way to discover more.

We'd be remiss if we failed to mention here—or relegated to a footnote—the hulking, ugly cave troll in online Tolkien spaces. In recent years there has been a rise in the appearance of new content on YouTube, blogs, and elsewhere from creators wishing to use Tolkien's work as a battle standard for their own noxious beliefs. Apparently brought out of hiding to take up arms against the much-celebrated diversity of casting in Amazon's *Rings of Power* series, these content creators—we will not utter their names here—will claim that they are defending Tolkien against revisionism and reinterpretation, when in reality all they're doing is defending their own racism, misogyny, toxic nationalism, and hate for people they see as different from them. The authors of this book have always, ever since we started our podcast in 2016, tried very hard not to gatekeep against *anyone*—and we won't question whether these people actually do love Tolkien like they say they do. But there are three undeniable facts about this rash (and it is a rash: an ugly, infectious, irritating rash) of hateful content that certainly make us go "hmm": (1) most of these racist and misogynistic content creators only sprang up in the past couple of years, after news started coming out about *The Rings of Power*, (2) their commentary about Tolkien adaptations is largely identical to similar comments made in other fandoms—such as Star Wars and the Marvel Cinematic Universe—in response to the emergence of diverse casting and themes in those universes, and (3) anyone who really pays attention to Tolkien's writing will recognize that it is love and togetherness, people from various backgrounds coming together to fight evil, that stands as the central ethos of the Middle-earth legendarium.[375] So we'll leave you to draw your own conclusions about whether these people who can't stop complaining about Elf-women wearing armor, or Hobbits who have dark skin, are true Tolkien fans or not. Most of the true Tolkien fans *we've* met are kind, generous, inclusive, and embracing of both the diversity of Tolkien fans across the world and the attempts by recent adaptations to bring more diversity to Middle-earth. We may not be perfect as a fandom, but most of us have good intentions; and we are trying to be better.

# Why Alan Loves It

Shawn and I have told our story at the beginning of this book: we met in a Facebook group; *The Prancing Pony Podcast* owes its very existence to the online Tolkien community. Our earliest growth was fueled by social media (mostly Facebook and Twitter); our biggest supporters get together with us on Discord; I've started a new project on YouTube (Today's Tolkien Times); and I share readings and more on TikTok. You may be holding a physical book in your hands[376]—but this all originates from, relies upon, and continues in, the online Tolkien community.

Perhaps the greatest joy of online content in the Tolkien fandom is the joy of finding your people. Each content creator attracts their own crowd—though there is plenty of overlap—so you can enjoy the content you choose while connecting with dozens, hundreds, or even thousands of other Tolkien fans

---

375  This isn't to say that there aren't some descriptions and treatments of race (particularly of Orcs, Dwarves, and the Men who follow Sauron) in Tolkien's works that are not problematic to modern sensibilities. As skilled a wielder of his word-hoard as Tolkien was, he was still a white man living in the early twentieth century, and although he famously hated Nazis (calling Hitler a "ruddy little ignoramus" in a 1941 letter to his son Michael, No. 45) and expressed compassion for Black people living under institutionalized racism in South Africa (in a 1944 letter to Christopher, No. 61)—which we hope means he was ahead of many of his contemporaries on matters of race—this does not excuse or erase the fact that he used some words and phrases to describe skin tone and other phenotypical attributes that leave people understandably hurt. A full treatment of race in Tolkien's works is well beyond the scope of this book and the experience of these authors; but we did approach the subject on *The Prancing Pony Podcast* in Episodes 114 and 192. An excellent scholarly study has been done by Dimitra Fimi in *Tolkien, Race and Cultural History*.

376  Unless, of course, you're not: we hope some of you are reading this on e-readers and others are listening to the audiobook.

at the same time. From small communities that follow a niche blog, all the way up to the massive YouTube channels, each group is both a community unto itself, and a part of the larger Tolkien fandom community.

Crucially, just as the field of Tolkien Studies has given opportunity to new voices and the democratization of academia in Tolkien, the ability to create and consume online content has democratized the fandom as a whole, giving voice to many who might not have had that opportunity as little as a decade ago. So I encourage you: find your spot, get your voice out there, and let the world see your love for Tolkien and Middle-earth.

# Why Shawn Loves It

As has been stated elsewhere (and often), Alan and I met online, in a Facebook group. When we launched *The Prancing Pony Podcast* in 2016, the early growth of the podcast came largely from social media exposure, and virtually all of the friends I have who are Tolkien fans are people I interact with online—except for occasional in-person meetups and moots. So I am definitely an active participant in the online Tolkien fandom, and proud to be both a creator and consumer of some fantastic online content related to Tolkien. If Lothlórien was "the heart of Elvendom on earth," then the heart of my fandom in Tolkien is online. It's where my people are, and always have been. As the kid in my high school who pushed all his friends to read *The Lord of the Rings*—and though they did read it, I was always a little annoyed that they never got into it as much as I did—it's great to find "your people" online, and it's no surprise that I have made some really good friends through the online Tolkien fandom.

Of course, that's all about Tolkien *community*, but community is one of the things I love the most about online content relating to Tolkien. Podcasts, YouTube channels, discussion groups, even Patreon pages for artists and writers (and yes, podcasters) tend to become nucleus points for communities: social media groups, Discord servers, and (as we've discussed earlier in this book) moots and online meetings. I've always said that meeting people and finding community has always been my favorite aspect of being a Tolkien podcaster, and it's also my favorite aspect of supporting other content creators online.

But, of course, it's only *one* of the things I love so much about all this great online Tolkien content. I suppose the other big one has got to be just how democratic it all is. You don't have to be a PhD, or a published writer, or a recognized name to start creating content. All you need is a computer (and maybe a microphone and a camera), a love for Tolkien, and an interesting way of expressing yourself...and you can start creating content that can find an audience. And so the vast amount of avenues for content out there has led to a diversity of voices: academics, yes, and professional journalists and writers, but also smart and passionate amateurs with a unique take on Tolkien's writing: young people reading through *The Silmarillion* for the first time, gamers, musicians, artists, web developers, people of color, women, and readers in parts of the world so far from Oxford and Birmingham that it would have been unthinkable that they could make a mark in Tolkien fandom even twenty years ago. And yes, even middle-aged dads who love quoting Monty Python a little too much can find a voice in this environment.

All this access has led to an outpouring of ideas from all over the world, from people of all sorts of different backgrounds, and though we've only begun to see where those ideas may yet take us, I am very excited to have the opportunity to watch it all happen. And I know that it will keep me busy learning for many, many years to come.

Why We Love Middle-earth

# AFTERWORD

As it turns out, writing a book is not *entirely* like writing a podcast: after all, if we wanted to "go long" and exceed our target 100-110 minute episode length,[377] we could just... keep talking. But it turns out that publishers expect a book to eventually, you know, *end*. Fret not, dear reader: there is a solution, and one I think we can all appreciate. We will simply have to write another one! To paraphrase film-Pippin: "What about second books?"

We don't know when this might actually happen – our families will, we hope and trust, want us both back after the long months of writing this one, and they'll have something to say about how much time passes before we do something this all-consuming again. But it is both our genuine hope and actual plan to write another book on Middle-earth and the Tolkien fandom.

In this eventual follow-up, we intend to dive deeper into the rich *themes* of Tolkien: hope and despair, fate and free will, fellowship and community, fall and redemption, death and immortality,[378] and so much more. As we have a chance to read newer books – *The Fall of Númenor*, and *The Battle of Maldon: Together with the Homecoming of Beorhtnoth* were both published during the course of the writing of this volume – we will include chapters on them as well.

And we'll get to explore even more adaptations! We both believe the BBC Radio adaptation, written by Brian Sibley, to be the gold standard of Tolkien adaptations, and we'll tell you why in the next volume. We'll cover

---

377 Those of you who have listened for years may laugh at this clock-based optimism, but that really has been the target episode length since the start of Season 2.

378 Serial longevity, actually, as we've pointed out earlier.

audiobooks, especially now that we have all three of the major works narrated by Andy Serkis, who voiced Gollum in the Jackson films. There's a new movie coming out next year, so *The War of the Rohirrim* will feature in the next book of ours, along with a little television project you might have heard of: *The Lord of the Rings: The Rings of Power*, which will be easier to write about with a few seasons under its belt. Finally, we plan to cover the long history of Middle-earth based games: both tabletop and card games (like the new *Magic: The Gathering* game) as well as video games like *The Shadow of Mordor* or *The Lord of the Rings Online*.

And the fandom – oh, there are so many more things we can talk about, and we will! Composers and musicians, visual artists, cosplayers, crafting, cooking, brewing: there are so very many ways to enjoy your Middle-earth fandom, and we'll bring as many of them to you as we can.

So join us again soon! In the meantime, we hope this book has been both informative and entertaining. And if it has, we hope that you'll recommend it or give a copy to a friend who is a Tolkien fan or is looking to take their first steps on the road to becoming a Tolkien fan, in the spirit of welcoming others into this Tolkien fandom we all love so much.

Well, folks... 100,000 words is far too short a time to spend amongst such excellent and admirable readers, but until next time: farewell, friends!

# ACKNOWLEDGMENTS

This book is the product of many months of writing, but also many more years of reading, talking, interviewing, podcasting, and independent research in our ongoing quest to learn as much as we can about J.R.R. Tolkien's life and works. Like Merry and Pippin when they were carried by Treebeard to the battle at Isengard, we stand on the shoulders of giants. So, Shawn and Alan would like to thank the following individuals who—directly and indirectly—helped make this book what it is.

First and foremost, we wish to thank our families for their patience, support, encouragement, and belief in us.

We wish to thank the many biographers and scholars whose work is cited in this book and has guided us in our approach to understanding Tolkien's world.

We also wish to thank the team of talented people who have come alongside us to help with many of the day-to-day tasks that *The Prancing Pony Podcast* requires. Team PPP, as we've come to call them, have been indispensable, especially over the months that we've written this book, as they have stepped up to take on more whenever possible. We express our deepest thanks, then, to (in alphabetical order because you're *all* important!) Megan Collins, Becca Davis, Phil Dean, Casey Hilsee, Katie McKenna, and Jordan Rannells.

To those who blew their horns and rode to our aid when it was most needed, reviewing parts (or all, in some cases) of the manuscript for accuracy and to provide feedback on how it was all coming together, we thank you: Jeremy Edmonds, Jeff LaSala, Chad Bornholdt, and James Tauber. Any errors or misstatements remaining in the book are solely the responsibility of the authors.

We also thank the many who contributed to this Númenórean effort with their comments and insights that are quoted in this book, including Sørina Higgins, Chad High, Andrew Ferguson, and Brandon Wainerdi. And there were also many who—quoted or otherwise—helped us keep our heads above water with encouragement, suggestions, and advice, and deserve our thanks as well: Shaun Gunner, Corey Olsen, Tom Hillman, and John Garth.

To the legendary individuals in the "too many slashes" Tolkien group on Facebook who participated in the Book Week posts so long ago: you all were our first followers, early inspirations, and companions in conversation, and we're grateful that so many of you have stuck it out with us for all these years. You know who you are, and we thank you.

We also wish to thank our editing team at Mango Publishing, including Brenda Knight, Natasha Vera, and Yaddyra Peralta. And to our illustrator, the incredible Emily Austin: thank you for helping these pages come to life.

*Shawn*: I would especially like to thank my wife, Lisa, an all-too-often silent partner supporting me in all I've managed to accomplish to get me to this point. For love, confidence, and trust; for counseling in my most difficult hours, and for being the island to which I return at the end of every difficult voyage. And to our children Lucian and Vesper, for showing maturity beyond their years in understanding the importance of this project and the podcast that spawned it. I appreciate you all more than these words can say.

I would also like to thank everyone who ever gave me a brutally honest comment in a writers' workshop, or a comment that I needed to hear about a podcast, that made me better at what I do. But also, thank you to those who praised and encouraged me, and gave me the confidence to keep growing.

And of course, thank you to every single person—from personal friends to podcast listeners and everyone in between—who reached out to me when I announced I would be stepping away as full-time co-host of *The Prancing*

Why We Love Middle-earth

*Pony Podcast*. I hope the volume in your hands is proof that I'm not *really* going anywhere.

*Alan*: I would like to thank my wife, Heidi, for her decades of support, encouragement, and persistent belief despite the odds. I would also like to thank our son Jai, and daughter Elanor, who have spent many evenings missing their dad as I write the book and the podcast. Now that the book is done, I hope I can say... "Well, I'm back."

I would also like to thank the incredible collection (cabal? company?) of co-hosts who joined me in Season 7 after Shawn stepped down in August of 2022. In order of appearance: Corey Olsen, Shaun Gunner, Don Marshall, James Tauber, The Nerd of the Rings, Marcel Aubron-Bülles, KnewBettaDoBetta, and Sara Brown. Thank you all for your willingness to jump in, work hard, and embrace the PPP community!

I have also had the support of friends from around the world who have encouraged me to keep going when it was hard, held me accountable when I needed to do the work, and reminded me to touch grass when I got too focused on the work. Sadly, naming any would almost certainly lead to forgetting to name one, and so I'll have to say... "You know who you are." And you do.

Finally, together we want to thank the incredible community of listeners that has formed around *The Prancing Pony Podcast*. For years now you have inspired us, challenged us, called us out, cheered us on, believed in us, and supported us. Especially to those of you who have supported us financially on Patreon, enabling us to take the time away from other priorities and tasks to constantly develop the podcast and, now, write a book. None of this would have been possible without your support. Thank you, and *eglerio!*

# ABOUT THE AUTHORS

**Shawn E. Marchese**

Shawn went down the hobbit hole in his teens and has been in love with Middle-earth ever since. He met Alan Sisto in 2015 and co-hosted *The Prancing Pony Podcast* regularly for six seasons. A native of Louisiana, he lives in Texas with his wife and two children, who seem to enjoy his dinner table retellings of stories from the First Age.

**Alan Sisto**

A California native, Alan has not yet escaped to the Shire, but nevertheless managed to begin *The Prancing Pony Podcast* with Shawn E. Marchese in 2016. He believes Tolkien can take over the world, and hopes to be a part of the process. He lives with his wife and two children, all of whom have been immensely long-suffering.

9 781684 812097